THE ROAD TO NUMBER 10

THE ROAD TO

Number 10

By Anthony Howard & Richard West

The Macmillan Company

NEW YORK

Contents

DA
591
W5
H6

Preface   7

1. The Third Man   13

2. Band of Brothers   44

3. The Lost Leader   64

4. The Queen's Commission   79

5. The Great Commoner   116

6. The Road Show   140

7. The Adman Cometh   160

8. To See the Queen   178

9. Quiz Game   192

10. Three Per Cent   205

11. Poor Dears   219

12. Enter Mr. Hogg   234

13. Into the Sticks   247

14. The Rains Came   267

15. In by Four   281

16. The Man Who Made It   300

Index   313

Preface

AS THE title of the English edition of this book implies, *The Making of the Prime Minister*, owes its inspiration to Theodore White's magnificent work on the United States election of 1960, *The Making of the President 1960*. Ours also describes how two great political parties chose their leaders, how those leaders matched up to one another, and how eventually one of them edged his way to victory. So much for the resemblance between our book and Mr. White's. The differences are as great as the differences between British and American politics. An American Presidential candidate is the master of a huge, highly organized machine for the winning of votes. From the moment of his entry into the first primary to the day his name appears at the head of ballot papers throughout the nation, he makes his appeal directly to the entire electorate of the United States. A British party leader, by contrast, is the victim of an antiquated and ramshackle vote-getting system devised and designed far more to get as many of his colleagues as possible back into the House of Commons than to lift him directly into Downing Street. From the day he starts bidding for the leadership of the party his primary target has to be the Parliamentary Party, not the public at large. It follows that a British general election is less immediately colorful, less obviously dramatic, and certainly less well organized than its counterpart in America. On the other hand, it can be below the surface equally subtle and fascinating.

This book is not an effort to rewrite British politics in American terms. Neither is it a psychologist's examination of election results and voting trends, nor even a sociological

7

study of why in October 1964 the British electorate voted the Labour Party back into office after thirteen years of Conservative rule. The Liberal Party, the color issue, the land and housing problem—all these matters are touched upon. But they are brought in only insofar as they impinged on the plans and strategies of the two major party leaders. Our book sets out to answer the hows, not the whys, of the general election.

The readers of a political book are entitled to know the personal views of the authors. Both of us are lazy supporters of the Labour Party and wary admirers of Mr. Harold Wilson. Yet even a random glance through the following pages will prove that we have not shirked issues or episodes that cast little credit on the Labour Party or indeed ones that show Mr. Wilson himself in an unfavorable light. This is in no sense an authorized study of Harold Wilson and, although we are deeply grateful to him for his unfailing helpfulness and frankness to us while we were engaged on the task of gathering material, there is certainly much in the final version with which he will disagree and nothing at all that he has either read or approved.

Throughout the twenty-one months from Hugh Gaitskell's death to Harold Wilson's election victory we have had constant talks with front and backbenchers of both political parties. We are grateful to them for their kindness and patience, and for their general eagerness to see that the truth should be told. We should also like to thank the many friends in journalism who have lent us their advice and suggestions. In particular we should mention both Mr. Gerald Kaufman and Mr. John Morgan of the *New Statesman* and Mr. Peter Jenkins of the *Guardian,* all three of whom generously read sections of the typescript for errors of fact and mistakes of emphasis. But above all we should like to thank Mr. Oliver Walston, now at the Princeton Graduate School, who worked alongside us during the two months of actual writing and cheerfully shouldered heavy burdens of research, interviewing, and revision.

None of these persons is responsible for any mistakes of fact that may emerge. There are few judgments contained in this book; but these, too, are our own.

December, 1964 ANTHONY HOWARD
RICHARD WEST

THE ROAD TO NUMBER 10

1. The Third Man

It's a choice between the bear and the fox—and in politics
there isn't one. You have to choose the fox.
    ROBERT MELLISH, M. P., *in the House of Commons bar during the
Labour leadership election*

THE Savoy Plaza Hotel in New York stands on Fifth Avenue
at 59th Street looking out over Central Park. It is not, by
New York standards, an expensive hotel, and few guests run
up a telephone bill of $168 in two days. But then in the third
week of January 1963 it had an unusual guest.

At forty-six Harold Wilson was no stranger to America;
indeed, three members of the Kennedy Administration had
been his pupils when he was a "boy wonder" Oxford don
before the war. And on this occasion, too, scholarship rather
than politics was the main purpose of his trip. He had arrived in the United States on Sunday, January 13, on a
private academic lecture tour—a tour that had, in fact, already attracted some adverse comment within the Labour
Party. Some enemies muttered that, with the Common
Market negotiations breaking down in Brussels, this was no
time for a "shadow" Foreign Secretary to be out of the
country.

But in the end it was not developments in Brussels that
brought Harold Wilson hurriedly home with less than half
his tour completed. It was a series of telephone calls starting
in St. Louis, Missouri, and culminating in two decisive calls
booked through the Savoy Plaza switchboard in the early
hours of Friday, January 18. After the second one, made at
8 A.M. American time*—the first had been at 3 A.M.—Wilson

* The time change does not worry Wilson. "Whenever I go to the States,"

13

finally made up his mind. "All right," he told his secretary, Mrs. Marcia Williams, "I'm coming back then. I'll be at London Airport tomorrow."

For Wilson it was not an easy decision to make—and one he had tried to resist. The previous night he had been interrupted while addressing a meeting of the New York Council of Foreign Relations to receive a call from London. But despite what he was told he had remained adamant: he would for the moment continue with his tour; to do anything else would only increase the anxiety spreading through Britain.

When Wilson had flown off from London Airport to Chicago the previous Sunday, Hugh Gaitskell, the Labour Party's leader for the past seven years, had already been lying ill in the Middlesex Hospital for nine days. But though his friends and colleagues were worried and puzzled about the nature of his illness—particularly as what had at first been described merely as "flu" was now officially termed "a virus infection"—no one suspected that his return to the hospital after Christmas would mean anything more inconvenient than a few months out of political action.

To meet the difficulties caused by that situation the Labour Party had already taken precautions. In the week before Wilson left for America a meeting had taken place of the five principal figures in the party, including the three who were soon to be fighting each other for the leadership. Although this meeting was presented in some quarters as having formed "a Regency Council," it in effect decided nothing more than that business should go on as usual. It was with this aim in mind that Wilson found himself encouraged to continue with his American tour as planned.

By the morning of Wednesday, January 16, it was clear that by going to the United States Wilson had placed himself

he once explained, "I always carry two watches. One with the local time, the other with the right time—that is, British time."

in a difficult and delicate situation. In the newspapers the small down-page communiqués on the progress of Hugh Gaitskell's mysterious illness (which as recently as the start of the week had been speaking of "a slight improvement") had become dramatic column-lead headlines blaring the word "anxiety" to the world. Nowhere is the prospect of death dealt with more mechanically than in the communications industry; and throughout the day elaborate stand-by arrangements were made on both television networks for mounting immediate memorial programs in the event of Gaitskell dying that night.*

The newspapers and the television companies were not the only people suddenly to perceive a new, unexpected turn in the political drama. The Labour Party's deputy leader, George Brown, had, like Wilson, been carrying on as usual by touring unemployment areas in the Northwest. Suddenly, on the evening of January 16, he abruptly cut short his tour, requested the use of an RAF plane from the Prime Minister and flew straight from Manchester to London—appearing late at night outside the Middlesex Hospital, where Hugh Gaitskell was now described as "battling for his life."

All this—and in particular the sudden intervention of his proclaimed and obvious rival, George Brown—Harold Wilson learned that night in a phone call made by his loyal secretary to St. Louis. His reaction was typically level-headed. He asked merely to have it arranged that he got a transatlantic call the next day from the party's respected and knowledgeable Chief Whip, Herbert Bowden. He would decide whether to carry on or return in the light of what Bowden advised. In the event Bowden's advice was clear-cut: he could not help by returning, and a sudden change of plan on his part might easily add to the atmosphere of panic that

---

* So meticulous were the BBC preparations that one peer of the realm (Lord Longford) was summoned out of a Chelsea cinema with the sepulchral whisper, "My lord, he's sinking."

was already threatening to spread throughout the Parliamentary Labour Party. Wilson—though now aware for the first time that a group of left-wing Labour M.P.s had already met and were individually trying to get in touch with him to urge his immediate return—decided to go on to New York, where anyway he had arranged to lunch that Friday with U Thant, the Secretary-General of the United Nations.

It was on his return from that lunch just after four o'clock on Friday, January 18, that Wilson learned what the BBC was simultaneously telling the British nation on its 9:15 P.M. news bulletin. Outside the Savoy Plaza hotel he found four American reporters together with an official of the British Information Services in New York. He was told that Hugh Gaitskell had died a few minutes earlier. The news made no difference to his plans: those he had decided on that morning in the light of the last bleak report he had got on the loss of hope for Gaitskell's life. But the fact that Gaitskell had died while he himself was still 3,000 miles away did mean none the less that he had been forced into the worst possible tactical position. His return to Britain the next morning could not now help but look like the behavior of a man reaching for the crown.

Such an impression would have mattered a good deal less if the roles had been reversed—if of the two public rivals for the succession it had been George Brown who had been in America and Harold Wilson who was on the spot in London. For of Brown's loyalty and allegiance to Hugh Gaitskell there was, and could be, no doubt; it was to be his strongest card in the three-week party struggle to find the new leader. Harold Wilson was in a very different position. Only just over two years earlier he had actually gone so far as to run against Hugh Gaitskell for the party leadership; and he had also somehow always seemed a strangely isolated figure during the days of Gaitskell's leadership of the party.

It was not that he actually betrayed political friendships

but more that he seemed to. Having resigned with Bevan from the Attlee Government, he refused to rebel with Bevan against the Gaitskell leadership of the Opposition. Having sided with Gaitskell on foreign affairs, he turned against Gaitskell on Clause Four. This devious line would not have mattered so much if Wilson, like Bevan, was an impulsive, passionate man who seemed to act from political fervor. But his frequent rebellions rang untrue in a man of such cold, sarcastic reason. Many people nicknamed Wilson "the little man." They distrusted his calculation and complained of his habit of murdering colleagues out of the side of his mouth. "I am the cat," he would often wryly remark, "that walks alone." This was no time to be caught sniffing the cream.

Immediately, on the night of January 18, Wilson did his best to destroy any such impression. His tribute to Hugh Gaitskell—describing him as being "to a unique degree the architect of Labour's expected victory" at the polls—was a model of generosity. It compared favorably with some of the far more egocentric statements made that night on British television by those who had been far closer to the dead leader. And the next morning, on arriving pink-eyed and seemingly dazed at London Airport, he was curt with those who asked what he took to be tasteless questions. In reply to inquiries about his own personal prospects of getting the leadership he simply replied: "I don't think we can begin to think about that when the leader has died only a few hours ago."

It was just the right note. Though Wilson himself, flying through the night from New York, had no chance of knowing it, the British press had that morning raised Hugh Gaitskell almost into the status of a national martyr. Bitterly and often unfairly attacked in his life, on his death Gaitskell received a mass anthem of admiration and affection unprecedented in the history of British political journalism. In this there was at least some kind of justice; for after all his

struggles, battles and even tactical errors Hugh Gaitskell
had at last attained a stature that transcended his formal
post as Leader of the Opposition. For the future of the Labour Party even this posthumous deification presented a
problem—brutally rubbed in by the *Observer* leader column
on Sunday morning: "In writing the epitaph of Hugh Gaitskell it is difficult to avoid writing also the epitaph of the
Labour Party he loved, so commanding a figure had he become." The second epitaph was premature.

When Wilson emerged from his Boeing 707 onto the
tarmac at London Airport, he was met by the most informal
reception committee imaginable: his wife, Mary, his schoolboy son, Giles, and his secretary, who had driven the family
car out to the airport. Having disposed of the press, the four
of them went to have lunch at one of the new hotels that
have recently sprouted along the road opposite London Airport. No press man bothered to follow them; their family
lunch in the dining room of the circular Ariel Hotel passed
unnoticed even by all the other customers.

Throughout this first weekend Wilson was to remain a
strangely unobtrusive figure. While George Brown, who had
bravely resumed his Northern tour (missing Wilson at London Airport on Saturday morning by a mere half hour), was
capturing the headlines with speeches at Durham and Newcastle, Wilson stayed quietly in his home in Hampstead
Garden Suburb, adding nothing to his original statement
that the party should stand firm by its policies and remain
fully united. It was, as it turned out, a wise decision. Already
at Newcastle on Sunday, January 20, George Brown, net-
tled by what he regarded as the hypocritical tone of the Conservative press, was sounding off in a way that scarcely
seemed appropriate to the mood of stunned shock that still
enveloped the Labour Party. "We shall be told," he declared,
"that the rest of us left behind are a pretty poor lot. Time
will show whether we are or not. But we can take comfort

in the fact that these chaps said all these things about Gait-skell and about Attlee before him."

It was just the kind of comment to gratify those who had already begun to organize Wilson's campaign for the leadership. The fact that George Brown was now acting leader of the Labour Party meant that in the next few days he was bound to have the central part in all the ceremonial drama—including the House of Commons tributes—following Hugh Gaitskell's death. In the subsequent leadership race this could hardly help but give him advantage over any other candidate who emerged; but any advantage would automatically disappear if Brown's performance fell short of expected standards.

And there was always a good chance that it would. Even his best friends do not say of George Brown that he is tactful. He had come into politics through the Transport and General Workers' Union and had learned in the rough school of Ernie Bevin and Arthur Deakin. From the union he had acquired not only his habit of calling everyone "brother" but a respect for organization and discipline. Totally loyal to Gaitskell throughout the party split on the bomb, he had tried to enforce the same loyalty on the rest of the party. As chairman of the Organization Sub-Committee at Transport House, it was he who had tried to expel dissidents from the party. He had especially angered the Left by his treatment of Lord (Bertrand) Russell, the celebrated and controversial philosopher-turned-propagandist. If Brown was a bogeyman to the Left of the party, he was not entirely liked by the Right. Some thought him overemotional, quick-tempered, rash in judgment. The upper-class salon socialists found him uncouth, and it was even whispered that he had changed his name. This particular lie is based on a misunderstanding. During his young days as a fur salesman for the John Lewis partnership there was another Brown in the same department, and the manager, to save confusion, ordained that

George should be known as Bruton. But he was certainly born Brown, the son of a grocer's packer, and he comes from mixed Irish and London stock. With bushy eyebrows, fluttering lashes and trumpeting tenor voice, he is one of the best orators in the country and a man of great intellectual force. Although Brown, in contrast to Wilson, got his support from the Right of the Parliamentary Party, all the polls showed him far more popular with the working-class elements of the population. His manner and personality were less liked by the middle classes, including the floating voters, and for this reason the Tories hoped he would get the leadership. Indeed this was one of the arguments that the Wilsonites used in their discreet, almost surreptitious canvassing.

It was Wilson's obvious course at this early stage to lie low—saying and doing virtually nothing. On his return home that Saturday afternoon he inevitably found himself being rung up by a large number of lobby correspondents all anxious to know what his own plans were. But though Wilson talked to each of them in turn freely and candidly—as he always has done to press men whom he knows—he was not prepared to authorize any firm announcement of his own intention to run for the leadership.

His decision had none the less been taken. Driving the Wilson family back along the Great West Road from London Airport, Marcia Williams, who had worked for Wilson eight years, finally plucked up her courage to ask the question that every political journalist in the country wanted answered. "I suppose this means you're going to stand for the leadership?" she said. "Yes," Wilson replied bleakly, "I expect so." The newspapers expected so, too. Only ten weeks earlier Wilson had run against Brown for the deputy leadership; and it seemed inconceivable that he would allow the man who had defeated him then by a margin of three to two now to slip unopposed into the actual party leadership.

In any case he really showed his hand that same night,

though it passed unnoticed by Fleet Street. Shortly after dinner Wilson came out of his house in the Garden Suburb, climbed into his gray Ford Consul car, and drove straight to an old friend's home in Well Walk, Hampstead, a couple of miles away.

In the small and closely guarded circle of Harold Wilson's genuine personal friends Thomas Balogh,* city banker turned Oxford economist, occupied a unique position. Alone among the various dons loosely attached to the Labour Party, his loyalty to Wilson had never wavered. In the darkest days when it had seemed that Wilson might well be eased out of the Labour hierarchy, Balogh had stood solidly behind him. Together the two of them—both involved in the Bevanite revolt of the early Fifties—had paced Hampstead Heath on Sunday mornings after the 1959 general election, trying to decide what defense Wilson would have if the revisionist right wing of the party succeeded in its privately declared objective of shifting him from his influential position as "shadow" Chancellor; and when Wilson finally did agree to move—to be "shadow" Foreign Secretary in the autumn of 1961—it was with Balogh that he most fully discussed the hidden threats and dangers of the change. It was, therefore, wholly appropriate that on this night—when he faced the greatest challenge of his political career so far—he should once again call on the man who had stood beside him in good times and bad.

In Wellside House, Hampstead, on Saturday, January 19, Wilson did not just find his host. Also there was the man who during the next three weeks was to organize his campaign for the leadership within the Parliamentary Labour Party, the volatile and brilliant Richard Crossman. Long afterward Wilson said, in justifiable irritation at press reports: "Look, a number of people appointed themselves my campaign

---

* Since October Wilson's chief economic adviser in the Cabinet Office.

managers—none of them asked me for the job and as far as
I am concerned they were acting on their own." But among
this company Dick Crossman—like Wilson himself a prewar
Oxford don turned professional politician—had probably the
strongest claim to having inspired the whole style and nature
of Wilson's campaign for the party leadership. That first
night Crossman laid down its broad lines. It was essential,
he urged, that Wilson himself (always suspected of too much
personal ambition) kept as far as possible above the contest.
He should neither canvass support nor solicit votes; all that
he must leave to his friends. And even they would conduct
the campaign not by taking initiatives themselves but rather
by trying to exploit any mistakes that the other camp made.

Crossman had realized that the greatest challenge facing
the Wilsonites was not so much support for any other candidate as suspicion of their own; this was bound to crystallize
sooner or later into a simple "Stop Wilson" movement.
Throughout the Gaitskell years Wilson's position in the
party had been ambivalent; and Gaitskell's sudden tragic
death provided the Wilson campaign with its biggest liability
—the fact that Wilson himself would never have been the
candidate of Hugh Gaitskell's own choice. It was, therefore,
vital that nothing should be said or done which could provoke the overwhelming majority of Gaitskellites in the party,
all of whom remembered only too well that Wilson had actually tried to defeat the late leader in his year of challenge
following the unilateralist victory at the Scarborough party
conference in 1960.

This Crossman analysis of the situation found striking con-
firmation in a second campaign meeting that was held two
days later—this time of the forces arrayed against Wilson.
On Monday, January 21, there assembled in Anthony Crosland's roomy, top-floor flat in the Boltons in Kensington most
of Hugh Gaitskell's closest associates and admirers in the
Parliamentary Labour Party. They were a strange company.

There was Crosland himself—bohemian, dashing and de-bonair, above anyone else the disciple whom Gaitskell loved; there was Mrs. Jennifer Jenkins, the wife of Gaitskell's other great friend in the House of Commons, Labour M.P. Roy Jenkins (who was to be away in the United States throughout the election); there were the three principal figures in the right-wing, loyalist Campaign for Democratic Socialism founded in 1960—its chief organizer Dennis Howell, its treasurer Dick Taverne, and its secretary Bill Rodgers—all of whom had been elected at by-elections to the 1959 Parliament; there were three other Labour M.P.s—a young trade-unionist, Reg Prentice, the wealthy accountant, Jack Diamond, and the journalist and commentator, Desmond Donnelly. The surprise people present were the chairman of the T.U.C. General Council, Fred Hayday, and the Labour Party's own Director of Publicity, John Harris.

This gathering certainly proved that Wilson in his bid for the leadership could expect to face tough and determined opposition, but it also revealed the essential weakness of that opposition. Most of the talk that Monday night in Tony Crosland's flat centered on whom the former loyal cadre of Gaitskellites should put up against Wilson—a discussion that was to drag on for a whole week and which in the end was virtually to wreck any chances that the "Stop Wilson" movement ever had. The obvious champion for the Gaitskellites was the party's deputy leader, George Brown, who had been Gaitskell's chief lieutenant for the past three years. Even that Monday evening, however, it became clear that some of those at the meeting had grave reservations about him as a potential candidate. Crosland himself was opposed and so, only slightly less vehemently, was John Harris. The doubts expressed at this meeting centered on Brown's prospects of being the right man to defeat Wilson. No one really resisted the conclusion that if a viable, fresh figure existed he might well have a better hope of victory than someone who had deliberately been chosen for the number-two position in the party and who, before Gaitskell's death, had seemed a very unlikely prospect indeed to succeed to the actual leadership. Forlornly even such names as Frank Soskice, Patrick Gordon Walker and Michael Stewart were put forward, only to be brushed aside by Crosland, who had already made up his mind that James Callaghan was the only worthwhile bet.

None of this was known to Brown himself, who that day had returned from the North assuming that as acting leader of the party he could count on the unqualified support of all the Gaitskellite members of the Parliamentary Labour Party. But Brown had no sooner arrived in his room at the House of Commons than he received his first shock of the day. Patrick Gordon Walker—always one of Gaitskell's staunchest friends on the Opposition front bench—came in to see him and warned him, in the course of a general conversation about the problems facing the party, that in certain circumstances he might feel it his duty to run for the leadership. For Brown this news was a bad blow. The emphatic support of a ruminative, reliable, cautious figure like Gordon Walker was essential to him, if only to reassure any doubts about his own impetuous temperament. But Brown nevertheless accepted that Gordon Walker had every right to make his own decision, and even thanked him for his frankness.

The incident nevertheless led Brown to make his first serious tactical mistake of the campaign. On the afternoon of Monday, January 21—through a message passed between their respective secretaries—he asked the other most frequently tipped potential contender for the leadership, James Callaghan, to come and see him. Their meeting took place in George Brown's room at 4:30 P.M., and it got off on the wrong foot from the start. What Brown naturally wanted from Callaghan was a guarantee of support and a promise not to intervene himself. In broaching the matter Brown candidly and openly told Callaghan of his conversation earlier in the day with Gordon Walker—and he was always afterward to believe that had he not done this Callaghan might have pledged his support from the beginning. As it was, Callaghan—hearing for the first time about the possibility of another third candidate—took the only course open to him: he told Brown that he must "reserve his own position," and even added that he had already been approached with a view to letting his name go forward for nomination. The strategy of the Wilson camp in letting George Brown make all the moves, while they just sat back, was beginning to pay off.

Brown's best chance of success obviously lay in a straight fight with Wilson—and his efforts to procure it seemed so far to have hindered rather than helped. Brown needed a straight fight for a variety of reasons. A simple, stark confrontation with Wilson and no one else would inevitably emphasize his own built-in advantage as the tenant-in-possession. That advantage was to be demonstrated that same evening when the Opposition "shadow" Cabinet met to consider its plans for the coming parliamentary session. Normally this would have been a purely routine meeting, but with the party leader dead it could easily have taken on a rather different complexion. In the event, this meeting—in which George Brown, as acting leader, took the chair as of right—scrupulously ignored the vacant leadership. It was only at the very end that Wilson and Brown in a brief conversation discussed the coming election.

What was said in this conversation was later to be hotly disputed, and certainly the two main contenders came away from it with different impressions of what had been decided. For George Brown it amounted simply to an agreement that the election should be fought cleanly and with the least damage to the party; Harold Wilson, on the other hand, saw it as a pact between each of them that either would loyally serve the other whichever was elected.

Two days later, on Wednesday, January 23, it was the Wilson version that found its way into three morning newspapers under the headline "LABOUR RIVALS IN UNITY PACT." This incident was to cause more suspicion than virtually anything else that happened in the entire contest. Not unnaturally George Brown saw it as an effort to undercut his own position—his fear being that once the impression got abroad that he would be perfectly willing to continue as deputy leader, he would inevitably forfeit his main tactical asset, the fact that he was already acting leader of the party. He lost no time in repudiating the story and in an interview with his own constituency paper, the *Derby Evening Telegraph,* expressly denied that he had entered into any pact with anyone. As an instant response, Brown's reaction was understandable enough; but Wilson saw it as a bad tactical error of judgment. Not only did it seem to make Brown appear as the candidate who was against party unity; it also— even more damagingly—effectively foreclosed his last chance of getting what he most wanted, a straight fight against a single candidate. Had he been content to grasp the public olive branch that had come from the Wilson camp, it would have been very difficult for any other candidate to enter the race and seem to be putting party unity in peril. As it was, the way was wide open for a "third man" to offer the party an alternative to a head-on collision between two long-publicized rivals. And one was soon to appear.

In the early days of the campaign it was the formal, official occasions that attracted attention—the tributes to Gaitskell and the adjournment in his memory of both Houses on Tuesday, January 22, the monthly meeting of the Labour Party's National Executive Committee on the morning of Wednesday, January 23, even Hugh Gaitskell's funeral that same afternoon in Hampstead Parish Church. But, as always, it was what happened on the periphery of these events that mattered most for the future. The fact, for example, that Harold Wilson had not even been invited to attend Gaitskell's funeral was a pretty clear indication of the degree of bitterness that still existed against him in the Gaitskellite camp. Had it been a purely private family affair this might not have seemed remarkable, but as the mourners included his main rival, George Brown, and a number of other leading Labour parliamentary figures (to say nothing of at least three ambassadors), his absence from the occasion could not help but look like a deliberate snub. Old wounds bled again in the National Executive meeting that same morning. After the 27 members of the Executive had stood in silent tribute to the former leader, Mrs. Barbara Castle—throughout the 1950's a persistent Gaitskell critic and a recognized leading left-wing member of the Executive—was rash enough to suggest some form of memorial to Hugh Gaitskell's memory. This proved altogether too much for right-wing trade-unionist, Jim Matthews, himself an old enemy of Barbara Castle's. He promptly accused the Left of "bloody crocodile tears," only to be told sharply by Tom Driberg, another left-winger, to watch his language and to refrain from swearing.

The incident of the alleged "unity pact" also cast its shadow over this edgy gathering of the party's Executive Committee. The meeting started at 10:30 A.M., and George Brown arrived at it five minutes late. No sooner had he sat down than a note was passed to him by his neighbor, Harry Nicholas, the Labour Party treasurer. The note was the result of a conversation Wilson had with Nicholas before the meeting started, and it read simply, "Harold Wilson thinks he owes you an apology." At first Brown was not pacified. "Thinks?" he scribbled on it. "He bloody well does," and tossed it back. A little later, however, Wilson came over to Brown, tapped him on the shoulder and beckoned him over to a corner. There he made it clear that he accepted full responsibility for the story, regretted the misunderstanding and offered his rival apologies. For Wilson it was, in Brown's eyes, uncharacteristically generous behavior, and he admitted later that evening that he had been impressed.

At this stage Brown's resentment was beginning to build up far more against James Callaghan than against his open rival. One of those who attended the meeting in Crosland's flat on Monday night had reported everything that had been said to Brown, and he had begun to suspect a plot against him even among those he thought his friends. In one sense Brown was certainly right: the original first gathering in Anthony Crosland's flat had led to two much more formal meetings of the "Stop Wilson" movement. Both meetings—held in Jack Diamond's flat in Greycoat Place, Westminster (conveniently near the House of Commons)—had been attended by at least four Opposition front-bench spokesmen, with a former Minister, John Strachey, in the chair. The problem at issue remained: which of the possible candidates stood the best chance of polling the maximum vote against Wilson? By now the argument had become a straight choice between the claims of Callaghan and Brown; and as the discussion wore on the supporters of each inevitably tended to take up more and more intransigent positions.

In any event this bold effort to introduce a "caucus" principle into British politics had in it an element of unreality. The safe delivery of a solid package of votes would have been welcomed by either Callaghan or Brown, but each in fact made his decision to run quite independently of the deliberations of camp followers. Brown's mind had been made up from the start; for the acting leader not to stand in the election would have amounted to a confession of inadequacy. Callaghan's position was more complex, but from the moment that two of his colleagues in the "shadow" cabinet (Denis Healey and Tom Fraser) waited upon him in his office in Bridge Street, Westminster, on Tuesday, January 22, and urged that it was his duty to stand, there was no going back for him either. On Wednesday, January 23—before even the second caucus meeting took place—he told Brown that the prospect of the deputy leadership did not attract him; and the next day, taking the press by surprise, he boldly announced that he was available for nomination.

The fact that the anti-Wilson forces wasted a week in discussing the respective merits of two rival champions—and, worse than that, that the news of their disagreements got abroad through the professional vigilance of the *Daily Express*—was to prove one of the decisive elements in the whole contest. Harold Wilson's supporters, while operating quietly and discreetly, had not been idle. On Wednesday night, while most of his opponents were gathered in Jack Diamond's flat hopelessly locked in disagreement, Wilson himself was less than half a mile away having dinner in the home of his own campaign manager, Richard Crossman. Even by that time Wilson was virtually certain that he would be faced with two rivals rather than one; that situation, he was convinced from the beginning, could only yield advantage to him. While the press kept insisting that the presence of a third candidate made no difference—in that whoever survived the first ballot out of Brown or Callaghan would inherit the votes of the other—Wilson saw that a split in the opposite forces could not be healed as easily as that. There would be bound to be a legacy of bitterness—bitterness strong enough to persuade them to vote for him on the second ballot instead of the rival right-wing candidate.

That night in Crossman's home Wilson's theory received its first vindication. After dinner he and Crossman were joined by the editor of the *Guardian*, forty-three-year-old Alastair Hetherington, who at that time rented an upstairs flat in the same house. Hetherington, asked to look in for a drink by Crossman, had no idea that he would find Wilson there; but, anxious that their meeting should be subject to no misunderstanding, he insisted that Wilson should first of all read a proof of next morning's leader in the *Guardian*, which he had happened to bring home with him. It was short, not much more than 500 words, and its sting lay in its tail. Discussing the qualities needed in a man who might in the nature of things shortly be Prime Minister, it mentioned "steady judgment, a reasonable consistency of policy, the courage needed to take unpopular decisions, administrative ability and robust health." Its last two sentences then ran: "Mr. George Brown, in spite of his great service and long devotion to the Labour Party, hardly measures up to all these requirements. There are other candidates who come nearer to doing so." If Hetherington had ever had any fear that Wilson would have welcomed a more robust endorsement, he was soon to lose it. Wilson was delighted, dwelling with particular satisfaction on the word "candidates" in the plural. It was just the sort of conclusion—as he instantly recognized—calculated to cause maximum friction between the supporters of Callaghan and those who were still remaining fiercely loyal to George Brown.

Nor was it just a matter of their supporters. The next day, Thursday, January 24, Brown and Callaghan met to talk together in Hugh Gaitskell's old room in the House of Commons, which George Brown, as acting leader, had slightly shyly moved into. It was not a happy interview. Callaghan began it by recalling that they had both agreed on Monday that the first priority was to defeat Wilson, and then added that he was now satisfied that he could do it whereas he did not frankly think that Brown could. Would he not, therefore, stand down in his favor? Not unnaturally, Brown was outraged by this suggestion, and he lost no time in pointing out that his own support was by any account twice as large as Callaghan's. That, Callaghan replied, was not the point: the real challenge lay in getting the extra votes needed for victory

—and here he was sure he was stronger than Brown, provided he was given a clear run. This only succeeded in making Brown even angrier than before, and the discussion ended with Callaghan bluntly saying that he would run in any case and that the party would simply have to choose between them as the best alternative candidate to Wilson.

How far this interview, about which he did not hide his indignation, was responsible for clouding George Brown's judgment can only be a matter for conjecture. But certainly in the next few days Brown laid the foundations of his ultimate defeat. He did it by alienating precisely the type of support that he was bound to need eventually if he was to win. There was, for example, his treatment of a young and able trade-union M.P., Reginald Prentice, who had been reported as wavering between Callaghan and Brown. That same night Prentice found himself summoned to see George Brown, who immediately challenged him about his intentions. After being put (as he described it) "on the mat," Prentice—although a member of the same union as George Brown and, like him, one of the Transport Workers' sponsored candidates—lost all his doubts. He made up his mind to vote for Callaghan and announced as much to a Sunday newspaper.

In retrospect it is hard to resist the conclusion that Brown exaggerated the threat that the Callaghan candidature presented to his own prospects. Nothing less explains the ruthlessness with which the Brown camp immediately went to work to destroy Callaghan's chances, even to the point of allowing it to be known that if Callaghan were to be elected, Brown would in no circumstances continue as deputy leader. In the short term this tactic certainly paid off: the Callaghan bandwagon never really began to move, and at the last moment before nominations closed on January 31 there were even strong rumors that Callaghan would not in the end proceed with his candidature at all. But the personal bruises that were inflicted during this period were not lightly forgotten and in themselves were largely the explanation of why in the end Callaghan's first-ballot vote of forty-one split in the ratio of two to one in favor of Harold Wilson.

On top of the damage done there was also, of course, the diversion of energy and distraction of effort. For a whole week Brown and Callaghan were running far more against each other than they were against the man they were both trying to stop, Harold Wilson. And the Wilson campaign certainly made the most of its opportunity. A leadership election within the Parliamentary Labour Party—proceeding, as it does, on the principle of eliminating candidates until someone has an absolute majority—may in its form be unlike most other elections held in Britain; but it is at least responsive to the same methods of vote-getting. While the "Stop Wilson" group continued to pursue the will-o'-the-wisp of prepackaging a vote to be delivered to either Brown or Callaghan (abandoning the project only when it reached total deadlock after an inconclusive "straw" poll on Monday, January 28), Wilson's own supporters went quietly and thoroughly about the task of traditional British canvassing. The essence of canvassing lies not in persuasion but in discovery; and it was because the handful of M.P.s working for Wilson accepted this that they enjoyed throughout the three weeks an enormous psychological advantage over their rivals. Where others were content to guess, they knew where their support lay.

They owed this knowledge largely to one man, who now emerged if not as Wilson's actual campaign manager then at least as a kind of "shadow" Chief Whip of the Parliamentary Labour Party. Throughout postwar politics the House of Commons has contained no more exotic figure than Colonel George Wigg. He served eighteen years in the ranks, was commissioned in the Army Education Corps during the war and was then elected Labour member for Dudley in 1945. In Parliament Wigg's speciality had been to find things out that were, deliberately, kept secret; and in the next three weeks he was to give to the task of locating Wilson's support within the Parliamentary Labour Party all the energy and skill that he had in the past lavished on such matters as the precise stationing of particular regiments within the British Army. As the backers of the other candidates chatted, persuaded and even bullied, George Wigg simply listened and watched. He marked a list of the 249 Labour M.P.s for all the world as if he were located not in the lobby of the House of Commons but on an American convention floor complete with walkie-talkie set. It was an exercise that he carried off with such professionalism and thoroughness that his final tally was to prove only three votes out on the actual result—far and away the most accuratè estimate made by anybody of the likely support for each of the three candidates.

The Wigg intelligence service provided a necessary part of the Wilson strategy. After the first meeting in Thomas Balogh's house on the day he returned from America, Wilson accepted faithfully that he must not appear overeager for power. George Wigg's listening post meant that ordinary canvassing was redundant; in cases of difficulty or doubt, waverers or potential hopefuls could simply be sent discreetly upstairs to have a quiet word with the candidate himself in the privacy of his room on the House of Commons upper committee floor. With such a high-grade information service at its disposal there was simply no need for the Wilson campaign to risk the kind of semipublic encounters—often leading to angry scenes—that all too often characterized the two rival camps.

Although the mood of Wilson's supporters became more and more confident as the days went by, the shrewder of them knew from the beginning that they faced one real task. An election with three candidates suited them down to the ground, if only because the division among their opponents was bound to ensure that their own candidate had such a commanding lead on the first ballot that he could hardly be beaten on any subsequent run-off. But the introduction of a fourth candidate could easily transform that situation. According to the Parliamentary Labour Party's rule book it would be he (provided he got enough votes to provide the margin for an absolute majority), and he alone, who went out on the first ballot. The intervention of a fourth candidate could thus provide the "Stop Wilson" movement with just the pause and opportunity that it needed in order to recover from disarray and regroup its forces for a final offensive ranged behind a single candidate. In the period before nominations closed on Thursday, January 31, this was the one prospect that caused any real anxiety in the Wilson camp.

They need not have worried; for faced with two possible courses, the Brownites chose the wrong one. Aware that an immediate straight fight was still their best bet, they preferred it to the alternative tactic of a fourth candidate. The factor which tipped the balance in making the decision was probably the knowledge that James Callaghan—though he had indicated his availability—had not actually put in any formal nomination as a candidate. In the last few days all the efforts of the Brown camp went into shying him off. One move was the deliberate "leaking" of a formidable roll of Brown's backers; another was Brown's own declaration that in no circumstances would he consent to serve under Callaghan; a third was the news purposefully put abroad that Patrick Gordon Walker—the most fancied of the potential fourth candidates—had now agreed instead to take the deputy leadership if George Brown were elected. The objective obviously was to frighten off Callaghan, but the result was to give both him and his supporters a new determination born of anger and resentment.

The methods employed in this phase of the campaign got the Brownites accused of strong-arm tactics. Tales spread of people being bludgeoned with threats or bribed with rewards; there were stories of thirty-eight Cabinet Ministers having already been appointed, to say nothing of five law officers. Undeterred, Callaghan put in his nomination papers. And Brown at last realized that he could no longer expect the automatic victory which initially he had considered his right.

The strain began to show—and not only in his relations with his colleagues. For its own period of internal turmoil the Labour Party had a dramatic political backdrop. As if the forced ending of the Anglo-American Skybolt project at Nassau in December and the highest unemployment figures since 1947 had not been enough, there now came the news of the final collapse of the Conservative Government's two-year effort to get into the European Common Market. A depressed Harold Macmillan appeared on both national television channels on the night of Wednesday, January 30, to make the Government's case and to explain the consequences for the future. Without overmuch encouragement from his colleagues George Brown decided that this had been in essence a party political broadcast and demanded, as acting leader of the Labour Party, the right of reply. The BBC, arguing that Macmillan had spoken as Prime Minister and not as party leader, turned him down flat; ITV invited him to appear and then, five hours before he was due on the air, tried to withdraw the invitation. The ensuing argument, which Brown insisted on conducting with Sir Robert Fraser, the Director-General of the ITA, led to lurid accounts of anger and threats. Although Brown's broadcast itself was successful —earning sympathetic press notices the next morning—the talking point among Labour M.P.s became the rough nature of the negotiations which had preceded it. Was this, it began to be asked, really the proper way for a Labour Party leader to conduct himself?

For Wilson the incident was invaluable, if only because reliability (at least in the political sense) had from the beginning been the most dangerous question mark hanging over his own candidature. The back-bench Labour M.P. who went round prophesying that if Wilson ever became Prime Minister he "would sell the country for 40,000 rubles" was certainly an extreme case, but at the top of the party there still survived grave doubts about how he would react to a great international confrontation like the Cuba crisis only three months earlier. These doubts largely explained why, when George Brown's supporters issued a list of their candidate's sponsors, it was literally impossible for the Wilson campaign to reply in the same coin. With the exceptions of Earl Attlee (the former Prime Minister), Bert Bowden (the party's Chief Whip) and one other member of the "shadow" Cabinet (Fred Lee), Wilson was virtually without support in the highest echelons of the party; for him to win it was essential that he should have the chance to make his appeal to the back benches—and a series of major debates in the House throughout the contest provided him with just the opportunity that he needed. Neither George Brown nor James Callaghan disgraced themselves in these debates, but there was not the slightest doubt that Wilson, widely regarded since the death of Nye Bevan as the most brilliant Commons debater, emerged with the greatest advantage. From the moment that he began a speech in his curiously flat North Country voice at the dispatch box, the message lying behind it came over: if the party, he seemed to be saying, really wanted a leader who could successfully discomfit the Government, then he was ready. Wilson's skill as a parliamentarian would have been an asset to him in any event, but events conspired to give him a bright opportunity.

There was nothing really unfair in this, for ever since he had stood against Hugh Gaitskell in 1960 (thereby sacrificing the deputy leadership which would otherwise have been his right) the weakest point of Wilson's personal appeal was his standing with his own colleagues in the House of Commons. With Gaitskell in command, the party could afford to keep him, as it were, in reserve in the number-three spot. But could it do the same with Gaitskell gone? Could it risk neglecting the claims of the one man within the party whose abilities paralleled and perhaps even surpassed those of Gaitskell himself? Fortunately for Wilson it was not he who had to pose the issue either directly or indirectly. In the last days of the campaign it was George Brown himself who brought it to a head. Of all the blunders that Brown made the worst was his clear indication that he could not accept Wilson as deputy leader. It confronted waverers within the Parliamentary Party with the price they would have to pay by choosing Brown as party leader. Eventually Brown saw his mistake and passed a message to Wilson that, provided he was prepared to take an immediate oath of allegiance to him on the moment of his election, he would not rule him out as a candidate for the deputy leadership. But by then it was too late; having put the first story around to a chorus of puzzlement and apprehension, Wilson's supporters could afford to put the second one about as an indication of the fear and nervousness that had begun to affect the Brown camp.

The ballot box—a large cardboard contraption with a slit in the top—stood about in one of the Opposition's Whips' rooms in the lobby for a whole week before it finally surrendered its secrets. But from the moment that it appeared, no one much doubted its verdict on the first ballot. Suddenly the steam seemed to have gone out of the Brown bid for the leadership; it was almost as if it had been recognized that the cost of beating off the Callaghan challenge had been a total exhaustion in conducting the second and main part of the battle. Even in the last three days Brown himself persisted in fighting on the wrong front; on Monday, February 4, he still could not resist sniping at Callaghan. Sitting next to him on the Opposition front bench at the end of a debate on unemployment, he suddenly said, "You must have a pretty good conceit of yourself to think that you can be leader of the

Labour Party. Why are you doing it?" "Because," Callaghan replied, "a lot of people think I'd make a better job of it than you." It was a brief exchange, but next day it was all round the Parliamentary Labour Party. In the view of the Wilson camp it had a good deal to do with Callaghan's surprisingly high vote.

When, in fact, the result was read out at the weekly meeting of the Parliamentary Labour Party on Thursday, February 7, it was only this big support for James Callaghan that came as any real surprise. Both Wilson and Brown had been warned five minutes before the crowded meeting in Committee Room 11 started at 6:30 P.M. that they would have to go on to a second ballot; but if the details of the figures were heard impassively by Harold Wilson, they clearly shocked George Brown, despite the fact that just before entering the room he had shown some premonition of what was to come by remarking, "I suppose I must go in and look brave, but frankly I don't feel very brave right now." That night Brown certainly needed all his courage; the result read out inaudibly by a veteran former member of Attlee's Government, James Chuter Ede, showed Harold Wilson with 115 votes, George Brown with 88 and James Callaghan with 41. Few of the 200-odd Labour M.P.s who heard the figures doubted what they meant. Short of a miracle nothing could now stop Harold Wilson being elected the following week; he, after all, needed only eight of Callaghan's eliminated votes for an absolute majority, whereas George Brown would have to pick up no less than 35 of them in order to attain victory. Of all the 249 members of the Parliamentary Labour Party Brown himself—once he had recovered from the initial shock —was about the only man who still seemed to believe that it was possible.

A born fighter, Brown that night held something of a council of war in his home in Dulwich. To his house came the two M.P.s who had worked hardest for him—his own

Parliamentary Private Secretary, Gerry Reynolds, and Desmond Donnelly, as well as a fringe back-bench supporter, Jeremy Bray, and a leading Transport House official, John Clark. Everyone except Brown seemed to find the effort to be festive a strain; what they did not realize was that their candidate's mind was already working on a counterattack that he proposed to launch the next day. "Tell me," he kept saying that evening without anyone realizing the significance of the question, "is there a big enough trade-union leader in town to swing this thing?"

For that it was already too late. Immediately after he heard the results of the first ballot, Harold Wilson left the House of Commons to go to dinner in Dick Crossman's house in Vincent Square, where his wife, Mary, had been waiting for him in case (in the event of an outright victory) she should suddenly be summoned to appear at Transport House. Eight votes had come between Wilson that night and an immediate victory press conference; but before he left Crossman's house that evening Wilson knew for certain that the date had only been postponed. Before the Commons adjourned at 10:30 P.M. the ever-vigilant George Wigg was able to report in Crossman's house that of the 41 voters for Callaghan, 12 had already pledged their second ballot preferences for Wilson. The news prompted Wilson to make one of his rare emotional gestures. Suddenly getting to his feet in the ground-floor sitting room in which Bevan himself had so often sat in the days of the Bevanite revolt, he raised his glass and proposed a toast to Nye Bevan's memory. The four other Labour M.P.s present—George Wigg, Dick Plummer, Anthony Greenwood and Crossman himself—had all in their time been Bevan disciples, and the symbolism of the gesture was not lost on them. The fight that they had vainly waged throughout the Fifties against the Labour establishment now looked at last as if it had been won.

For the moment, though, nothing was being taken for

granted. In the week between the two ballots the main anxiety of the Wilson camp was that nothing should be said or done that could at the last moment rob them of victory. Enormous effort went, for example, into getting the *Observer* to withhold publication of a profile of Wilson until Sunday, February 17, when whatever it said would not matter. But there were some things naturally that could not be controlled. When Wilson appeared on a platform at Blackburn in Lancashire on Saturday, February 9, he was firmly introduced to an enthusiastic audience as "the man whom we all hope in a week's time will be designated our next Prime Minister." It was an assumption Wilson's closest supporters approved but not one they wanted to have too publicly emphasized.

The Wilson camp knew of the lengths to which George Brown would go in order to keep the contest alight. When the figures for the first ballot were announced on Thursday night a number of Labour M.P.s thought Brown might accept that the final verdict was bound to go against him and therefore withdraw from the contest, conceding victory to Wilson. It did not take long for them to be disillusioned. No sooner had the *Daily Mirror* called for "a brief announcement from Mr. Brown" than one was issued, but not in quite the terms that the *Mirror* had had in mind. Instead of being conciliatory, it was combative; far from amounting to a concession, it was almost a declaration of total war. The election of a new leader of the Labour Party, Brown declared, was not just a matter of individuals and their personal abilities; it was bound to involve also questions of principle and of attitudes on vital issues. If the statement had actually mentioned Hugh Gaitskell by name, it could hardly have made the point more clear. The Labour Party found itself asked to remember who had stood at Armageddon—and who had not.

A certain air of mystery was to attach itself to this statement, for in the next few days, to the obvious relief of the

Wilsonites, Brown did absolutely nothing to follow it up. The explanation was simple enough: Brown's first instinct when faced by the prospect of defeat had been typically belligerent. As the "intellectuals" in the Parliamentary Labour Party had let him down, he would appeal above their heads to his own side of the movement—the trade unions. At first Brown seems to have thought he could get some kind of "round robin" signed by various influential union leaders; but his proposal withered in the bud the moment he put it to his own closest supporters. Patrick Gordon Walker—his own first choice for deputy leader—was horrified; he and others gradually bore in on Brown that his proposed last gamble could not help but result in his committing the one unforgivable sin in the Labour movement—that of splitting the party. In face of the unanimous advice Brown reluctantly abandoned the idea of a last desperate throw and prepared himself for the inevitable.

In doing so he had at least one consolation. By now there was widespread sympathy for his position throughout the party. In voting on the second ballot Labour M.P.s found themselves the victims of contradictory pulls. They wanted to give Wilson a big vote of confidence that would show the party's unity under his leadership; yet they also wanted to avoid inflicting humiliation on George Brown, who had, after all, held the fort through four of the most difficult weeks in the Labour Party's history. In the event the twin influences produced a result that could hardly have been better balanced. The second and decisive ballot—declared on the evening of Thursday, February 14—gave Harold Wilson 144 votes to George Brown's 103.

When the results were read out in Committee Room 14 of the House of Commons, Brown, as acting leader, was in the chair. It would have been a bitter moment for any politician; for one so emotional as Brown it was almost unbearable. He needed all his tremendous stock of courage to steel himself for the short speech customary on these occasions. He congratulated Wilson, made it clear that he accepted the party's verdict and announced that he proposed now to withdraw for a period into the background so that the new leader's impact should not be blurred in any way. As for continuing as deputy leader: "I will have to consider my own position," Brown concluded.

Wilson, on his feet to a great ovation as soon as Brown had sat down, lost no time in trying to eradicate any ominous impression that Brown's last remark might have seemed to carry with it. He wanted George Brown to continue, as he was sure the whole party did; he would do everything in his power to persuade him to do so. The party needed Brown's energetic, dynamic qualities, and he thanked him for the way in which he had deployed them in leading the party during the past month. It had even occurred to him that it might be best in the future if the party were to operate permanently on a troika basis. Certainly, he said, in the past month while three candidates had been running for office the party, far from falling apart, had actually grown in strength and appeal, as all the polls confirmed. Wilson's speech could hardly have been surpassed in magnanimity, but for the moment it failed in its purpose. Sitting silent, Brown gave no sign that his mind had been in any way changed; he was still reserving his future position.

This was to be the only failure in what otherwise was an evening of triumph for Wilson. As soon as the party meeting in the House of Commons was over, he left for Transport House to hold his first press conference as leader of the party. Struggling his way through the crowds around the entrance, he made his way with his wife to the platform from which in the next twenty months he was to speak in a variety of changing moods. On this first occasion, however, the mood was clear from the start: all modesty and awe. "You will understand," he began, "that at a time like this even somebody not normally at a loss for words finds it a little difficult to find words to express himself." It was the first sign of the emergence of a new Wilson—no longer the confident "cheeky chappie" of the past, but a statesman of maturity and even of humility.

Old enemies said that Wilson's apparent humility was merely another mask. Even they might have changed their minds if they had seen him later that night at a private celebration party in Pimlico. All the old faithful were there: the men, and two women, who had stuck by Wilson during his dark days in the party. As the little band of politicians waited for Wilson to come from the TV and broadcasting studios, there was a note of hyperemotion in the small talk, a twang of hysteria in the laughter. When Wilson arrived at 10:30 P.M. and had shed the inevitable macintosh and had lit the inevitable pipe, his host, Ben Parkin, a Labour back-bencher, rose to speak and to propose the toast. Parkin spoke well and with feeling; but after a few minutes he seemed to have lost his audience. All eyes had turned to the other end of the room where Wilson sat. It was strange, out of character, almost incredible, but without doubt true: the ice-cold Puritan who now led the Labour Party had allowed himself the rare luxury of tears.

2. Band of Brothers

You go to an elementary school, you become an Oxford don
and are reasonably happy with people of every—what is called
—social class, provided they've got something to say.
I think, you know, the whole progress of education, as far as
it's gone, should be turning this country into a genuine
classless society.

HAROLD WILSON, *traveling down in the train from Liverpool to
become Prime Minister on October 16, 1964*

TWO immediate tasks faced Wilson once he had won the
party leadership. The first was to patch up quarrels within
the Labour Party. The second was to impress his face, views
and personality on the British people. Of these two tasks
party unity took priority.

On the night his defeat was announced Brown, too, had
attended a party, if necessarily a less cheerful one than that
given for Wilson. After the meeting at which the result of the
poll was announced the hard core of last-ditch Brownites had
left the House of Commons and made their way to a flat in
Pond Square, Highgate. It belonged to Maurice Hackett, an
employee of the Central Office of Information and a brother-
in-law of Brown's. Once during the actual contest Brown had
jovially announced he would install him in Downing Street
as press relations adviser once he became Prime Minister. But
no one, now, was in the mood to recall jokes like that. Instead
the five or six former Gaitskellite M.P.s discussed earnestly
what they could do to exert a moderating influence within a
Labour Party now led by Wilson.

In the middle of the discussion Brown suddenly announced that initially at least they would have to do without
him. He was going away for a holiday, and nothing his

44

friends said could shift him from his intention. Early the next morning—Friday, February 15—he left his home in Dulwich and, avoiding newspaper reporters, drove with his wife to London Airport, where a flight had been booked for them both under assumed names to Glasgow. Even this flight was the result of a last-minute change. The original one booked had been canceled when Brown discovered, to his horror, that Frank Cousins was also traveling on it. Brown wanted secrecy in which to lick his wounds. And for the next five days—to the mystification of colleagues, the press and all but a handful of close friends—he vanished.

For his hideout Brown had chosen a house belonging to friends on Lake Menteith in Perthshire; his whereabouts were known only to half a dozen people who did not even include the Opposition Chief Whip, Herbert Bowden. Before he went Brown had left with Bowden a long letter—written in anticipation of defeat before the final result was announced—in which he had tried to make his personal wishes clear. On the morning of Friday, February 15, Bowden showed this letter to Wilson, who, although he was relieved to discover that Brown was, after all, ready to continue as deputy leader, immediately dissented from Brown's other suggestion, that he should become "shadow" Foreign Secretary as well. "It wouldn't possibly do," he told Bowden. "Think of what the Tories would make of it." And Bowden agreed.

While Brown was away in Scotland, Wilson busied himself with mending fences and building bridges within the party. His first major decision—to offer the "shadow" Foreign Secretaryship (which he himself had held for the past two years) to Patrick Gordon Walker—was quite deliberately designed to reassure the Gaitskellites within the party. It succeeded triumphantly, not least because the left wing of the party made no effort to smother their yelp of pain.* By the week-

* A Labour front-bencher who approved the choice described Gordon Walker as "the best Selwyn Lloyd we've got."

end Wilson had decided his entire "shadow" Cabinet and was already confiding his new appointments (Denis Healey to Defense, Charles Pannell to Works and Dick Crossman to Science) to close friends. But he could not announce anything until Brown returned from hiding, if only because the knowledge that two of his former most ardent champions, Gordon Walker and Pannell, had deserted his cause and had accepted posts under Wilson might well have been enough to provoke Brown into resignation.

Brown's absence, increasingly played up by the newspapers, was becoming a severe political embarrassment for the new leader. On Tuesday, February 19, Wilson decided that he had no alternative but to try and put a stop to it. He spoke to Brown's secretary, told her how much he admired her loyalty in not revealing Brown's whereabouts but added that, for the good of the party, she must telephone Brown right away and ask him to ring back the same morning. Shortly before lunch Wilson got a call from Brown, who insisted that he was not taking part in any plot against him and agreed to continue as deputy leader subject to their having a long policy discussion when he got back.

At the time Brown undoubtedly hoped that this discussion would include the question of his own appointment as "shadow" Foreign Secretary. What had disturbed him more than anything else was the mounting rumor in the press that the job was to go instead to his own former faithful henchman, Patrick Gordon Walker. It was this which led him to ask Desmond Donnelly to find out what happened to the letter which he had left with the Chief Whip: why was everyone keeping so quiet about it since it explained the whole position? Unfortunately, Donnelly took this telephone call to mean that he was authorized to release the contents of the letter to the press, and he lost no time in giving the information to the *Evening Standard*. The result was disastrous. No new party leader could possibly have been expected to give way to such an "ultimatum," which inevitably was the way in which George Brown's letter was presented in next morning's newspapers.

Wilson, of course, had known from the beginning that he would have to resist Brown's expressed wish for the foreign affairs spokesman's role, and neither Brown's public absence nor Donnelly's private intervention made any difference to his decision. The effect of both, however, was to dismay and distress Brown's own friends and supporters within the party. "He's making even those who voted for him ashamed of what they did," said one leading Brownite.

By the morning of Wednesday, February 20, even Brown had got the point. When his close friend Lord Walston offered to fly up to Scotland and talk to him—Brown's friends feared that he might do something irredeemable like holding a press conference in Scotland denouncing Gordon Walker's appointment—Brown agreed instead to come back to London himself. He caught an after-lunch plane from Glasgow's Renfrew Airport and was photographed in flight by an enterprising photographer from the *Scottish Daily Express*, which shrewdly had kept a continuous watch on Renfrew Airport for the past few days. He had asked Lord Walston to meet him at London Airport, but Walston pleaded that he had that evening to attend a meeting of the Agricultural Committee of the National Executive. "They'll nationalize the land if I'm not there," he explained. So in his place Brown was met by the ever-faithful Donnelly, who had driven out to London Airport in a large limousine belonging to the David Brown Corporation, a large engineering firm of which Donnelly is public-relations adviser. In the chauffeur-driven car Brown was whisked straight to the House of Commons, but even so he arrived just as the first meeting of Wilson's "shadow" Cabinet was breaking up. That night Brown and Wilson spoke only briefly together, but they agreed to meet for a more serious negotiation the next day. Brown then drove home by himself, his Hillman Minx car (which Wilson, characteristically, had been alert enough to notice) having been parked that morning by one of his daughters in Palace Yard.

The following morning the successful and the defeated candidates for the party leadership had a two-hour talk together, and by the end of it the breach had been healed. Brown accepted that he could not have the "shadow" Foreign Secretary's job, agreed instead to become the Opposition's principal spokesman on home affairs and made no difficulties about continuing as deputy leader. That evening he appeared on BBC Television's "Gallery" program and confounded his critics by his calm. Was there not, he was asked, a real gulf between Wilson's views and his own? Brown did not waste time with hypocrisy. "It would be very stupid of me," he replied, "to pretend that Mr. Wilson and I have always looked the same way at issues, but I came out of my meeting with him this morning believing that we can make it together—and together we'll certainly make a better government than we have at the moment." What about his wanting to be "shadow" Foreign Secretary? Well, yes, he'd certainly wanted it—"but if I was in the driver's seat, I'd have had it my way. As he's in the driver's seat, he has it his—and maybe he's right too."

The capitulation was complete, and it meant that within a week of Wilson's winning the leadership all his former critics had rallied behind his banner: Brown, Gordon Walker, Callaghan, Pannel, even Strachey. There were a few, admittedly, on the extreme right of the party, like Desmond Donnelly and Woodrow Wyatt, who persisted in opposition to Wilson. But they were unimportant and unheard. At the same time the extreme left of the party applied to return to the fold. The five M.P.s, including Michael Foot, who had been deprived of the whip under Gaitskell's leadership asked for it back the day after Wilson took over. He heard the request coldly, even though at the beginning of his campaign he had promised a group of left-wing Labour M.P.s, including Stephen Swingler and Anthony Greenwood, that once elected he would try and facilitate the re-entry of the five. He let it be known that if the rebels were to get the whip back, they would have to make firm promises of future loyalty. It was a small but revealing sign that Wilson established in the leadership would be less inclined to the Left than Wilson as a candidate bidding for power.

From then on until the Labour Government, there was scarcely a breath of criticism of the new leader from within the Labour Party. There was not one carping article from the Right, nor one outburst of heckling from the Left. The Labour Party conference held in Scarborough that October was a positive love feast. The C.N.D. dissidents were reduced to a few clusters of gloomy individuals on the Ocean Parade. In the hall, where a desperate Gaitskell three years before had sworn to "fight and fight and fight again" (against part of his own party), the resolutions were passed with monolithic unity. The old, right-wing miners' union leader, Sam Watson, grumbled bitterly: "It's too soon after 1960. Do you remember then how the C.N.D. were parading in front of this hotel? Now look at them. They're all sitting inside. The King is dead. Long live the King."

But such muttered resentments were rare either from Left or Right. Both sides stifled their deepest feelings rather than give offense to Wilson. When the German Social Democrat leader, Willy Brandt, spoke at a Sunday rally, the left-wingers who once called him a "Nazi" managed some faint applause. The greatest gesture of peace from the Right came on Wednesday, with George Brown's speech. Toward the end he suddenly said of Wilson: "Though I had my doubts six months ago about the way we reached our leadership decision . . ." The rest of his words were drowned as the whole audience rose in a mighty ovation. Touched, or at least pleased, by this tribute. Harold Wilson stepped over and seized Brown by the hand. There were many damp eyes in the hall at this very emotional, very well-timed demonstration of loyalty. Never, perhaps, in its sixty years of life had the Labour Party been quite so united and confident. Much of the credit for Labour's optimism belonged to the hard work done by Wilson since February.

In the three months following his election as leader Wilson made thirty-two major weekend speeches, a trip to Washington and a multitude of broadcasts, including such off-beat appearances as a talk "About Religion." He took the offensive on every issue. When Macleod, soon after Wilson's election, brought out a pamphlet on nationalization, *Entitled to Know,* Wilson replied with a reiterated endorsement of Clause Four, the controversial article on public ownership. He opposed the Government over its handling of the Vassall spy case, Dr. Beeching's proposals for modernizing the railways, the new nuclear agreement and even such seemingly nonpartisan matters as the Radcliffe Report on security. He seemed to go out of his way to provoke his political opponents. On March 17, for example, he joined in a long, wet and cold rally in Trafalgar Square to denounce apartheid. After sitting through speeches by Barbara Castle, the Bishop of Southwark and others he made a firm pledge to stop the export of arms to South Africa and to outlaw racial discrimination at home. For good measure he denounced the newly revealed color bar at the Walsall Labour Club. This speech embarrassed some cautious front-bench colleagues and did not pass unnoticed in such places as Smethwick.

Later that month the then Lord Hailsham told a meeting of Young Conservatives: "There is no doubt that the untimely and tragic death of Hugh Gaitskell will change the whole ethos of the Labour Party. A new and far more destructive and irresponsible mood is abroad. Mr. Wilson could not stem it if he wished, and my impression is that so

far from wanting to stem it, his object will be to encourage it
and lead it." The Labour Party would have called Wilson
aggressive rather than irresponsible or destructive; the whole
country had come to agree on the new leader's fantastic verve.
By late spring he had become the most talked-of politician
in Britain.

The commentators, the cartoonists and the TV producers
all vied to explain and familiarize this apparently gray man
with his everlasting pipe and Gannex macintosh. This was
the normal treatment given to politicians. The unusual
feature was Wilson's willingness to endure the intrusive pub-
licizers. Ever since he applied for a job on the Manchester
Guardian after graduating from Oxford (he withdrew his
application on being offered a research job with Beveridge),
he had sought out the company of journalists, got to know
them by name and found them useful. When visiting Manchester in the early Fifties he would often ring up the
Guardian and ask if any reporter on duty would care to
come round to his hotel for a drink. He understands the profession of journalism far better than most of the people who
interview him, and he proved equally adept at TV. "You can
almost see his mind working," said an admiring BBC director
in 1963, "saying to himself 'head left to camera—smile—now
full face for zoom.' If it's a filmed shot you seldom need more
than one take." He soon became almost as friendly with all
the TV interviewers as with the journalists. Most British
political leaders have been friendly with certain editors,
newspaper proprietors and broadcasting controllers; Wilson
is almost the first to have been friendly, in the American
fashion, with ordinary rank-and-file journalists.

In return, the press and TV created an instant legend. So
eager was Wilson to co-operate with this myth-making that
he consented to spend a whole day, March 9, on behalf of
Granada TV paying a visit to the scenes of his youth in Huddersfield. It so happened that at this time a by-election cam-

paign was under way in the Colne Valley division just west of Huddersfield. It was the first by-election since Wilson got the leadership and he was none too sure of success in a seat with a strong Liberal tradition and a popular Liberal candidate. By tradition in British politics no party leader goes to speak at a by-election, but Wilson was glad of a good excuse to meet the party workers there. And he had just this excuse. The little village of Milnsbridge, now included in Huddersfield West, was part of the Colne Valley constituency when Wilson was born on March 15, 1916, at 4 Warneford Road.

To know Milnsbridge and the Colne Valley is to begin to know Wilson. There have been woolen and some cotton mills here since the start of the industrial revolution, but the industry remains scattered among many small towns and villages, each snuggling around one or two mills at the foot of the hillside. A sharp ten-minute climb takes you up onto moorland where soot-blackened sheep scamper about in the mist. Every street scene has a backdrop of grimy hills and dribbling mill chimneys, sometimes lit with extraordinary beauty, as when a huge orange moon rises up like a nuclear fireball. The brown Yorkshire stone never crumbles. The mills and even the looms inside them have hardly changed since Victorian times. If the locals do not actually talk of "trouble at t'mill" they often complain that mills are "playing" or idle in face of foreign competition.

For every mill there seem to be three pubs and four chapels: Elim, Salem, Bethesda, Zoar. The rigid nonconformity of the area explains why Colne Valley has never had a Conservative M.P. in its eighty years as a constituency, although socially it is not strongly working class. One of the first dozen Socialist M.P.s, Victor Grayson, won the seat at a by-election in 1907 that rocked the stock exchange. A roaring twenty-five-year-old, he believed in revolutionary socialism and the abolition of sexual ties. At one point in the campaign he sat on a lighted cigarette, burning a hole in his own trousers, after which he told hecklers: "It's not that I don't dare turn my back on you, it's just that I don't want to shock your Yorkshire Puritan susceptibilities by showing you too plainly what I think of you." This astonishing man lost his seat to the Liberals at the general election and disappeared without trace in 1920, but if he should ever return from the Outback or the Yukon, as some locals still fancy, he would find little change in the Colne Valley.

Nothing had changed much at Milnsbridge, Wilson's birthplace. He went to visit both the houses where he had lived as a child ("I see they've still got the London Pride"), revisited both his old schools and went to a match at Leeds Road football ground. For the benefit of the TV cameras Wilson pulled out the grubby *Chums* series photograph of the 1922 Huddersfield Town team that he has kept in his wallet over the years. Various old friends were eager to re-open the friendship. "We used to call him Willy Wilson," a Huddersfield stockbroker, Harry Cliffe, revealed. "He was always top of the class when I was bottom." "He was troop leader of Kangaroo Patrol," said Bert Parken, an engineering worker, "and he always used to provide that extra little bit of something, even when we were kids. When we were scouting and came up against some little difficulty, he used to be able to get round it." The return of the hero provoked some jealousy in the old Milnsbridgeans. "He didn't really know Harold well," they will mutter about one another.

Here in Milnsbridge, Wilson seems to merge into the crowd. It is not just that many old childhood friends smoke pipes and are called Harold. It is not just the atmosphere of the chapel, the scouts and Sunday school. Even the dourness and sardonic wit are typical of the district. They never smile when they tell a joke; and even when Huddersfield F.C. scores a goal, the crowd scarcely consents to cheer. That arch supporter, Harold Wilson, did not even bother to take his pipe out of his mouth in the moment of victory.

The Wilson family were lower-middle rather than working class. His father Herbert had come to Milnsbridge from Lancashire to work as a chemist with an explosives firm. A devout Manchester *Guardian* reader, he was in those days a Liberal and once campaigned for Winston Churchill at Oldham. Later he turned to the Labour Party, and this change of faith was confirmed by a long spell of unemployment in the early Thirties. In any case, social divisions are not as deep in Huddersfield as in the south of England. There are great contrasts of wealth, but employer and employee probably speak with much the same accent and share much the same culture. This is important to an understanding of Harold Wilson, who is often accused of class bitterness. In fact his dislike of Eton, London high society and the landed gentry is a regional characteristic. It would be shared by most of the true-blue members of Huddersfield Chamber of Commerce.

The following year there were critics within the Labour Party who blamed Harold Wilson for having fostered the cult of his own personality. Certainly by October 1964 the Labour Party itself had been slightly eclipsed by the personality of its leader. But to blame Wilson for seeking publicity early in 1963 is to use false hindsight. He believed then, as did most of the Labour Party, that Macmillan would hold the general election in October that year, 1963. Therefore Wilson had only seven months to build up a reputation and stature equal to that of Gaitskell, who had been leader of the Opposition for seven years. Certainly Wilson was right to expect an autumn election. By that time the Government might have dragged the economy out of its winter difficulties. The public is always more satisfied with the party in power after the holidays. And above all Wilson realized that an October election was necessary to Macmillan himself. The Conservative leader was unpopular with much of his own party, but even his bitterest critics would not be troublesome if an election was imminent. Therefore as long as Macmillan kept them guessing about the date, he could stop them bringing about his overthrow.

This had been Wilson's plan: a summer of big speeches and TV talks and newspaper interviews, followed by an election in mid-October followed by four or five years in power. But all his plans were swept away by the fantastic events, not in themselves political, which came to be known as the Profumo Affair. These events swept Wilson right off the front pages to make way for the curious, tragic, hilarious, evil, salacious and lunatic stories which for three months made Britain what she had not been since Victoria's days—the news center of the world. From the communal farms of the Ukraine to the near-beer drinking huts of the Congo, the names of Profumo, Keeler and Ward became famous. Visitors to Skopje, soon after the devastating earthquake in July, were pestered for information about "Miss Killer." The story inspired films, romances, a new hair style and a boom in osteopathy. The sad, bad story is the subject of many books and need not be retold in full. Two Indian authors, B. S. Verma and J. K. Vaish, in their book *True Love Story of Keeler* (Verman & Co. P.B. No. 51, Saharanpur, U.P., India), give a poignant if exotic account of that first fateful meeting between Profumo and Keeler by the swimming pool at Cliveden: "Profumo gazed at the lusty body of Keeler. Her body was reflected lush in her lustrine fine and thin suit. For a moment he was intoxicated when his thirsty eyes drank from the luscious lips of Miss Keeler. He could not balance himself but begged for leave." Shortly afterward Ward asks Keeler to put Profumo under her spell: " 'Your fangs are much effective. You have magnetic eyes, even stones are affected by them. Keeler, you have wonderful, dynamic personality.' " He introduces her also to Commander Ivanov, who promptly succumbed to her charm: " 'Darling, I am fortunate to find you. You are a wonderful girl. Should I expect your favor in future?' said the Commander under a light intoxication."

But when the tryst was kept, Ivanov "drank badly and be-came sentimental and passionate. He embraced Miss Keeler and drank some from her lips. Keeler had guessed all this all beforehand and she got pleasure out of him. She too kissed him and found him lying passively along herself. He seemed quite serious and exhausted. Perhaps either he was remem-bering his young Russian wife or was imagining the fearful face of Khrushchev." And so the romantic tragedy draws to a close in a prison cell where Ward "could not stand the cruelty of the world and his colleagues. He thanked all of them and once finally bowed before the portrait of Lord J. Christ and begged pardon. He took a bottle of some slow but dangerous poison in the trembling and shaking hands . . ." And so ended one of the few authentic folk stories of the twentieth century.

For the man whom Verma and Vaish called "Harold Wil-son, the opposite leader," the Profumo scandal was a mixed political blessing. He was probably one of the first people outside Keeler's circle to hear the story. On November 11, 1962, his friend and watchdog Colonel Wigg received an anonymous telephone call while he was visiting a constituent, Councillor Friend, in Stourbridge. The caller, who knew that Wigg had been busy investigating the security aspects of the Vassall case, said: "Forget about the Vassall case; you want to look at Profumo." Wigg paid no attention until, later that evening, it suddenly occurred to him: "How the hell did they get the number?" Only his wife knew that he was visit-ing Councillor Friend—unless he had been followed. And why Profumo?

On January 2, Wigg for the first time heard the nature of the rumors concerning Profumo. An old acquaintance and former Labour M.P., John Lewis, had met Christine Keeler, who was then in the news because of her part in the forth-coming trial of John Edgecombe, her former lover. She told Lewis about her relationships with Profumo and the Russian naval attaché, Ivanov. Worried about the security aspects of this story, Lewis told Wigg, who at the time was skeptical. Wilson was told the rumor by Wigg a day or two after his fight for the leadership of the party. On March 10 he discussed it again in a private talk with Wigg, whose dossier on the affair was thick and, as it proved, accurate. Although Wilson advised him against raising the rumor during the coming debate on the army estimates, he gave the impression that Wigg should feel free to do what he thought wise. On March 21, three Labour M.P.s—Wigg, Barbara Castle and Richard Crossman—all asked questions about the affair while the House was debating the case of the two journalists who had been jailed for refusing to name their sources at the Vassall tribunal.

Later that night Profumo was interviewed by William Deedes, the Minister without Portfolio; the two Law Officers, Sir John Hobson and Sir Peter Rawlinson; the Leader of the House, Iain Macleod; and the Chief Whip himself, Martin Redmayne. As a result of this meeting Profumo issued his famous statement next day denying any impropriety with Keeler. Apart from Profumo himself and the *Guardian* ("It would be grossly unjust not to accept his words at face value —they ought to end the talk"), few politicians or journalists believed he had got away with it. There was good evidence that he had lied and most people believed that this would be revealed, most probably by Keeler. As it happened, Stephen Ward was the man who blew the gaff. The police were investigating his private life and he wanted to ingratiate himself with the authorities by telling all he knew of Ivanov. On March 26 he went to see Wigg at the House of Commons. He revealed how he and Ivanov had tried, during the Cuba crisis, to arrange mediation between the United States and Russia. He told Wigg of how he had personally written to Wilson. The letter was, indeed, in Wilson's file. Armed with this letter and full report of Wigg's talk with Ward, Wilson went to see Macmillan. The Prime Minister affected not to be anxious, although later he agreed to an inquiry by "the appropriate authorities."

From the end of March onward, the facts of the Profumo scandal had become so widely known that their truth was believed by almost everybody but the Prime Minister. The rumor grew not only day by day but hour by hour in verbal additions. On May 7, Ward took a decision which made Profumo's exposure inevitable. He went to Admiralty House, where Macmillan was living while 10 Downing Street was under repair, and spoke to Timothy Bligh, the Prime Minister's Principal Private Secretary. He claimed that Profumo had been lying about his relationship with Keeler. As the police investigations grew ever more prying, Ward grew ever more frightened. Perhaps hoping to blackmail the Government into laying off the police, he repeated his charge against Profumo both to the newspapers and to the Home Office.

On June 1, while spending a Whitsun holiday in Venice, Profumo realized that the game was up. He confessed to his wife, returned to England and gave in his resignation. The news broke on Wednesday, June 5. The miserable Profumos vanished into obscurity to the accompaniment of a chorus of sanctimonious and hypocritical abuse. Perhaps the most disgraceful aspect of the whole scandal was the way that Profumo's former political friends deserted him in his mental agony. One should record the few honorable exceptions: John Hare (now Lord Blakenham), Iain Macleod (although he had never really been much of a friend) and Randolph Churchill.

During the uproar of the next week, it seemed to many politicians that the Government would be brought down. But the man who stood to succeed to office spent most of the next ten days on a visit to Russia.

Wilson returned from talks in the United States and Canada on June 6 and left for a week in Russia on Saturday, June 8. This was in reply to an invitation accepted by Gaitskell the previous year. The Wilson party changed planes at Copenhagen, and it was here that he first disclosed his private views on the Profumo affair. He made clear his attitude that the Labour Party was interested only in the security aspect of the Profumo affair. A reporter queried this. "Surely," he asked, "you didn't really believe that the Russians would have used Keeler and Ward to extract information from Profumo? Didn't this kind of under-the-bed spying go out with the Victorians, when the spy asked at what time the Lancers were leaving the fort?" To which Wilson replied: "But the Russians *are* nineteenth century. You wait and see when we get there." However, he said, and was proved right, that "Ward isn't the sort of man that the Russians would use as an agent. He's too unstable. But he was definitely used as a tool. Of that there is no doubt whatsoever."

At this stage Wilson was deeply suspicious of Macmillan's role in the Profumo affair. He had seen the Premier talking to Profumo behind the Speaker's chair in the Commons Chamber on the last day before the Whitsun recess. He assumed that they were discussing the Keeler affair. Wilson did not believe that the Profumo affair would bring down the Government, at least not for some months. He did think that Macmillan might be forced to resign, in which case "churchwarden Butler would serve as caretaker."

During their stay in Moscow, Wilson and Gordon Walker occupied the two suites in the National Hotel, which had been Lenin's headquarters in 1918. But for much of the time they must have felt that the real revolution was going on at home without them. The Transport House press officer telephoned three or four times a day with the latest news. Late on Monday evening, while Wilson was drinking solemn toasts with some Soviet officials, an aide came up to tell him that a visitor had arrived with yesterday's English newspapers. For the last few toasts Wilson's face was a mask of impatient misery. When the meeting at last broke up he hurried up to

the visitor, grabbed the bundle of newspapers with a muttered "thank you" and sped to his room 115 like a Rugby
wing three-quarter who has just taken a pass near the enemy
touchline. There was something almost grotesque about this
nineteenth-century room, with ormolu mirror, grand piano,
sculptured nude and nymphs on the ceilings and a view on
to the walls and domes of the Kremlin. Here almost every
evening Wilson, Gordon Walker, their four aides and a
dozen British journalists gathered for eager conference or
chat. And invariably, after a short review of the day's talks
with the Soviet leaders, the conversation, so far from home,
would turn to the latest antics of Ward, Keeler, Profumo,
Ivanov, Macmillan and Hailsham.

Yet in retrospect it was the serious side of the Russian visit
that had more bearing on Wilson's general election campaign, because Britain's relationship with the U.S.S.R. was
to become an electoral issue. Both party leaders claimed to
be better suited to deal with Mr. K., and the Conservatives
were repeatedly to allege that Wilson was weak in his attitude
to the Russians. In fact the tour showed him thoroughly skillful at foreign affairs.

In many ways he knew Russia much better than any other
politician. This was his eleventh visit to the country. Even
in the prewar days of Spain and the Popular Front, Wilson
was never attracted to Communism, but he has always been
interested in Russian prerevolutionary history. The devious
machinations of Tsarism find an echo in Wilson's own personality; he is openly fascinated by Rasputin, who figures in
many speeches. As president of the Board of Trade in the
Labour Government and, later, as the representative of a
timber firm, he had come to know much about modern
Russia. His trade talks with Mikoyan in the Forties are something he never tires of recalling. The two men would argue
up to seventeen hours at a stretch. During one dispute, Wilson had his plane started up to show he was prepared to

break off talks if he did not get satisfaction. For relaxation in Russia he saw *Swan Lake* sixteen times and once got up a cricket team by the Volga where he became "the only bowler ever to have been dropped at square leg by a member of the NKVD." The game was denounced in the Stalinist press as "lakeside orgies and pirouettes."

By the second day of his visit Wilson had impressed resident British journalists by his knowledge of Soviet ways and personalities. Even then he knew who were the coming men —such as Brezhnev, Kosygin and Polyanski—and he knew a great deal about them too. He posed with Marshal Malinovsky after a chance encounter at the ballet. "You notice I didn't smile," said Wilson to a TV producer afterward. He was well aware whom not to be seen smiling with.

Wilson's first meeting with Khrushchev on this visit came on Monday. They had met on several occasions before, including the famous Labour Party dinner to Khrushchev and Bulganin during their tour of Britain in 1956, when, after a stand-up row with George Brown, Mr. K. had declared his preference for the Conservative Party. And in fact there was a minor row in the Kremlin this Monday. At the press conference afterward, Wilson said that the Soviet view and ours about Berlin were quite different, although the difference had been amicably expressed. But Gordon Walker on Thursday said that Khrushchev had "been very angry although I don't know how much of this was real. Maybe he expected a Labour Government to be weaker on this subject." Next month Wilson recalled this first meeting with Khrushchev: "At one point he was banging the table and accusing me of wanting war." But he and Khrushchev agreed about the possibilities of a ban on all except underground tests. Indeed by the time the tripartite test-ban agreement had been initialed in late July, Wilson was to say: "If any credit goes to Britain for this it is to our delegation in June. We suggested the idea of a ban except for underground tests and Khrushchev wasn't

briefed for that." Whoever deserved the credit, Macmillan
and Home were to claim it.

On Wednesday, Wilson went up to Leningrad for the day
and returned on the night sleeper. Until 2:30 A.M. he was
taking part in a filmed TV talk in the compartment. Up at
six, he went onto a series of meetings with trade officials, yet
still found energy for a bravura display at a lunch given for
him by Soviet journalists. It was the first lunch of this kind
for a Western politician. The questions and answers were off
the record to newspapers, but many of the host journalists
were astonished by what they heard. In answering a loaded
question about the American alliance, Wilson replied
through his interpreter: "We are allies of the Americans and
we are loyal to our allies although sometimes it is necessary to
be frank about our disagreements, just as you have to be frank
about your disagreements with"—and here he stopped for the
interpreter—"the Albanians." Even the dimmest of the two
hundred Russians there must have taken this reference to
mean the Chinese. About half frowned; the other half
laughed. All looked around desperately to see which reaction
was expected. One party hack was so needled by Wilson's
joke that he asked a pointed question about the United
Nations. Whereupon Wilson launched into a denunciation of
those nations—and he made it clear that he referred to the
U.S.S.R.—that did not pay their UN subscriptions. Several
of the audience tried to interrupt but were shouted down.
The great majority of the audience gave Wilson an exceed-
ingly warm hand at the end. A Reuters journalist, who had
spent some years in Moscow, said: "It must have been a
fantastic shock for seventy per cent of the people here to hear
a Western mind at work. After listening to Wilson, I intend
to vote for him."

On Friday, June 14, Wilson had a second and much more
friendly talk with Khrushchev. This was the day that the
U.S.S.R. sent up astronaut Bykovski, shortly to be joined

in space by Valentina Tereshkova. Solemn newscasts, the bleep-bleep of space messages, and the first few bars of the "Internationale" crackled from scores of loudspeakers hung in the Moscow treetops. It was Wilson's good fortune that he had just arrived to meet Khrushchev when the news of the space shot was ready to be announced to the world. "Correspondents come back," said Mr. K to the Western photographers, and had them take his picture with Wilson, waiting for further news of the space shot. Thus Wilson became identified with the one newspaper and TV story which was capable, that weekend, of pushing the Keeler affair into second place.

The Labour Party was lucky in that Monday June 17—the day Parliament reassembled after the Whitsun recess—was a Supply Day; it could therefore choose the subject for debate. There was only one subject it wished to raise: security, or, in other words, the Profumo affair. When Wilson arrived back from Russia and Poland on June 15 he settled down to a weekend of preparation for the attack. He read and reread the dossier built up by Wigg and others and prepared a long, cold but deadly indictment of Harold Macmillan. He had always been anxious to keep clear of the moral aspects of the scandal and to concentrate on the security risks. When the speech was prepared and the House assembled on Monday, Wilson remarked with grim satisfaction to a colleague: "We've got him on toast."

3. The Lost Leader

. . . let him never come back to us!
There would be doubt, hesitation and pain.
Forced praise on our part—the glimmer of twilight,
Never glad confident morning again!

    NIGEL BIRCH, M.P., *quoting Browning, at the end of a savage
attack on Harold Macmillan during the Profumo debate on
June 17, 1963*

THE Profumo affair dealt a fatal blow to Harold Macmillan's political reputation and career. In the eyes of many Conservative M.P.s, perhaps even a majority, he was guilty not of negligence but of slackness. His administration seemed to have grown tired. It was accident-prone. Few people blamed him for having believed Profumo's lie to the House about his relationship with Keeler. But why, they asked, had an amiable but essentially frivolous man like Profumo been given the job of War Minister in the first place? Why had Macmillan never been told that the Cabinet Secretary in 1961 had warned Profumo against Ward? Why had it never been made clear which Minister had responsibility for security? And why, above all, had Macmillan not immediately ordered a special inquiry in May when rumors were rife all over London and Harold Wilson had passed on his dossier of the affair?

Some of these questions were unfair. In his attitude to the rumor about Profumo, Macmillan was heavily influenced by the aftermath of the Vassall affair. Here most of the press innuendoes had proved to be unfounded. In particular the stories that had gone the rounds about a junior Minister, Thomas Galbraith, whose resignation Macmillan had over-hastily accepted (and, some people believed, actually demanded), had been shown not to have a shred of substance to them. It was at least understandable that Macmillan should have been determined not to make the same mistake again, even to the point of bending over backward to avoid committing a second act of injustice to a Government colleague. There was also another—and even more personal—excuse for Macmillan's apparent lethargy. For all his cavalier charm he had always been unusually puritanical by the standards of the age and indeed of his own younger colleagues. Long before the Profumo episode broke his hatred of any discussion about sex had been a standing joke among those who worked with him. For him to have had to interrogate Profumo about his private life would have been an experience almost too distasteful to be endured. Yet inevitably critics fastened upon this failure to take the course which any prudent employer in any other walk of life would almost certainly have faced. Had he, with all the authority of a Prime Minister, actually interviewed Profumo there would always have been the chance that he would have shamed him into speaking the truth. As it was, his decision to leave the task to his Chief Whip left him wide open to the charge of professional slothfulness, even though he was really guilty of no more than personal reticence.

This same old-fashioned feeling for propriety largely explains Macmillan's subsequent decision—made within three days of the Profumo debate—to agree to the Labour Party's demand and set up a full-scale inquiry into (among other things) "rumors affecting the honor and integrity of public life." "The Denning Inquiry was one of the very few things I had a row with Macmillan about," Iain Macleod was later to recall. "I was against it from the beginning and believed we ought not to give an inch to all the filthmongers. But I can remember now going to see him on the Thursday before he announced it. He was in a terrible state, going on about a rumor of there having been eight High Court judges involved in some orgy. 'One,' he said, 'perhaps two, conceivably. But eight—I just can't believe it.' I said if you don't believe it, why bother with an inquiry? But he replied 'No. Terrible things are being said. It must be cleared up.' "

For a fortnight after the Profumo debate Macmillan's hold on office hung in the balance. "My spirit is not broken, but my zest is gone," he had told a friend on Monday, June 17— and his subsequent public appearances seemed to prove it. At a garden party held in his own constituency of Bromley on Saturday, June 22, he moved like a sleepwalker around the coconut shies, the raffles and the lucky dips. As he posed for a photograph with the tiny daughter of a constituent, one of a group of young hecklers hissed into his ear: "Take your hands off that little girl. Don't you wish it was Christine Keeler?" No flicker of anger or even of comprehension crossed his face.

When he appeared the following Wednesday in all the robes and dignity of a University Chancellor at a Gaudy (reunion dinner) held at Christ Church, Oxford, he seemed unable to take anything in. As his car drew up in Oxford's largest quadrangle he made no effort at all to acknowledge the crowd of people who had come to greet him. Instead he shuffled forward like a man of ninety, gazing unseeing into the middle distance; during dinner he frequently closed his eyes—once or twice appearing to nod off—and throughout the after-dinner speeches he sat impassive as a waxwork, not even registering the slightest reaction when his own Minister of Education (Sir Edward Boyle) paid a warm and generous tribute to his lifelong encouragement of young men.

But if Macmillan at first had all the energy and fight drained from him, the same was certainly not true of his supporters. These included, improbably, Harold Wilson himself, who took the opportunity that week to lecture the Conservative Party in Parliament about its behavior. "At this moment of time," he declared at Walthamstow, referring to the coming visit of President Kennedy that weekend, "we read of the 1922 Committee engaging like a group of aboriginal savages in a frenzied ritual dance with only one end in view—to obtain the Prime Minister's head as a sacrificial offering to expiate the collective anxieties of the Conservative Party." This was to be a favorite Wilson theme throughout the summer—and very few Conservatives ever suspected his motive. The bulk of the party felt they were not going to have their own Prime Minister patronized by the Leader of the Opposition; they would reward him for his uncalled-for interference by keeping Macmillan in office. It occurred to virtually no one that this was exactly what Wilson wanted and that the whole purpose behind this type of speech was to make it as difficult as possible for the Tories to dislodge Macmillan and substitute an alternative (and possibly more dangerous) national candidate for the election.

In private Wilson never bothered to conceal how much he wanted Macmillan as his electoral opponent. It was not that he had no respect for him—in the week of the Profumo debate he was to describe him in a newspaper interview as "the cleverest politician of our age"—but he rightly saw him as a Sugar Ray Robinson of politics—a champion well past his prime providing a sitting target for a younger challenger with quicker footwork, faster reactions and nimbler ring craft. Yet if Wilson's clear preference was for Macmillan continuing in office, he was also skeptical of the claims of the various other candidates. Whenever Butler's name was mentioned he would produce his joke about "the churchwarden turned caretaker," adding "Poor Rab, he's got the worst liability you can have in politics, the look of a born loser." Nor was he much impressed by Maudling. "If he does get it, I'll tell you one thing, he won't last long as Leader of the Opposition: he's not nasty enough for them." Heath he'd never thought much of: "After all, what's he got behind him, just the Common Market failure"; while Hailsham he dismissed with the simple, savage comment: "Quintin? We'd murder him." Only one possible candidate frightened him. Like Hugh Gaitskell before him, Wilson never wavered in his belief that Iain Macleod was easily the Tories' best electoral bet as their next leader.

He had, however, little need to worry about him. The Profumo affair had dished both the former favorites for the succession. The bachelor, Edward Heath, was heavily if irrationally dropped by his supporters, while the unlucky Macleod paid the price for having been one of the five Ministers who had helped Profumo draft his personal statement in March denying any impropriety with Keeler. The decline of these two contributed to the revived prospects of R. A. Butler. A friend of Butler's had remarked early in 1963 that "Rab can only be Prime Minister if Harold is knocked over by a bus." The Profumo affair was almost that bus. Disappointed in his confident hope of the Premiership in 1957, Butler now looked like getting revenge for his rejection six years earlier.

His claim on the office was powerful. To R. A. Butler (even his wife calls him Rab) belongs most of the credit for having transformed a prewar Conservative Party of landowners, laissez-faire capitalists and retired army officers into a modern, technocratic, middle-class liberal party. After the electoral disaster of 1945 he and Lord Woolton took over the party organization and brought its ideas more or less into line with postwar British realities. Thanks to Butler's teachings, the new Conservatives forgot their dogmatic beliefs in the free market at home and imperialism abroad. They accepted the need for welfare legislation and even came to terms with a mixed economy. As a result Butler was stuck with two labels that made him unpopular with much of the Tory Party: he was a "pinko" and an intellectual. In White's or Buck's or the Beefsteak Club the second of those is probably the more opprobrious insult.

With his mind restlessly attached to contrivance, compromise and innovation, Butler had served his party and Britain well in a variety of top government jobs. During the spring and summer of 1963, when the country was torn apart by the Profumo affair, he toiled diligently—and with almost miraculous success—to reconcile the opposing factions in central Africa. His talents for diplomacy were useful, too, in the domestic methods of party politics. He is the master of the ambiguous promise, the meaningless communiqué, the quick lick of soft soap. In the House of Commons he would frequently interrupt one of his own debating speeches—just at the point where the Opposition was beginning to get angrily restive—with entirely irrelevant references to old-age pensioners and disabled war veterans so that the enemy were obliged to relapse into sympathetic nods of agreement.

Yet Butler's worst enemies have always been within his own party. The Churchills, the Macmillans and the Cecils, the powerful blue-blooded clans, think him "wet." His public school, Marlborough, was too bourgeois and "churchy." He does not much enjoy shooting or racing, though he occasionally—out of a sense of what is expected of a Tory leader —allows himself ludicrously to be photographed at both. To the landed gentry and the retired military, whose influence still survives in the upper reaches of the Conservative Party, Butler is quite simply a prissy liberal. Typically it is still held against him that he supported the Munich pact; yet the same charge is not made by Tories against Hogg or Home, who were equally identifiable Municheers. What with them would, at worst, be considered an error of judgment is with Rab taken as yet one further infallible indication of "wetness."

Despite all these liabilities it was generally recognized throughout the late summer of 1963 that if Macmillan left suddenly in a time of crisis the Queen would be almost bound to send for Butler. He was the only respected sheet-anchor in the Conservative fleet. He enjoyed majority support in the Cabinet. And, perhaps most important of all, he had a fund of good will behind him from the middle and professional classes, whom the Conservatives could affront only at the cost of imperiling their electoral chances. To block Butler it was essential for Macmillan to delay the moment of his departure in order to build up another candidate.

At first it looked as if Macmillan would not be able to choose that candidate—that his successor would, in effect, be foisted upon him by his own enemies within the Parliamentary Party. Almost immediately after the Profumo debate of June 17 Reggie Maudling began to emerge—at least in newspaper terms—as the main threat to Macmillan's continuance in power. In a way it was a surprise choice. Maudling—the British Erhard, as someone once unkindly described him—had always given the impression of looking out on the world with a relaxed, languid grin; even at important conferences his habit of sitting slumped in a chair and the permanent blue shadow across his heavy chin often combined to suggest that instead of sitting up all night working on government briefs he had just wandered in from watching a floor show in a night club. He looks lazy and, therefore, quite unfairly, has often been accused of being lazy.

It was not until Macmillan appointed him Chancellor of the Exchequer at the early age of forty-five in July 1962 that anyone really woke up to just how swift and assured his rise in politics had been. Not quite upper class by Conservative standards—he had gone to Merchant Taylors' School before winning a First in Greats at Merton College, Oxford—he became the first of the postwar, new-wave Conservatives to occupy one of two great traditional offices of state. But even after his well-received first Budget of April 1963, doubts persisted about his political dedication. Even these, however, deserved to disappear in the light of a conversation that Maudling held with a Cabinet colleague that first week after the Profumo debate. Asked to come around to an informal gathering of Ministers to discuss Macmillan's future, he refused point-blank. "No," he said, "I don't think I could possibly do that —after all I am a candidate for the succession."

At first Maudling owed his position as a candidate far more to the efforts of other people than to his own standing and reputation within the party. The promoters of his cause were a group of back-bench Tory M.P.s marshaled and organized by the aristocratic but turbulent young right-winger, Lord Lambton, an opponent of Harold Macmillan's ever since the withdrawal from Suez. With his dark good looks, dark glasses and dark hair curled around the edges, Lord Lambton the heir to the Earldom of Durham and therefore immune from the normal chip-on-the-shoulder Tory attack) had all the air of the conspirator of romantic political fiction as he moved around the lobbies pressing Maudling's claims on his colleagues.

But his efforts none the less were highly practical. On June 18 and 19 Lambton—and the rest of the Maudling campaign staff, including safely middle-class, middle-of-the-road M.P.s like John Hall and William Clark—conducted the first of a series of polls on Tory back-bench opinion. The results of these polls consistently and probably accurately showed a clear majority of feeling for Maudling as the man most favored to take over the party. The figures were shrewdly made available to the *Daily Telegraph,* which, being now anti-Macmillan, was only too glad to publish them without at any time disclosing the source. The weekly publication of these polls right through to the adjournment of Parliament at the end of July certainly helped to consolidate a growing opinion that Maudling, rather than Butler, was the natural choice as successor. The first poll set the pattern of the rest to come. Out of 50 Conservative M.P.s asked who should be the next Prime Minister, 21½ (the half indicates a split preference) said Maudling, 8 Hailsham, 6½ Heath,

4 Butler, 3 Enoch Powel, 1 Iain Macleod and 1 Lord Home.

The identity of the one man who spotted the winner perhaps deserves recording. If there were any medals for prescience in politics, one should surely have been pinned on that June day on Sir Otho Prior-Palmer, the back-bench Brigadier who for nineteen years represented the safe Tory seat of Worthing in the House of Commons.

After Maudling had lost the fight for the succession he said ruefully, "No politician can be held responsible for his supporters"—and in spite of the urgent efforts to give it respectability his campaign gathered most support from right-wing extremists and notorious fractious dissidents. This was not really surprising; the main aim of those who came out into the open at this stage was not so much to get Maudling in as to get Macmillan out. It is often said that Maudling threw away the Tory leadership by not taking stronger action at a time when Macmillan's overthrow could almost certainly have been procured. But, in reality, his fundamental mistake was a different one. By assenting to, though not encouraging, the activities of his curious supporters he turned himself into the front runner much too early on. From the end of June onward he could not go forward; he could only go back.

One man who spotted this was a now revived Harold Macmillan. Protected by his friends, like the two Tory joint chairmen, Lord Poole and Iain Macleod, through the original dangerous days of shock, the Prime Minister had by the beginning of July rallied sufficiently to start making plans for the future. At no time did these plans include his being succeeded as Premier by Reggie Maudling; but if the worse came to the worst they did involve a readiness to hand on the torch to someone else. Right through to the time he was forced to resign by what he was later to call "an Act of God," Macmillan's secret design—recognized by his friends if not admitted to himself—was to stay in power if he could; but if it proved impossible for him to go on being king, he was determined at least to be a king-maker.

Accordingly, as early as the middle of July he first planted in Hailsham's mind the idea that he should begin to think in terms of succeeding him in the Premiership. Macmillan's cue for doing this was a crucial Cabinet decision taken in the second half of July. The Peerage Bill—the product of Anthony Wedgwood Benn's two-and-a-half-year fight as a Reluctant Peer—had passed through the House of Commons early in the summer. But while the Government majority in the Commons had voted down an Opposition amendment urging that the principal provision of the bill—allowing a peer to renounce his title—should take effect not on the date of dissolution but as soon as the Royal Assent was given, a coalition in the Lords between Labour peers and dissident Conservative ex-Ministers had carried it. The result was an embarrassing Cabinet meeting. Superficially it was a question of tactics: to stick to original Government policy and put up with a tiresome delay in their legislative program, or to accept the Lords' amendment and endure the indignity of having seemed to evacuate a position taken up from the Treasury bench in the Commons.

But no one in the Cabinet Room that July morning was under any illusion what the decision also involved in terms of the succession. If the Lords' amendment was accepted and peers were enabled to renounce their titles before the general election, then Hailsham—or, for that matter (as someone casually remarked), Home too—could immediately become an active candidate in any pre-election leadership contest; if the amendment were resisted they would both in effect be ruled out. Understandably the argument swung back and forth, but, partly because the other possible contenders felt inhibited from getting involved and partly because Macmillan had already made up his mind which answer he

wanted, it went—as a Maudling supporter later ruefully put
it—"the wrong way." The Cabinet decided not to fight the
Lords' amendment, and, though no one realized it at the
time, the scene had been successfully set for both the first
and second acts of the leadership drama to come. Three
months later, when that drama had been played out, Wedgwood Benn on October 24, 1963, became the first ex-peer
to enter the House of Commons. He was given a great all-
party ovation, but one man on the Government front bench
found himself unable to join in. He was Reggie Maudling,
who correctly recognized in the youthful, slight figure of the
newly elected Labour member for Bristol Southeast the man
who bore the prime responsibility for robbing him of the
Tory leadership.

At first it seemed as if neither Maudling nor Butler had
much to fear from the Cabinet's reversal of its previous decision. The effect on Hailsham of Macmillan's encouragement of his candidature was to put an end to any slight
chance he had ever had of getting the leadership in an orthodox way. Always excitable, he now became exuberant; never
anything but talkative, he now became compulsively gar-
rulous. By the middle of September Lord Poole—throughout
this period Macmillan's closest confidant—felt he had to report to Macmillan that there was no longer a hope of getting
Hailsham as his successor: the majority of the Cabinet, he had
to explain, simply would not wear him. Far from being disappointed by this news, Macmillan seemed almost encouraged
by it; if the party would not accept Hailsham—the only figure
among his colleagues in whom he detected his own combina-
tion of a Tory democrat's political flair with romantic *pan-
ache*—then might not the best chance of an electoral victory
be found in his staying in office after all? For the moment the
matter was left open, but those who saw Macmillan at the
time had very little doubt of the direction in which his mind
was moving.

All Macmillan's plans were continually thrown out of gear by the aftermath of the Profumo affair. The trial, conviction and suicide of Dr. Ward at the end of July caused new disgust with the Government. It seemed to the public at the time, and to commentators afterward, that Ward had been made a whipping boy to distract attention from more important and influential sinners. Several of the police witnesses switched sides during the course of the trial; there was no real evidence that Ward was a pimp except in the most rigid sense of the word; the Judge's summing-up came in for much criticism.

As summer dragged on into autumn, Macmillan would have liked to put the Profumo affair behind him. But it was bound to crop up again, thanks to Macmillan's own mistake. By setting up an inquiry under Lord Denning, he had guaranteed a new burst of publicity and scandal even if, as happened, he was exonerated. To make matters worse, Denning himself attracted publicity. To pose for a press photographers' session was all right. But unfortunately their pictures, when blown up, showed that the letter on his desk was a request to an important Cabinet Minister to discuss a rumor about his private life. The reporters who kept watch outside the Denning inquiry offices were astonished by the range and variety of the witnesses that he interviewed. Many of them talked to the press about what they were asked and how they answered. The pert Mandy Rice-Davies described Denning as "awfully sweet—quite the nicest judge I've ever met or hope to meet." Another female witness at the Ward case explained afterward why she had not told Denning the names of her clients: "I never would. It is a matter of honor that you don't name your clients. My business depends on trust. It takes a long time to build up a clientele of my standing." After explaining to Denning that she did not have intercourse but indulged in practices such as whipping, she was asked why clients went in for these practices. "I told him I supposed it went back to their nannies. Bus drivers and people like that who don't have nannies don't ask you to whip them."

Each day's newspapers brought more titillation. The Duke of Argyll's divorce case was dragged into Denning's inquiry, and the listeners in the public gallery in Edinburgh's Courts of Session learned that a Cabinet Minister had agreed to an examination of both his feet in order to prove he was not the "headless man" in one of the Duchess's photographs. To the nation's moralists, such as the editor of *The Times,* the Government seemed corrupt. To the ordinary citizen it was now just ludicrous.

As Macmillan had hoped, the Denning inquiries cleared all his Ministers of the rumors in circulation. He firmly believed that this would prove the most publicized aspect of the report and he therefore hoped it would be given maximum space in the newspapers. He arranged that the document should be published at midnight on September 25–26 and he doubtless anticipated the long queues outside the Stationery Office bookshop in Kingsway. It might have gone according to plan but for a most unfortunate leak. On September 19, a whole week before publication, the *Daily Mail* had a sensational headline—"MINISTERS CLEARED"—and then: "but the security aspect of the Profumo affair is a far different matter." Conservative back-benchers were delighted with the news, but Wilson at least saw that it damaged the Government. He had already been shown the report at Admiralty House, and he admitted, on September 25: "I was worried. It was partly the point about *comprendre et pardonner,* and it was partly a fear that the press would concentrate on 'no scandal.' But as soon as I saw the *Daily Mail* last Thursday I knew we were all right. Of course I had a bloody great row with the Prime Minister about it, but no one was happier that the leak had occurred than I was. It meant that when the report finally came out, the newspapers would have to concentrate on the political aspect, which is what I wanted them to do." In his actual meeting with Macmillan, Wilson had said: "Prime Minister, this is a very serious matter. It's a clear leak and it must come from your side—and what's more from somebody who is no friend of yours. I demand instant publication." When Macmillan hesitated, Wilson went on: "You may not be a politician but you're a publisher and you know it can be done. Look at Hansard and *its* printing."

The newspaper headlines on the day of the publication of the report were just as damning to the Prime Minister as Wilson had anticipated. "It's Dynamite," said the *Daily Express*. "Premier Failed," "Mac Blamed," said the *Daily Telegraph* and *Daily Sketch*. The report which in fact cleared his Government's reputation was made to sound like a personal indictment. To this day it is not certain who leaked the Denning Report. Whoever was the culprit, the victim was Harold Macmillan.

During the autumn of 1963 Harold Wilson naturally appeared to the nation and to the Conservatives to be plotting the downfall of Harold Macmillan. In fact he was doing everything possible to keep him in power. He wanted to see him discredited, not deposed. When the Labour Party met for its annual conference on the weekend after the Denning Report, Wilson's very first speech was designed to guard Macmillan from his enemies in the Conservative Party. The Labour Party was united and confident, he told a rally on Sunday night, while across the floor of the House they had a party disunited, demoralized, leaderless, unable to agree on who their leader should be or even on the procedure of selection. The strategy of the Tory High Command was clear: they were seeking a sacrifice, a scapegoat on whom all their ills could be blamed, and for the role they had selected the very man in whose shadow they had climbed to power. If they succeeded, Wilson prophesied, there would follow "a massive campaign of de-Stalinization which will make the activities of Mr. Khrushchev at the Twentieth Congress look like the efforts of a well-intentioned amateur. What they did to Baldwin, to Chamberlain and to Eden is nothing to what they have in store for the latest in the series of those who are deemed to have outlived their usefulness." The true purpose of this speech, to stop the Tories changing their leader, was probably understood by only two men in Britain, the only two men of outstanding political cleverness: Harold Wilson and Harold Macmillan himself.

4. The Queen's Commission

It's a great thing, you know, to get the Queen's Commission.
Yes, that's what counts—the Queen's Commission.
   HAROLD MACMILLAN, *Daily Mail*, January 5, 1959

FOR months it had been said—if with increasing despair by
Macmillan's Tory enemies—that the party conference would
prove decisive. And in the end it was, though not quite in
the way that anyone had foreseen. When the special 1:35 P.M.
Tory conference train drew out of Euston on Tuesday, October 8, the half-dozen Cabinet Ministers on board had, it was
noticed, cut things rather fine. Most of them had arrived
with as little as five minutes to spare; but what the lesser
passengers on the train did not know was that since 10 A.M.
that morning the Cabinet had been closeted in its most crucial
meeting since the Profumo crisis.

Having waited till the very last moment, Harold Macmillan had decided to confront his colleagues with the issue
of the leadership. (The previous night both Lord Home and
Lord Poole—against the advice of Macmillan's own family
—had plainly told him that it was his duty to retire.) He
faced the challenge with his usual dexterity and aplomb. Had
anyone, he asked, got anything he wanted to say about
whether or not he should fight the next election? The hush
perhaps betrayed embarrassment rather than enthusiasm, but
at least the Prime Minister was provided with his cue for
saying, "There has got to be a decision and I must announce
it at Blackpool." No one (even after Macmillan withdrew,
which he immediately tactfully did) seems to have inquired
what exactly this was supposed to mean, but it was generally
assumed that the Prime Minister had signified his intention
of carrying on.

79

The expressions on the faces of the various Cabinet members as they hurried along Platform 14 that Tuesday lunchtime displayed relief rather than resentment. At the time some of them, as they were later to confess, had their reservations as to whether the right course had been taken; but their uppermost thought almost certainly was that after a highly damaging six-month period of uncertainty and speculation, something at last had been settled. As the train moved slowly out of Euston—and the newspaper photographers were taking their last long-distance telephoto-lens pictures—some fairly festive lunch parties had begun in the front ministerial carriages.

In Britain there is nothing like a nonstop express train for making one incommunicado from the outside world.* Short of a railway signal to halt the train there is virtually no way of getting messages passed to particular passengers, however distinguished. But, in fact, the question does not seem to have arisen. That wet Tuesday afternoon, as the diesel locomotive plowed its way up through Warrington, Wigan and Preston, only one Cabinet Minister—and he had remained in London—was told that the Prime Minister might not, after all, be able to fulfill the plans that he had outlined to the Cabinet that morning. At five o'clock Butler was summoned from his office in the Treasury to 10 Downing Street to be told in strict confidence that the Prime Minister had been suffering some considerable pain for the past twelve hours; he would be seeing his doctors in an hour or two for a medical examination and he would then know if he was fit enough to make the journey to Blackpool later in the week.

The Cabinet Ministers traveling to Blackpool—and they included such senior figures as Iain Macleod (joint chairman of the party and leader of the House of Commons), Edward

* The radio telephone used a year later by Harold Wilson was an entirely new departure. No such instrument had ever been installed before on a British railway train.

Heath (the Lord Privy Seal and formerly Britain's Common Market negotiator) and Henry Brooke (the Home Secretary) —were left in complete ignorance of all this. Even when they arrived at Blackpool's Imperial Hotel they were given no indication that anything might be subject to change in the battle plan for the conference which had been discussed in the Cabinet room that morning. A crowded press conference at 7 P.M. thus found Iain Macleod—who throughout the week was to act a little unhappily as an uninformed master of ceremonies—replying confidently to a rapacious American questioner: "I am quite certain that the Prime Minister on Saturday will make the position about leadership absolutely clear." When one or two other reporters gamely tried to press for information on what had really been said at the Cabinet meeting, they found themselves brusquely snubbed. "You are wasting your time on this one," Macleod somewhat impatiently pointed out. "What is discussed in Cabinet is never revealed or commented upon." But conscious that it had nevertheless been given a wink, the press conference soon broke up, and as they pushed their way out the journalists agreed almost without exception that they were in for a dull week, until on Saturday afternoon Macmillan formalized what Macleod had already indicated.

The Ministers were now in a more cheerful frame of mind and they went off to spend a matey evening with the party's troops-on-the-ground, the constituency agents. This dinner— which is the annual political equivalent of the regimental officers' visit to the sergeants' mess—is traditionally addressed by a senior Cabinet Minister. This year it was the turn of one of the party's new men, Edward Heath, the hero of the previous year's Common Market conference at Llandudno. Present to hear him alongside Iain Macleod were the other joint chairman, Lord Poole, one other Cabinet Minister, Bill Deedes, and a number of officials from the Central Office, including the number three in the hierarchy, Lord Aldington. With their departure through the swing doors, the conference headquarters hotel became bare of celebrities, and most of the press corps turned to the ever-difficult task of getting a good meal in Blackpool.

There was fine fare at the agents' private dinner in the Blackpool Casino; but for five of the guests peace of mind lasted only as long as the soup course. At two minutes to nine, when the fish had just been served, a waiter approached Iain Macleod at the top table and told him that he was wanted on the telephone. The joint chairman of the Conservative Party—who in the best commanding officer-R.S.M. pattern was sitting alongside the chairman of the Conservative Agents' Association—registered some irritation and asked that the caller leave a message or ring back later. A moment or two later the waiter returned and whispered in Macleod's ear that the call came from his sister. "That's extraordinary," Macleod replied. "I had only one sister and she died years ago." Impatiently the waiter was waved away. Twenty minutes later Macleod's own Central Office secretary—having traveled down by taxi from the Imperial Hotel—burst agitatedly into the room. "Oh, Mr. Macleod," she said, "I've been trying to get you to come to the telephone without giving anything away. Downing Street wants to speak to you urgently." This time Macleod got up and left the room.

A few minutes afterward—no longer a jovial, festive figure —he returned to the top table, made his apologies to his host and beckoned to his Cabinet and Central Office colleagues to join him outside. There, in an anteroom, they were told that the Prime Minister had suddenly been rushed to the hospital with a blocked prostate gland, that he would not be able to come to Blackpool and that he would be out of action probably for two months. The public announcement, Macleod added grimly, would not be made until 9:30 P.M. and until then they would have to go through with the dinner as if nothing had happened. The five of them then trooped back to their places of honor at the top table and did their best to behave as if nothing of any importance had occurred. They were not entirely successful. Ted Heath was to confess later that evening that the agents' chairman's wife sitting next to him had reproachfully remarked: "Mr. Heath, are you feeling well? You're not very talkative, and you're eating nothing at all. Is there anything I can get for you?" "I'm afraid," he had to reply lamely, "I'm always nervous before a speech."

Meanwhile in London things had moved very quickly. Macmillan had known that something was wrong very early that morning, before even the Cabinet meeting took place. Not having been able to sleep, and suffering from a familiar ailment, he had asked his staff to call a doctor at 4 A.M. Shortly before 5 A.M. Dr. Frederick King-Lewis (his son's doctor though not his own) drove around from his flat in Chester Street, Belgravia, to Admiralty House. He was with the Prime Minister for an hour and a half, but he at first regarded the matter as one calling for only routine treatment. After this visit the Prime Minister apparently felt better, and, though Edward Heath, who called on him shortly after breakfast, took away the distinct impression that he was not looking at all well, he had rallied a bit by the time the Cabinet met. The alert Sir Keith Joseph said later in the day that he had "rarely seen the old man in better form." This, however, was by no means the view of all the Cabinet—the Chancellor of the Exchequer (who traditionally sits opposite the Prime Minister in Cabinet meetings) even being heard to comment as the Ministers went out: "You know, this man is far too ill to make the journey to Blackpool."

In fact, of course, at the Cabinet meeting Macmillan had made an oblique reference to what had occurred. His apparent (though not, in fact, specific) decision to soldier on was, he had emphasized, dependent on his getting a clearance from his doctors. Few of his colleagues, however, took this reserva-

tion very seriously. In every statement about his future intentions, from the time of the 1922 Committee luncheon
right back in April, Macmillan had always included the sav-
ing clause "provided my health and strength remain." It
had seemed a reasonable condition for a man of sixty-nine;
but this time he had clearly given it more than its usual
meaning. Just how much was shown later that evening when,
after a consultation with two other doctors, including his
own, who had come down from the Lake District, Macmillan
was driven from Downing Street to the King Edward VII
Hospital for Officers in Marylebone to await an operation.
He had meanwhile informed Lord Home as well as Butler.

It naturally took some time for the news of all this to get
around in Blackpool. The original news flash went out on
television and radio just after 9:30 P.M., but at 10 P.M. in the
bars of the headquarters hotel party officials were still unaware of what had occurred. Even when told, one group of
area press officers stoically refused to believe it. But the bleak
and grim-faced return of the ministerial guests from the
agents' dinner soon put the matter beyond doubt. Within
minutes, Iain Macleod had called his second press conference
of the evening—this time anxiously explaining that when
he had said earlier that the Prime Minister would make the
position "absolutely clear" on Saturday he had, of course, no
foreknowledge of what might occur. He added, somewhat
pathetically, that he could not be expected to say anything
about future arrangements as he did not yet know anything
about them. So shattered was Macleod—through the previous
months always Macmillan's champion—that he rejected all
blandishments to appear on television that evening and lost
no time in disappearing up the staircase to his first-floor
suite. It was left for Ted Heath—already booked by the BBC
to answer questions on his speech at the agents' dinner—to
pick up the pieces as best he could on a late-night political
program.

Macleod's sense of numbed shock was by no means shared by the people who now gathered in bars and corridors. In contrast to the successive medical bulletins about Gaitskell nine months earlier, the news of Macmillan's illness was received by much of his own party with almost a sense of relief. For month after month the question mark had hung over this one man, and the party had come to accept that only he could decide the future. Now it looked very much as if the decision was going to be taken out of his hands; and after the ritual expressions of regret even the dedicated Conservatives came to realize that this might be good for the party. The drift and uncertainty were over; now they were forced to act.

The talk in the conspiratorial groups that night was tough rather than sensitive, but it was also realistic. For the basic problem still remained: if not Macmillan, then who else? First, and most obviously, there was R. A. Butler.

The sixty-year-old First Secretary of State had remarked casually during a TV profile of himself only the night before, "I have had quite enough good luck to suit myself or anyone else." And for once it did indeed look as if Rab Butler's luck was in. It had, after all, always been said that if the Prime Minister were to be run over by a bus, then Rab would have to be the automatic beneficiary. Now that—for the second time—that seemed to have happened, it was hard even for Rab's opponents to see how his claims were going to be resisted. This time—even his enemies agreed that first night—Rab was not going to be easy to beat.

But whom should they run against him? In politics it is hopeless to match like against like. To win a victory against the odds it is imperative to gamble on contrast. For years, in the eyes of Tory constituency workers, Butler's polar opposite in the Tory Party had been fifty-six-year-old Quintin McGarel Hogg, 2nd Viscount Hailsham. Tempestuous where Rab was temperate, colorful where Rab was colorless, reckless where Rab was restrained—Hailsham was adored for having modeled his career on Churchill as Butler was despised for having followed the placid precedent set by his first mentor, Stanley Baldwin. Those who were ineradicably opposed to Butler's becoming Tory Party leader knew at once what they must do. Somehow or other Hailsham must be persuaded to set sail even though (as the shrewdest of them perceived) he might eventually end up as no more than a fire ship. And Hailsham, who still regarded himself as Macmillan's own choice for successor, was eager to try for the job.

Other names were mentioned. The clear choice of the Conservative back-benchers in Parliament, the Chancellor of the Exchequer, still remained a runner, but it soon became obvious that at least in the conference arena Round One was going to be fought out between Butler and Hailsham. The first shot was, in fact, fired by the Hailsham forces the next morning. Whether by accident or design Hailsham arrived on the Winter Gardens conference platform a tactful few minutes after the rest of his ministerial colleagues. Immediately there was a great shout and clapping of hands and banging of feet from the delegates. The conference was in no doubt of its favorite candidate. If the enthusiasm and ecstasy of the rank and file were the test of a Tory leader, Hailsham had made it. But they are not.

The real battle that first day did not take place in the conference hall. It was fought instead in a first-floor suite of the Imperial Hotel. In naming Butler to act as his deputy Macmillan had (some suspected deliberately) left one loose end untied. What was to happen about the annual mass rally —always traditionally addressed by the leader—due to be held on Saturday afternoon? As he arrived in Blackpool from London at 6:15 P.M. on Wednesday, October 9, Butler clearly believed that he must deliver this vital speech or risk getting nudged out of the leadership contest. He was, therefore, relieved to learn that the executive of the National Union of

Conservative and Unionist Associations—that strange, amorphous body that comes to life once a year to organize the annual Conservative conference—had just finished meeting and was proposing to invite him as acting Prime Minister to take over the speech at the annual rally. For once no victim of indecision, Butler immediately tried to get this proposal ratified by his Cabinet colleagues since the National Union had said that its invitation was conditional on Cabinet approval.

Having taken possession of the suite that had originally been booked for the Prime Minister, Butler summoned a meeting of all available Cabinet ministers. At 7 P.M. a round dozen assembled in his sitting room while Mrs. Butler tactfully withdrew, first to go to a press party downstairs and then to sit patiently waiting on a hard-backed chair outside, in the first-floor corridor. Before Butler brought up the subject of Saturday's meeting he conveyed one piece of news to his colleagues that took them all badly by surprise. He understood, he said, that it was the Prime Minister's wish, in view of the uncertainty both about the length of his absence and his prospects of complete recovery, that "the normal processes of consultation" should now begin about the selection of a new Conservative leader. In fact at that stage Butler already knew that the Prime Minister's retirement was to be announced the next day, but he had been sworn to the strictest confidence, which he did not break till the next afternoon when he warned in advance two of his closest supporters in the Cabinet.

It was bad luck for Butler that he had to pass on the Prime Minister's message at this moment. It meant that everyone present now knew that the question of who should speak at Saturday's rally was clearly involved with the question of choosing Macmillan's successor. Whoever got the job got a head start in the race. The argument over the National Union's invitation was therefore a hard-fought one and the meeting dragged on for an hour and a half: Butler was not finding it easy to get what he plainly regarded as his right. The Cabinet Ministers present split up almost straight away into opposing camps. In favor of Butler's taking the rally were those like Henry Brooke, the Home Secretary, Enoch Powell, Minister of Health, and Keith Joseph, Minister of Housing, who were to be his supporters for the next ten days; against his doing it—or at least in favor of cancellation—were those who eventually were to cost him the leadership: Iain Macleod, Reggie Maudling, Frederick Erroll, as well as his own implacable personal opponents like John Hare, Christopher Soames and Ernest Marples.

To all this, however, there was one exception. The most ardent Butlerite of them all—the Minister of Education, Sir Edward Boyle—caused some offense to his own champion by strongly urging upon him that he should be content merely to make a speech at the end of the Saturday-morning session and should not insist on being the central figure in the annual revivalist ritual of the mass rally. After the meeting was over—and Butler had had his way mainly by his own firmness—Sir Edward found himself being congratulated by one of Butler's opponents on having been the one person taking part in the meeting who had displayed disinterestedness. It is more likely, however, that the youngest Minister present (at forty Sir Edward was still the baby of the Cabinet) had shown something else—a shrewd political cunning. He realized that from Butler's own point of view, taking over the Prime Minister's mantle at the rally, far from helping him, might actually damage his cause. Whatever Butler's gifts and abilities were, they did not include oratory or histrionics; Boyle's fear that Butler's performance on Saturday might merely show up his limitations as a political leader turned out in the end correct.

Meanwhile the Hailsham supporters had not been idle. Their own candidate did not attend the meeting where Butler had won his point that evening. He was fulfilling a long-standing speaking engagement at the neighboring seaside resort of Morecambe. There, unaware of the news that Butler had told his other colleagues, he was sending a boisterous message to Harold Macmillan to "get well quick . . . so that when you come back, as you will do soon, we can hand back to you a Government and a party in good order." Hailsham's record of somewhat loud loyalty to Macmillan had been a constant factor throughout the crisis; there can be little doubt that while he was saying all this he meant it.

He was already, however, being flatly contradicted by one of his own more raucous supporters. That same evening the brash Conservative back-bench television personality, Sir Gerald Nabarro, was announcing to a constituency meeting in Bolton: "Britain cannot be led and governed by a sick septuagenarian." Having dismissed Butler as "donnish, dignified and dull," damned Maudling as "manly, matey and moneywise," Sir Gerald went on to declare that the mantle of the Premiership "should fall on Lord Hailsham, who has fire in his belly."

This was clearly an unauthorized one-man outburst, though it inevitably made its impact on the newspapers. The real work for the Hailsham candidature was being carried on more discreetly in the hotel corridors and the conference-hall lobbies by a group of young Conservative M.P.s who had turned themselves almost overnight into a campaign staff. Prominent among them were the wealthy proprietor of the *Spectator,* Ian Gilmour, who had always up till then been associated with the progressive wing of the Conservative Party; Peter Walker, a young city tycoon, who had formerly been national chairman of the Young Conservative movement; and Anthony Royle, the rich and elegant Parliamentary Private Secretary to the Minister of Aviation, Julian Amery, who later emerged in his own right as the chief Hailsham campaign organizer. In addition Hailsham had at his side a young advertising executive, Denis Walters, who had been his personal assistant when he was chairman of the party and was now prospective candidate for the safe Conservative seat of Westbury. At this stage Hailsham was the only likely candidate backed by an active organization.

But in spite of their best efforts on the second day of the conference, the atmosphere had noticeably simmered down. For the first—and, as it turned out, the last—time the conference hall itself came to life with two brilliant demagogic speeches from Iain Macleod in a debate on Conservative principles and philosophy. As the joint chairman's odd but compelling counter-tenor voice rang out through that vast Empress ballroom ("And will we win? Of course we shall") it seemed just possible that this tensest-ever gathering of the Conservative Party might yet be transformed into what it was always intended to be—the springboard for the general-election campaign.

That same afternoon all such hopes were dashed. At 4:30 P.M. Lord Home appeared in the conference hall for the first time, and during the following half hour the platform was seen to be filling up with Ministers who, the observant noted, seemed to be having some sort of note passed to them. As soon as John Boyd-Carpenter, the Chief Secretary, had finished a rambling dissertation on rates, Lord Home got to his feet. He had, he said, a message from the Prime Minister. In his flat, thin voice the Foreign Secretary then read out a 300-word letter in which Harold Macmillan explained that, whatever his previous feelings, it would not now be possible for him to carry the physical burdens of leading the party at the next general election. He therefore hoped it would "soon be possible for the customary processes of consultation to be carried on within the party about its future leadership," and he made it plain that once these were completed he would place his resignation in the hands of the Queen. Lord Home added just one pious phrase of his own

—that Mr. Macmillan had "once more shown that his whole concern was for the nation and the party"—and immediately there was a great burst of applause from the entire hall.

Partly, no doubt, this was meant to underline Lord Home's tribute, but there was also relief at the end of uncertainty. In fact the decision had been taken over twenty-four hours earlier. On Wednesday afternoon Home and Poole (who had flown down specially to London) visited Macmillan, then still awaiting his operation in the King Edward VII Hospital. The original medical advice to the Prime Minister was that he must expect to be out of action for two or three months; and in face of that he recognized that he could scarcely carry on as an absentee Prime Minister in a period just before a general election. Macmillan's friends were later to say that had he been pressed to remain in office he would probably have done so, especially after he had learned from his own surgeon (too late to stop the conference message) that he might, after all, expect to be back at his post in as little as six weeks. But, in fact, the reverse happened. Far from being urged to stay, Macmillan was encouraged by Home and Poole to go. They grasped the sad fact that still eluded Macmillan: his illness provided the first cue for an honorable exit from office since the humiliating Profumo debate on June 17.

Once Macmillan accepted that he must resign, he made Home and Poole promise to read out the announcement as soon as they reached Blackpool. He was afraid that if the announcement was left until later, people would say that his illness was only a sham. Unfortunately for the Conservative Party the time and place of Home's announcement meant that the curious "processes of consultation" would, for the first time, be carried out in the hurly-burly atmosphere of the annual conference. The quarrels and feuds would leak to the press; the devious Ottoman intrigues of the party would be changed into a kind of mass political beauty contest. "If only we had had the sense to hold the news up till Saturday,"

Poole was to say ever afterward, "the whole thing would never have got out of control. I should never have allowed Home to read that letter out on the Thursday. The trouble was we'd both promised Macmillan that we'd do it then. But keeping that promise was probably the biggest blunder I ever made in politics."

Sure enough, the battle for power was launched that same evening. When a Prime Minister announces that he is going to resign he can normally count on capturing all the next day's main headlines. In the event Macmillan got them only in *The Times* and the *Telegraph*. The rest all bore such banner legents as "Hailsham Shock," "Enter Mr. Hogg," or simply (in a tabloid) "Call Me Mister."

Whether Macmillan had intended it or not—and the Hailsham supporters insisted right to the end that he had—the immediate beneficiary of the Prime Minister's letter was Lord Hailsham. Absent from the platform when the letter was read out—he was meeting his wife and one-year-old daughter at Preston station—he learned of its existence from Peter Goldman* only when he arrived back at the Imperial Hotel shortly after 5 P.M. Once told, his reaction was instantaneous. He rushed upstairs and seized a copy of the letter from one of the Downing Street secretaries who had arrived in Blackpool. "This is it," he remarked a moment or two later. "It's now or never." It was obvious straight away—though strenuous efforts were made to dissuade him, especially by Lord Aldington—that his mood was "now"; and that night the big chance came.

Unlike the Labour Party, the Conservative conference does not go in for "fringe activities"—tea meetings, brains trusts or evening rallies. But every year the Conservative Political Center—a kind of intellectuals' pressure group within the party—holds one evening meeting that is complementary to

* Director of the Conservative Political Center.

the party conference without being part of it. This meeting is addressed annually by a Cabinet Minister and always provides an opportunity for the delivery of a testament of political faith. This year's speaker was Hailsham, whose claim to be one of the party intellectuals had been established years before by his book *The Case for Conservatism*—a powerful tract in a style midway between Edmund Burke and Barry Goldwater.

Long before he arrived at the Pavilion Cinema to find 2,500 Conservatives packed inside and another 1,000 ticketless trying to storm the entrances, Hailsham had decided what he must do. He would go through with his prepared speech on the theme of "National Excellence" and then, at the end, when he came to reply to the vote of thanks, he would make a purely personal statement declaring his decision to renounce his peerage.

In the event the prepared speech was a flop. Hailsham stuck doggedly to his script, frequently fluffing his lines and often badly miscalculating his timing. After about an hour the audience grew restive; but in that gathering that evening Hailsham would have been a hero if he had simply read out the telephone directory. When eventually he sat down, the cheers rang boldly out. A few minutes later he was back at the front of the platform. This time there was no prepared text, and the nervousness and hesitation were part of the orator's equipment. "There is one other thing," he began with an unfamiliar diffidence, "that I feel I ought to say to you. I hope you will bear with me if I put it in my own words."

The rest followed inevitably. After a tumultuous demonstration (which put one outraged Conservative M.P. in mind of "the politics of the Nuremberg Rally") Hailsham—as befitted the first man ever in British politics publicly to place his own name in nomination to be Prime Minister—found himself at the center of a volcanic eruption of emotion.

It reached its peak when just after midnight he made a char-
ismatic appearance at the Young Conservatives' Ball. Like
Barry Goldwater at the Cow Palace in San Francisco nine
months later, this odd, emotional peer had become the party
darling. But the Conservatives, unlike the Republican Party,
do not elect their candidate by a convention.

For a few flickering hours Hailsham did indeed seem to
have the light of star dust, the strut of triumph, the throb of
destiny. Yet that Thursday night he had taken the only
initiative that was open to him, and its impact, though formidable, aroused an equally firm opposition. On radio and
television that evening he was referred to in icily disapprov-
ing tones by Iain Macleod; later that night the forgotten man
of the contest—Reggie Maudling—told everyone within earshot, "You know, if you asked the Cabinet to raise their
hands for Quintin I don't think a single hand would go up";
and the next morning that most orthodox and respectable of
Conservative newspapers, the *Yorkshire Post,* wrote flatly
that Butler would be the next Prime Minister and dismissed
Hailsham's promise to give up his peerage as "an unnecessary, a deplorable distraction." In the small hours of Friday
morning even Hailsham himself confessed to Lord Aldington—the man who had most strongly advised him against
taking such a melodramatic course—"You were quite right.
It is all over. I am finished."

If he had failed to take the party by storm Hailsham had
at least burst the whole contest wide open. Each of his rivals
was now forced to follow his example, and they all suddenly
started to fight for the prize. Butler gave a clumsy, self-pro-
moting interview to the *Daily Express;* Maudling at last
came out on television to say that he was willing to accept
the Premiership; the wily Macleod hinted at a possible Home
candidature in an effort to divert the Hailsham enthusiasm.
That Friday, in fact, marked the first moment when Home as
a candidate began to be taken seriously. It was partly due to

Macleod and partly to that senior influential back-bencher, Nigel Birch, who, having destroyed the previous leader, now set himself the task of defeating both the front-runners for the succession. Arriving in Blackpool that Friday afternoon, he left no doubt as to how he intended to do it. To a journalist he remarked almost casually, "Oh, I'm an Alec Home man. There aren't any other possibilities. He's *going* to get it."

Only that morning the Foreign Secretary—always an idol of the annual conference—had enjoyed an oratorical triumph with his speech on foreign affairs. At that stage the delegates were probably all the more generous in their applause as they still looked upon Home as the one Olympian figure above the stresses and strains of mundane personal conflict; but whatever the motive, the fact now stood on the record that Home—in the midst of the parade of recognized candidates—had got almost as big an ovation as Hailsham. True, he had offered a prize "to any newspaperman who can find any clue in my speech that this is Lord Home's bid for the leadership," but in retrospect even that began to look not quite as innocent as it had sounded. In any event the suspicions of Home's intentions increased that night when he gave an interview on BBC television. For a prospective king-maker he showed a marked reluctance to take his own eyes off the crown, a fact that was noted somewhat bitterly by the other potential "third man" in the contest, Reginald Maudling (who himself had made a good but wholly ineffective speech on economic policy that same morning in the conference hall). Coming out of the studio in which they had both been interviewed, he remarked: "I do admire the political skill that our aristocracy has now acquired. It seems to me that he wants the job and that it's all over." It was one of the few true prophecies of that week.

By no means everyone saw as clearly as that. The next morning found a competing clamor of headlines. Some papers claimed that support for Hailsham had grown, others that he had fallen behind in the race, and one at least (the *Daily Telegraph*) flatly contradicted itself between editions —"Support for Hailsham Grows" being changed at about 2 A.M. to "Support for Hailsham Wanes." The effect of all this was to leave the final day of the conference in a frayed state.

For one thing, the conference realized that by transforming itself into a political beauty contest it had by no means established its right to a real or substantial voice in "the normal processes of consultation." Ministers and M.P.s were becoming convinced that the sooner the arena was transferred to the calmer, more rational atmosphere of London the better it would be for everyone. It was in that spirit that Butler came to make the final speech to the conference—the opportunity he had fought so hard to be given—on Saturday afternoon. This was Butler almost defiantly plain—making no concessions at all to the hysterical atmosphere of heroes and hero worship in which he found himself. As he wound his labyrinthine way through all the aspects of Government policy he appeared anxious to remind his audience of only one thing: that it was the Conservative Party's task not just to find a magnetic leader but rather to choose a Prime Minister who understood and grasped the whole reach and span of an already decided political program. This was Butler's basic strength; and his speech, skillful if pedestrian, emphasized it.

It was not, however, what the 4,000 representatives had come to hear. His audience made that crudely obvious by reserving all its enthusiasm for the chairman of the meeting, Lord Home, and yielding Butler only the applause that politeness—perhaps guilty conscience—required. Yet Butler had made a deliberate decision. His sights when he sat down were plainly fixed on the coming—and, as he believed, very different—struggle that lay ahead in London. He had at least survived a week in which he had been forced to fight on his most vulnerable flank. In his own milieu of Whitehall and the Cabinet Room he could begin to assert his claim.

He certainly lost no time in doing so. The next day, Sunday, October 13, Butler admitted a Press Association photographer to his country home in Essex and posed, looking dignified, reticent and relaxed, on a chintz sofa. The picture, which came out all over Monday's press, summed up Butler's campaign for the leadership. To be seen to be striving after it would have removed his one great advantage over all his rivals. Where they needed to press their claims (while Butler was being photographed in silence, Maudling and Hailsham were giving "live" newspaper interviews) he was content to let his case, as it were, rest: his record of service to the state, the fact that he was now once again acting Prime Minister, the public's sense of familiarity with him—none of these things, in his view, required any proclaiming. But, more than that, his own mood was one of supreme confidence. In a passage, deleted at his own request from the "Panorama" profile of him on the previous Monday night, he was asked: "If you failed to succeed Macmillan, to what would you ascribe your failure?" He answered: "But your question is absurd—I *am* going to be Prime Minister." And at least in the early part of the week that firmly represented his view.

He had good reason for holding it. The fact that the Prime Minister was still recovering from the sedative after-effects of his operation in King Edward VII Hospital necessarily meant that Butler was now the central public figure in the drama. It was he, having taken up daytime residence in Downing Street, who was now going to receive the other Ministers; and, more important even than that, he was surely bound to be the conduit pipe between the sick, retiring Premier and the rest of the Government. Significantly, though, Macmillan did not immediately summon Butler to his bedside. Instead, having held consultations with both the Government Chief Whip (Martin Redmayne) and the Lord

Chancellor (Lord Dilhorne), he sent him a letter. In it the outgoing Prime Minister explained that in his present state of health it would be wrong for him personally to recommend any successor to the Queen; as an alternative he recommended that the Cabinet should agree to a procedure which in his view should establish which candidate really enjoyed the maximum support. At the time Butler saw nothing suspicious in this proposal. Indeed he cheerfully read Macmillan's letter to the assembled Cabinet the next morning and got them to agree to it.

Macmillan's suggestion had been that four official "straw" polls should be held as quickly as possible—one for the 350-odd Conservative members of the House of Commons, one for the roughly 200-strong active Unionist peers in the House of Lords, one for the 20 members of the Cabinet and one for the 150-odd officers and executive of the National Union—to establish the feeling of the constituencies (it was noticeable that parliamentary candidates were left out, but no one seems to have protested about this at the time). Once the evidence had been collected, Macmillan undertook to present it to the Queen so that she might exercise her prerogative in the light of a demonstrated party preference. Now Butler had doubted from the beginning whether Macmillan would ever yield him any personal endorsement; he himself had referred to Macmillan as "an aging, foolish old man" in an interview with a journalist at the end of September. Therefore this proposal of an entirely novel method of giving advice to the monarch may well have come as a relief. He might not be markedly in the lead in any one of the four suggested polling areas, but he assumed that he was easily the strongest all-round candidate. Many Cabinet colleagues agreed with him.

What Butler overlooked was that with this one act of acquiescence he had forfeited his single solid asset. From now on, instead of being the tenant in possession, he was simply just another candidate for the succession. It was to Macmillan that the results of the various polls were to be presented, and it was Macmillan who would weigh and evaluate them, put them together and present them to the Queen. As if to demonstrate the point—or perhaps to rub it in—Macmillan did indeed ask Butler the next day (Tuesday, October 15) to visit him, before the Cabinet meeting took place; but he was also scrupulous to invite, after it was over, each of the other three main surviving candidates (Maudling, Home and Hailsham), as well as the two increasingly remote outsiders (Heath and Macleod). In retrospect Butler correctly recognized this as the decisive moment when fortune turned against him.

At the time, though, its significance was not perceived, even by his rivals. In fact the real tribute to the initial strength of Butler's position was the collective belief of all his opponents that he was the man they would have to beat. Long afterward the shrewder of the Hailsham supporters were to claim that they had deliberately put this view around on purely tactical grounds, as they had been convinced from the beginning that Butler was the one candidate their own champion *could* defeat. But in the immediate post-Blackpool atmosphere there was not much opportunity for that kind of sophistication. Each of the three challengers to Butler by now had his separate campaign staff who knew that they had a job of work to do and that there was not much time in which to do it.

In the Maudling camp the return to London had caused a considerable recovery of confidence. Admittedly their candidate had flopped badly at the conference but he himself was not too worried: "Now that we have returned to London it will be apparent that this is a matter which will be decided by deliberation and not by decibel meter." Maudling, in fact, started the week in a mood of jaunty confidence. Traveling back from Blackpool by train, Iain Macleod assured him

once again of his personal allegiance and of his political conviction that in the end he must emerge victorious. Macleod's
shrewd tactical brain had grasped the central point: that a
right of veto was bound to operate against both Butler and
Hailsham. It would be wielded by the intransigent opponents
of each. The preservation of party unity must demand the
emergence of a compromise candidate. To the last, Macleod
had wanted Macmillan to stay. As soon as this became impossible, he plumped for Maudling. He was now certain that
Maudling would get the job and nothing that happened at
Blackpool—not even the glint in Home's eye—had altered
Macleod's professional political appraisal of the situation.

But that Saturday afternoon in the railway carriage Macleod suffered a shock, which ought perhaps to have shown
him the warning light. Slightly embarrassed, Maudling confessed to him that when he had been asked for his views at
Blackpool by the Lord Chancellor (who was then conducting what afterward passed into official terminology as "the
poll of the Cabinet") he had replied that, although in no
circumstances would he serve in a Government headed by
Hailsham, he would accept office under Butler or, for that
matter, under Home. The effect of the latter name upon
Macleod was certainly electric. He launched into a tirade on
the impossibility of a 14th Earl being a Tory leader in the
second half of the twentieth century, basing his case largely
on the damning, dispiriting effect that such an appointment
would have on the people he really cared about in the party
—the classless Young Conservatives and the working-class
Tory trade-unionists. The vision of Home leading the party
would, he argued, make a mockery of everything that they
had tried to achieve since 1945 in broadening the base of
Conservative appeal. But though Macleod was angry he was
not yet alarmed. To him the very notion of Home being
Prime Minister was still inherently impossible. This was
later his defense for having at one moment at Blackpool

rashly floated the Home candidature to a journalist in a diversionary effort to damage Hailsham.

Macleod would certainly have taken Maudling's confession more seriously had he known one of the best-kept secrets of Blackpool. Some time after lunch on the Friday of his foreign-affairs speech, Home had been waited upon in his hotel room by a deputation of four influential Conservative M.P.s. They were Selwyn Lloyd (Macmillan's sacked Chancellor), Martin Redmayne (the Government Chief Whip), Nigel Birch (Macmillan's arch-enemy) and Colonel Lancaster (a back-bench member of standing and seniority). They had one simple question to put to the Foreign Secretary. Although they quite recognized that he was not an active candidate for the succession, they asked him to give them an assurance that if a draft were forthcoming Home would not refuse it. Without too much hesitation Home gave them what they wanted. If the party genuinely desired him to lead it, he would step down from the Lords and become Prime Minister in the Commons. Indeed Home did more than that: Later in the day he made arrangements to see his doctor in London on the following Monday so that he might have a complete medical checkup.

It is doubtful if any of the four recognized at the time quite what they had done. For (unknown to them) only three days earlier Home had given an assurance to all his Cabinet colleagues which most of them were to remember vividly and resentfully throughout the twelve months of his premiership. "I wish to make it clear," he had told his fellow members in the Cabinet Room at the pre-Conference meeting on Tuesday, October 8, "that in no circumstances am I a candidate." It may not have been quite the famous Sherman statement of nineteenth-century American politics: "If nominated I will not accept, if drafted I will not run, if elected I will not serve." But for most of Home's colleagues it remained throughout the crisis the main basis for their belief that—whatever the pressures put upon him—the Foreign Secretary simply could not, without notice to them, slip his moorings as a nonstarter. The only people who knew for certain that he had already done so were the four who had waited upon the Foreign Secretary that Friday afternoon; and it very much suited their purposes to keep this information to themselves. What they wanted—and what in the end they got—was a victory for their candidate with scarcely a shot being fired against him for the simple reason that nowhere until the very last moment was he definitely visible in any of his opponents' sights.

This was especially true of the Hailsham camp. They were throughout the coming five days the most highly organized and the most noisy, but they did not suspect the danger from Home until much too late. From the moment of the return to London (which most of them made expensively by airplane) the Hailsham campaign staff faced a problem. At Blackpool their candidate had used up almost all his political ammunition; how could they keep the guns firing? Their answer was a policy of intense activity, some of which had started on the previous Saturday afternoon at Blackpool. Before he rose to address the final afternoon rally, Butler found himself handed a pile of telegrams. No doubt thinking that they were congratulatory messages from well-wishers he opened them. Instead of good wishes he discovered angry admonitions: "Must win election for sake of country, stand down for Hogg, Andrew Kerr"; "Make way for Hailsham and win respect of all, Percy Clark"; "We hope to hear you recommend Hogg for Premiership, Young Tories, Scunthorpe"; "Back Hailsham and win glory, Eileen Harryman"; "Quintin, please, Randolph."

The last one, of course, was the giveaway. Each of them had been sent just after noon from the bar of the Imperial Hotel by Randolph Churchill, who, having narrowly resisted the temptation to pin a "Q" button on the ample posterior of Lord Dilhorne, the Lord Chancellor, now set about a much more subtle campaign of psychological warfare. Randolph Churchill has always been one of the most attractive, if unrecognized, political "naturals" in Britain; and in his *The Fight for the Tory Leadership* he has already given his provocative but entertaining account of the whole Conservative leadership crisis.

He modestly did not include in it his own quite important role. If the Hailsham campaign had from the beginning a degree of American political "professionalese" entirely lacking in those of all his rivals (except in a much more dangerous, diffident English way in that of Home's), it was largely due to the energy and activity of this former Prime Minister's son. Having been in January 1957 about the only journalist in Britain correctly to tip Macmillan as successor to Eden, Randolph Churchill immediately set to work to justify his second prophecy (published in the *News of the World* on Sunday, October 13) that the next Prime Minister "will be Mr. Quintin McGarel Hogg, formerly Lord Hailsham."

Randolph Churchill was by no means alone in his personal journalistic prophecy or in his vicarious political ambition. Indeed the amazing—and for a number of his present Opposition colleagues the alarming—thing about the Hailsham crusade for the leadership was how near it came to success. The timing and the setting for it had, of course, been exactly right. In no other week of the year could Hailsham have got his candidature off the ground; but at Blackpool, surrounded by his own public (the party militants), performing in his own natural arena (that of oratorical excess), and basking in the arc lights of publicity (Hailsham was since the death of Aneurin Bevan the only natural-born "celebrity" in British politics), he had certainly succeeded in making his claim look a plausible one. Nor was it based entirely on publicity. Reggie Maudling, for example, was certainly wrong in declaring at Blackpool that Hailsham had no support in the Cabinet. In

Conservative politics the blood line is all-important. An excitable Hailsham lieutenant, Peter Walker, announced at one point: "We've got the Churchills and the Devonshires; now all we need is the Cecils." He may have been exaggerating, but the remark reveals an important aspect of Tory thinking.

Astonishingly, in October 1963 a respectable proportion of the whole Tory "Establishment" was, in fact, working for Hailsham. In the Cabinet (quite apart from Macmillan himself, who characteristically abandoned his promotion of the Hailsham cause only when he became convinced that even in a new situation it could not succeed) there were originally both Sir Winston Churchill's sons-in-law, Duncan Sandys and Christopher Soames; outside it in the party organization there was Iain Macleod's opposite number as joint chairman, Lord Poole, whose wife at Blackpool had made no secret of the fact, even once in Mrs. Butler's hearing, that "Oliver is breast high for Quintin"; while outside the Government and the party organization were virtually all those whom Maudling himself baptized "the blue-blood-and-thunder boys"— the buccaneering Tory "grandees" who traditionally meet together in the most neolithic of all London clubs, White's in St. James's.

The Tory Party is still predominantly the betting party, and not the least triumph of the often wealthy backers of Lord Hailsham lay in keeping the price offered on his candidature at Ladbroke's (the large firm of London bookmakers who ran throughout the crisis a much publicized book on the Tory leadership stakes) consistently above that of Maudling and, until the very last moment, ahead of that of Home as well. But basically the prizes that the Hailsham campaigners went out after were the wrong ones. The backing of the moneyed interests in the city, the endorsement of the magnificos within the party, even influence over the Palace— all these trophies, though still not to be sniffed at, would have looked a good deal more glittering in 1923 than they did in 1963. A party that has successfully brought the Bantu of the professional and middle classes into the higher reaches of its decision-making can never afterward—if the point now needs any underlining—afford to operate as if they did not exist.

It was symbolic that the Maudling supporters had as their rendezvous the definitely middle-class Junior Carlton Club; nearly all the Hailsham councils of war took place in the defiantly upper-class White's. The part that Hailsham himself (always proud to be called "a Tory democrat") played in this strategy was probably small. Very early on he decided "to sit tight and leave it to my friends who are much more efficient than ever I had supposed." But at least he bears the responsibility for the prevailing tone of truculence by having at the beginning passed the word to his supporters that if he did not get the job "no one should count upon me signing on for the next voyage."

Strong-arm tactics, which tended to rebound soon, became characteristic of the approach of Hailsham's supporters. A member of the Cabinet was shocked to discover that Julian Amery (Hailsham's campaign manager) was prepared to warn him in semipublic, "You're making a big mistake if you think that our people will ever back a Rab Government." Perhaps, though, the person who suffered most from this kind of approach was Iain Macleod, whom for some reason the Hailshamites had expected to have in their camp along with the other joint chairman, Lord Poole. They found instead that he was doing his best to "wreck" their activities. At one stage Macleod was even stormed at in White's Club by the young and affluent Tory back-bencher by whom he is now employed—Ian Gilmour, the proprietor of the *Spectator*. But despite the fact that many of his friends (and practically all his former most devoted supporters in the Commons like Gilmour himself) were involved in the Hailsham campaign,

Macleod held out against all threats and blandishments with the uncompromising statement, "I'm not rowing in that crew."

The other potential supporter whom the Hailsham forces allowed to get away turned out in the end to be an even more vital figure. Prominent on the platform at the Hailsham declaration meeting at Blackpool had been Selwyn Lloyd, who bore no love for Butler or Maudling. The first he rightly suspected of helping to get him removed from the Chancellorship in July 1962; the second had actually taken over his old job. Selwyn Lloyd was therefore regarded as natural Hailsham campaign material. In fact at Blackpool he had already committed himself to Home; but throughout the early days back in London the former fallen Chancellor maintained contact with the Hailsham camp. He met Hailsham personally at least once, but normally communicated through a twenty-one-year-old undergraduate—the son of the then Conservative member for Bury St. Edmunds, Sir William Aitken—who happened to be the president of the Oxford University Conservative Association; and one of the more quixotic episodes of the week was the summoning of an emergency meeting of that vital body with the purpose of sending a message to the Conservative Central Office insisting that Oxford youth was solid for Hailsham. Yet Jonathan Aitken's importance in the leadership struggle was not so much as an active participant—not for nothing is Oxford the home of lost causes—but rather as a funnel of communication.

Throughout, the Hailshamites had the best intelligence service. They were operating on a social as well as a purely political net. For instance, Duncan Sandys was thought to have finally pledged himself to Hailsham's cause when he took the elder of Julian Amery's sons to a conjuring show. So it was fitting that in the end they should have been the first people to get the real news. At 10:25 P.M. on Wednesday, October 16, the telephone rang in Randolph Churchill's home at East Bergholt, which had become the communications center of the Hailsham campaign. On the line was a sad and disappointed Jonathan Aitken. Selwyn Lloyd, he reported, had just seen Home; he had committed himself irrevocably to Home's cause and had been told by him that he was now prepared to come downstairs from the House of Lords and accept the leadership. Half an hour later the telephone rang again. Hailsham himself, who only a few hours earlier was reported firm and confident, had to be told the worst. "I have," Randolph Churchill began by saying, "bad news for you." "Well, come on, tell me. I can take it," the candidate replied. He was then given the substance of Aitken's message. Hailsham's response displayed a greater political prescience than that of any of his followers, who right to the end had insisted on calling Home "a nonstarter": "I always saw it happening," he said wryly. "I'm afraid this means the end of my political career. I could not continue it under such conditions."

Butler heard the news the next morning in the form of an advance warning from the Lord Chancellor. The warning was a friendly one, since the official pretense had to be maintained that the decision would really be made only when Macmillan had weighed all the evidence of the four "straw" polls.

The Maudling followers, on the other hand, got no wind at all of what had happened. That same evening they were holding a fairly cheerful campaign meeting, and the very next morning Maudling himself—who throughout the crisis had been treated by the senior members of the Government far more as a junior Cabinet Minister than as a serious candidate —required a tip-off from Iain Macleod (who had got the news from his wife) even to learn that the decision was likely that day. Maudling promptly confirmed Macleod's information in a telephone conversation with the Lord Chancellor (Lord Dilhorne), who varied it only to the extent of saying that the final decision would probably not be known for twenty-four hours. Macleod's reaction was firm, clear and unsuspecting; they must, he advised, play for time. Still absolutely ruling out Home, Macleod committed himself to the view that if the decision were made in the next twenty-four hours it must mean that it was going to be Rab, but that if somehow they could work for delay "you must be seen to be the only choice." Buoyed up by this conversation held in the Chancellor's room in the Treasury, Maudling invited Macleod to join him and his wife at lunch at the Mirabelle, where they wasted the next crucial hours.

By four o'clock Maudling was back in the Treasury when the "scrambler" telephone rang. It was Iain Macleod: he had just heard from William Rees-Mogg, the political and economic editor of the *Sunday Times* and probably the best-informed of all Conservative journalists, that Home had been chosen and that he would go to the Palace the next day. At first neither Maudling nor Macleod believed it. They reassured each other by agreeing that "press leaks" had been wrong before and could be again. Macleod, however, took the information sufficiently seriously to propose a meeting that evening. And Maudling agreed, asking only if he could bring with him Frederick Erroll, the president of the Board of Trade, who happened to be in his office at the time. The meeting, Maudling characteristically added, would have to be late, as he was due to dine that evening with Lord Cobbald (the Governor of the Bank of England).

Once again, therefore, valuable hours were lost, though Maudling did visit Macleod's flat briefly before dinner where he found Sir Edward Boyle, Enoch Powell and Lord Aldington all miserably chewing on the news, which now seemed to have been confirmed. None of these had quite such cause to be mortified as the one Minister who appeared on television that evening. Toward the end of the afternoon Reginald Bevins, the Postmaster-General and one of the few elementary-school-educated members of the Conservative Government, visited Television House in Kingsway to record an interview on the British telephone service for the "This Week" program. Not unnaturally the conversation afterward turned to the question everyone was talking about—who would materialize the next day as the new Tory leader. The one name that Bevins (member for the Toxteth division of Liverpool) would not entertain even as a possibility was Lord Home's. "Look," he said with some degree of prophetic foresight, "the most important man in my constituency is my agent, and he insists that we couldn't expect to hold a single seat in Liverpool if a fourteenth Earl were chosen.* It'd be electoral suicide for us—they must know that."

But apparently they didn't. For even as Bevins spoke, those responsible for organizing the four "straw" polling stations—in the Cabinet, the Lords, the Commons and among the constituency parties—were reporting their returns to Macmillan in the King Edward VII Hospital. In the morning they had each separately visited the Prime Minister in his first-floor room at the hospital to tell him what their respective sounding had established; and in the afternoon Macmillan took the wise precaution, to avoid any suspicion of the books having been cooked, of having them repeat in front of each other what their various canvasses had shown. For this purpose Macmillan was brought downstairs from his room to the Matron's office, where, still lying in bed, he received collectively the Lord Chancellor (Lord Dilhorne), the Chief Whip in the House of Lords (Lord St. Aldwyn), the Chief Whip in the Commons (Martin Redmayne) and the joint chairman of the party (Lord Poole). One week later Redmayne was to lift the veil a little on what the Prime Minister had been told that afternoon by announcing in a public speech at Bournemouth that Home had been the common choice of all four

---

* Bevins's agent was almost right. At the general election the Tories lost four of the six seats they had previously held in Liverpool, including Bevins's own.

polls—though he admitted that among Conservative M.P.s his lead had been narrow."

But this was not the first occasion on which Redmayne released this information. At midnight on the same day that the results of the polls were presented to the Prime Minister he was using them for his own purposes in argument with four Cabinet Ministers. Macleod's proposed meeting of "rebel" Ministers had finally been arranged at the home of Enoch Powell (the Minister of Health) in South Eaton Place. There just before midnight—in addition to the host, Powell—assembled Iain Macleod (the joint chairman of the party and leader of the House of Commons), Frederick Erroll (the president of the Board of Trade), Lord Aldington (Special Assistant to the joint chairmen in the Central Office) and, hot from his party at Lord Cobbold's in a dinner jacket, Reginald Maudling (the Chancellor of the Exchequer). To this gathering the Government Chief Whip was summoned by telephone. At the time he was naturally suspected of being part of the abortive conspiracy. But in fact Redmayne had been a Home supporter since the previous Friday at Blackpool and was present only as the official channel of communication to the Prime Minister.

Playing the traditional part of a Chief Whip with "rebels," Redmayne at once did his best to persuade them that their cause was hopeless. Without giving exact facts or figures he assured the five that Home had been the leading choice among all the segments of the party that had been consulted. He reminded them, too, that the procedure they were now disputing was one which only two days before (at the Tuesday Cabinet meeting) the four Ministers present had all endorsed. At last seeing the noose that the whole Cabinet had put its head into, Maudling and Macleod tried to cut free of it by asserting the overriding rights that any Cabinet must have in selecting a new Prime Minister. All right, they argued in effect, perhaps Home was the party's choice, but that did not necessarily mean that he was the ideal Prime Minister. If, even as the favorite, he could not unite the Cabinet, surely there was a case for re-examining the claims of the runner-up, who, they urged, could. Redmayne had been summoned only after Hailsham had on the telephone made it perfectly clear that he too was violently opposed to Home and was now ready—even eager—to serve in a Cabinet headed by Butler.

For the five men in Powell's house that night this change in Hailsham's attitude had naturally seemed decisive. There had been three public contenders for the leadership, and two of them had now agreed to serve under the third. What need, they kept pressing Redmayne, was there to take the matter any further? The crisis was surely over now that both Butler's main rivals had agreed to accept him as leader of the party and Prime Minister. So confident, indeed, did they all now feel that one of them—Lord Aldington—even went to the length of ringing *The Times* to make it clear that the whole situation had changed and that Butler was now almost certain to be summoned to the Palace the next day. This telephone call largely explains why *The Times*, in a lonely alliance with the *Daily Worker*, persisted the next morning in backing Butler's claims. Though aware of the earlier stories about Home, *The Times* took the view that they had been superseded by the "exclusive" information provided by Aldington.

Yet even Aldington was soon to have his doubts. As the meeting broke up he offered a lift home to Redmayne, who had come round from the whip's office in Downing Street by taxi. The whole purpose of having Redmayne at the meeting had been to enable him to pass on the information he had learned at it, both officially to the outgoing Prime Minister and informally to the Palace. But as Aldington drove down Whitehall, Redmayne said something that conveyed unmistakably that he did not seem to regard the situation as having been in any way changed by what had happened. It was enough to alert Aldington's suspicions. Early the next morning he himself telephoned Sir Michael Adeane, the Queen's private secretary, only to learn that no inkling of what had occurred had yet reached the Palace.

Getting the message through to Harold Macmillan mattered rather less, though Butler was by no means the only man to suspect that the outgoing Premier was never told the real importance of the meeting in Powell's house. Yet if Macmillan was never made aware that both Maudling and Hailsham had withdrawn their claims in Butler's favor he at least knew from newspaper headlines like "Cabinet Revolt" or "Midnight Cabinet Drama" that something had gone wrong. Far from giving him pause, the effect was to make him more determined than ever to press ahead. From his hospital bed he had a telephone call put through to Home. The Foreign Secretary was uneasy: "Well, I thought I was coming in to heal, not to wound." But Macmillan pressed him to keep up his courage: "Look, we can't change our view now; all the troops are on the starting line. Everything is arranged. It will just cause ghastly confusion if we delay." Just after 9 A.M. Macmillan sent his formal letter of resignation round to the Palace by the hand of his private secretary.

Right at the beginning, before his operation, Macmillan had let it be known that he wanted, if possible, to delay his actual formal resignation so as to go to the Palace in person to deliver up the seals of office. The growing tensions of the week, and the vision of the Tory Party publicly tearing itself to bits, made it clear that this would not be practicable. But, so far as Macmillan's regard for constitutional protocol was concerned, the next best thing happened. As he could not go to the Queen, she came to him. At 11:30 A.M., in spite of the fact that a month before she had canceled all public engagements on the ground of her pregnancy, Queen Elizabeth arrived at the hospital and was ushered into the Matron's office, where her Prime Minister of the last seven years was lying propped up in bed. While declining to give formal advice on his successor, Macmillan then read her a long memorandum which he had prepared the previous night after hearing the results of the polls and offered her a copy to take away with her. The Queen accepted it, but she had apparently already got the message. On returning to the Palace at noon, she immediately sent for the 14th Earl of Home, who drove out of the Foreign Office at 12:15 P.M. and was back home having lunch in Carlton Gardens by one o'clock with the royal invitation to form a government in his pocket. At the same time a depressed but still not wholly despairing Rab Butler was publicly and defiantly lunching with his wife in the dining room of the Carlton Club. To those who came up to sympathize, he complained of only one thing: Macmillan's apparently willful refusal to telephone him that morning despite a request made through Lord Dilhorne.

If any proof were needed of the toll that the past ten days had taken on the normal instantaneous Tory instinct to rally round a new leader it lay in the fact that, unlike Churchill in 1940, Eden in 1955 and Macmillan himself in 1957, Home did not feel able immediately to accept the Queen's Commission. Instead he asked for time to discover whether or not he commanded sufficient support to form an administration. Although in the end he was shown to have erred on the side of caution, Home's wariness was understandable. He did not know it then, but even before he was driven to the Palace the three other contenders for the leadership—together with Iain Macleod—had met together in the office that Rab Butler occupied in the Treasury. They joined in one last desperate throw to block the Foreign Secretary's accession. There, in the strangest *renversement* of all, Hailsham repeated in front of Butler what he had already told Maudling on the telephone the previous night—that he was now prepared to serve under Butler and that he would throw him any support that he had. He urged Maudling to do the same, not apparently being aware that Maudling and Butler had had just such a compact ever since the previous July. At this midmorning meeting Hailsham was far the most intransigent of the four in his opposition to Home's appointment; he was the first to fall in with Macleod's suggestion that they should insist on having a collective confrontation with Home as soon as possible.

But Home, showing an unexpected political cunning, was clever enough not to fall into that trap. He began seeing his new prospective Cabinet at 2:30 P.M., and as in January 1957 poor Butler was the first summoned. But he managed to ward off a meeting with his three main rivals together until he had got positive pledges of support from well over half the rest of the Cabinet. Up to that point neither Butler (who had been offered the Foreign Secretaryship straight away) nor Maudling (to whom Home's first question had been "Will you go on as my Chancellor?") had given an inch; each of them emphasized when they saw Home separately early in the afternoon, and again when they confronted him together shortly after 7 P.M., that they reserved their positions—Maudling, though, at this stage making it clear to Home that he had abandoned his own candidature in favor of Butler's.

Ironically, it was only when the four-cornered meeting took place that the situation was transformed. It was then that the united front of the triumvirate broke, with Hailsham announcing that he had agreed to serve and urging his two colleagues to do likewise. Neither Butler nor Maudling had had any advance warning of this development and they were both naturally taken aback at Hailsham's sudden change of front. They might have been less surprised had they known of the pressure put on Hailsham that afternoon by Julian Amery, who was shattered to learn that his own candidate had actually pledged his support to the abhorred Butler.

The Hailsham capitulation marked the end of the leadership crisis. Though Butler and Maudling asked for the night to think things over, they agreed as they were leaving 10 Downing Street and preparing to get into their cars that it was now really all over. That night there was no effort to organize any further last-ditch resistance to Home (indeed the only significant activity came from Maudling, who tried vainly to persuade Macleod and Enoch Powell not to throw their careers away, and from Butler, who did exactly the same—this time successfully—with his own most dedicated supporter, Edward Boyle). At 10 A.M. next morning—Saturday, October 19—Butler went to Downing Street and accepted the Foreign Office. Shortly afterward—an hour earlier than the time they had agreed the night before—Maudling was also summoned. He was told that Butler had agreed to serve as Foreign Secretary. Would he now—for the fourth time of asking—agree to continue as Chancellor? The youngest and, as it turned out, toughest contender said "Yes"—and the crisis was over.

Shortly afterward a smiling, triumphant 14th Earl of Home left Downing Street for the Palace, kissed hands and became, if only for a few flickering aristocratic days, the first peer to be Prime Minister of Britain since the third Marquess of Salisbury resigned in 1902. But his first message was certainly democratic—if in the best sporting public-school tradition. He told a crowd of 700 sightseers in Downing Street who had assembled to cheer his return from the Palace: "We are going to work together as a team to win the next election. I hope now that everyone on this fine Saturday morning can forget about politics except me."

5. The Great Commoner

To have gone out after him in those early days
would have been rather like shooting a wounded stag.
HAROLD WILSON, *December 1, 1964*

THAT first weekend a considerable section of the public
found themselves asking "Lord who?" There was nothing in
the new Prime Minister that seemed easily identifiable. Admittedly he was tall, thin and elegant, but so were scores of
hereditary peers. At first his name, if only because of its odd
pronunciation, was a good deal more memorable than his
face. The long mouth and the large teeth could not save it
from anonymity; the half-moon spectacles only blurred the
impression of the stare. Probably the most startling thing
about Home which the public learned that weekend was the
discovery that he had first entered the House of Commons as
long ago as 1931 and had been continuously in office ever
since Churchill formed the first postwar Conservative Government in 1951. What on earth had he been doing all that
time? Why until now had no one felt it necessary to take
much notice of him?

There was, of course, an explanation. Men like Home are
born to a certain role in the Conservative Party, and it is rare
for them to depart from it. "Alec Home is today's Lord Salisbury," Iain Macleod had remarked only six months earlier;
and his whole career had indeed until this moment con-
formed to the pattern of the inside figure of influence rather
than the external man of power. Even as a young back-
bencher in the Thirties he had made his impression on the
people who mattered rather than on the party as a whole. As
Lord Dunglass he had become in 1936 Parliamentary Sec-

retary to the man who was soon to be Prime Minister, Neville Chamberlain. Malicious—and perhaps envious—M.P.s said at the time that Chamberlain had appointed him only to get the use of his shooting and fishing rights during weekends in Scotland, but in fact Chamberlain had been impressed by his vigorous defense of the principle of the Means Test during a stormy debate on unemployment assistance. In his turn Dunglass much admired Chamberlain and even went so far as to grow a Chamberlain mustache in imitation of his master. To this day he makes no apologies for Chamberlain's Munich Agreement.

His attitude then was in fact very much of a piece with his later outlook. A hatred of Communism has always been the mainspring of Home's philosophy. When laid up for two years during the war with spinal tuberculosis he made a detailed study of Marx and Lenin, even reading *Das Kapital* (a book which Wilson proudly confesses he has never got beyond the first two pages of). The only time in his whole political career that Home ever spoke against his party was in 1945 when he criticized the Yalta Agreement on the ground that Churchill had given too much away to the Soviet Union.

Home's parliamentary career was abruptly interrupted at the end of the war. In 1945 he lost his seat of Lanark to the local stationmaster and was not re-elected until 1950. The next year, 1951, his father died and he succeeded to the earldom and had to leave the Commons for the Lords. In October of the same year he was given his first ministerial office as Minister of State at the Scottish Office. It was said at the time that the Prime Minister, Winston Churchill, did not even know Home by sight. Certainly he then seemed to have no dreams of high office. "It seemed rather stodgy just to stay at home and live on your money and look after your estates," he later explained when asked why he had gone back into politics. His first job was a comparatively junior one for a

middle-aged man with over fifteen years political experience
in both Houses behind him. And it was not till four years
later that he entered the Cabinet. When Eden became Prime
Minister in 1955 he appointed Home to the Commonwealth
Relations Office. Because of the Central African Federation
problem this was a controversial department, and throughout
his tenure of it Home was to be suspected of being less
sympathetic to African aspirations than at least one of
the Colonial Secretaries—Iain Macleod—alongside whom he
worked for almost a year. At this time he could frequently be
heard repeating, as if he had just heard them, the old settlers'
clichés about Africans: "They didn't even discover the
wheel," "You've got to go out there to really understand
them," or "We've had two thousand years of civilization." He
went so far as to say in 1959: "Britain and South Africa are
two countries on the same side in the essential task of secur-
ing the safety and the liberty of the free peoples of the
world." Once in 1959, when voted down by the Oxford
Union on a motion in favor of Central African Federation,
he remarked that Oxford had not used to be like that. "But
mind you," he added, "they tell me that most of the right
people were on the river."

If Home's views were antique, they were usually decent; it
was not what he thought that offended the Labour Party.
They were still outraged by the suspicion that the Prime
Minister had been chosen, in Wilson's words, "by a machinery of aristocratic cabal producing a result based on family
and hereditary connections." Indeed Home's very manner
seemed to aggravate the suspicion. His aloof self-confidence,
his patrician voice and his air of disdain when meeting
strangers were contrary to the expected qualities of a democratic leader.

As he shuttled all that weekend between his flat in Carlton
Gardens and his new residence at 10 Downing Street, Home
wore a smile of utter confidence. But his problems were

quickly revealed when at 6 P.M. on Sunday he announced his Cabinet. A whole day earlier it had been known to at least two newspapers that neither Iain Macleod nor Enoch Powell was prepared to serve; and when the formal list of twenty-three Ministers was made public (showing only four new members) both their names were absent. If these two had been merely tired Cabinet war horses, their absence could easily have been glossed over. But in fact both Macleod (rightly) and Powell (wrongly) had always been considered emblems and symbols of modern reconstructed Conservatism. The effect of their rebellion inevitably backed up the charges made by Wilson against Home's appointment.

The new Prime Minister got his chance to reply to them when he made his second television appearance on the night of Monday, October 21. This time he was to be interviewed —a form of broadcast which he prefers to straight solo camera talks. Looking the opposite of a staid and stuffy aristocrat— once or twice his face even broke into an urchin smile—he put up the performance of the handsome, confident cricketer that he had been in his youth. Even the fast-ball questions (Butler's disappointment, Macleod's and Powell's withdrawal, his own self-confessed ignorance of economics) were dealt with crisply and neatly, and he eventually brought off a full on-drive in the direction of the Leader of the Opposition. Asked whether a 14th Earl was not specially vulnerable to attack by the Labour Party he replied reflectively: "I suppose Mr. Wilson is really, when you come to think of it, the fourteenth Mr. Wilson. I don't see why criticism should center on this. Are we to say that all men are equal except peers?" It was a boundary stroke, and the crowd cheered. Harold Wilson showed his irritation by protesting in private that the statement was meaningless: he wasn't the fourteenth Mr. Wilson anyway.

Home's coronet created all kinds of difficulty. On the day he accepted office the new Prime Minister had let it be known

—though Harold Wilson immediately branded it "an act of impertinence"—that he would prefer the new session of Parliament not to start until he could take his own seat on the Treasury bench; and, following his first full Cabinet meeting on Tuesday, October 22, the announcement was made that the reassembly of Parliament was postponed for a fortnight. Simultaneously it was made known that the 14th Earl of Home was also divesting himself of his earldom and three baronies in the peerage of Scotland, his barony in the peerage of the United Kingdom and his additional barony in the English peerage. He was able to keep one handle to his name, since in addition to his hereditary honors he was a Knight of the Thistle. Purely an order of chivalry, this involved no disqualification from sitting in the Commons.

All these moves were the required preliminaries to Sir Alec (as he overnight became) finding a seat and getting elected a member of Parliament. This difficulty had been troubling the Conservative Party ever since the beginning of the leadership struggle. Lord Hailsham, in the first phase of the contest, had been offered a choice from no less than four seats by self-abnegating followers among the ranks of Conservative M.P.s. None of these four was the constituency which offered the quickest and surest route for a peer to get back into the Commons.

At the beginning of the parliamentary recess the previous obscure Conservative member for the safe Scottish constituency of Kinross and West Perthshire had died. Apart from the highly risky marginal seat of Luton, vacant since the previous June, this was the only constituency for which the Speaker of the House of Commons could issue a writ for election during the recess. By-elections in any other seats conveniently made vacant by resignation would have to wait even for starter's orders until the House reassembled.

The Conservatives in Kinross showed no signs at first of wanting to get involved in matters of London *haute poli-*

tique. They succeeded in getting the writ issued for their by-election on the morning of Thursday, October 18, when the question of the future leadership of the Conservative Party was still publicly unresolved; that same night a young Scottish brewer, George Younger, whom they had chosen as candidate even before the former member died, was formally adopted at a meeting of the local association. The next day the local Conservative agent, who from the time of Blackpool onward had firmly discouraged all inquiries about the availability of the seat to either Home or Hailsham, announced that there was no question but that Mr. Younger's candidature would go forward.

But on October 19, while Sir Alec was kissing hands at the Palace, Younger was communing with his conscience. The first public sign of this was the cancellation of a meeting due to be held that night at Killiecrankie. By next day, a Sunday, Younger's mind was made up. It is highly unusual for the Conservative Party, still less its Scottish version, the Unionist Party, to conduct political business on the Sabbath. But this was an emergency, and for once rules had to be broken. After several hours hard chewing in the Glasgow Conservative Club, the officers of the Kinross association and the chairman of the Scottish Unionist Party were able to announce that Younger's offer to stand down had been accepted. There was an exchange of letters—modest from Mr. Younger, grateful from Sir Alec—and the new Premier had been presented with the third safest Tory seat in Britain.

Although Younger stood for, and won, Ayr at the general election, he was at the time so sick at heart he could hardly bother to look for another constituency. His feeling of deprivation was understandable. Sir Walter Scott once wrote that if you asked any Scotsman to name the most beautiful county in the land he would put his own county first and Perthshire second. Even the Labour Party admits that the country is good to look at. On the October morning when the first wave of politicians and Fleet Street men arrived, it was looking its best. The triangular Schiehallion mountain range soared into a duck-egg blue sky, set off by leaves of all shades from russet to veridian. The fields were dotted with pheasants pecking about in the stubble; grouse tittuped across the moorland roads; while in their houses and lodges dozed the lairds and gentry of Perthshire: Lord Ancaster of Drummond Castle, Major Bowser of Argaty, Lord Doune, Sir James Denby Roberts of Strathallan . . .

The constituency itself is one of the largest in Britain, covering over 2,000 square miles from Kinross in the southeast to Kinloch Rannoch in the northwest. Its immense size and sparse 33,000 electorate led later to the suggestion, much resented locally, that it was populated mainly by sheep. Sheep— and during the next three weeks reporters. The sight of a Prime Minister fighting a lonely by-election battle on the hustings was without precedent in twentieth-century British politics; and Home, for British journalists, had that extra dash of newsworthiness that attaches to the aristocracy.

At first the press had little to do except examine claims to attention of Home's five opponents. Sir Alec himself, still preoccupied with the task of completing his Government, did not journey up to Scotland until October 25, when, having first stopped off at his border home, the Hirsel, he then drove on to "Andy's Place" in his new constituency. This was the white-washed house of Major Andrew Drummond-Moray in Comrie, which was to become for the next fortnight both by-election headquarters and Cabinet Office.

Once arrived, Sir Alec wasted no time. Pausing only to hand in his nomination papers, he opened his campaign the next day in the cattle-auction room in Perth. There, in his first major speech as Prime Minister, Sir Alec at once began to lay down the policy departures and personal style of his premiership. The last celebrity to appear in that same sanded ring had been an Aberdeen Angus bull which had been knocked down for £63,000 a few weeks earlier. Sir Alec, not to be outdone, was dealing in hundreds of millions. Having plainly decided that the new reign should be launched by a little judicious window dressing, he upturned the economic cornucopia and shook out before the electorate the fruits of their patient abstinence during the aftermath of the credit squeeze. While Reginald Maudling was sounding a quiet warning in his own constituency about the possibility of the boom getting out of hand, Sir Alec in Perth was promising 400,000 houses a year, £3,500 million for higher education and £800 million for hospital building inside ten years. Later he threw in £1,000 million to be spent on roads before 1969 and £400 million on schools before 1968. Not surprisingly all this bonanza led one Conservative newspaper, the *Sunday Telegraph*, to ask sharply whether the new Prime Minister was "wise to underplay everything that distinguishes Conservatism from contemporary Socialism."

Personally as well as politically Sir Alec made it clear that day in the Perth cattle market that he would never be a predictable public performer. He departed extensively from his prepared handout; sentences vanished in a mist of subordinate clauses; verbs oscillated from singular to plural; and he bewildered most of his audience by insisting that the world had three times in the past three years stood on the brink of war.

The next day, Sunday, Sir Alec attended the Episcopalian church in Comrie. More in hope than in expectation of a story, the press filed in with him only to be smitten by a spectacular thunderclap of outraged morality from a visiting preacher.

It was certainly strong stuff and Sir Alec called it a "jolly good sermon." "We have all been shaken up," Canon Boxer roundly declared, "by news of violence, racketeering in slum property, to say nothing of the sale of national security and the doping of race horses." But for the representatives of the newspapers, including one or two which had, in Canon Boxer's phrase, "paid huge sums for horrible details and bestial memoirs," the events of the spring and summer already seemed a world away. And the slight, tweedy figure of Sir Alec himself was remote from the raffish world of Rachman and Profumo. Even before Home arrived in Perthshire his true-blue constituents had taken to him as Premier and M.P. "Yes, the Denning Report's arrived up here and we've all been paying our seven and sixpences," said one Perthshire businessman. "Poor old Macmillan—he was past it. Now Lord Home, he may not be able to do the twist, but he's with it. A few months ago we were all assuming that we were in for another spell of Socialist misery under Mr. Wilson. But now it doesn't look half so certain."

Sir Alec already was grooming himself as the Rodney Stone of politics, the gentleman amateur who was going to show up "the fourteenth Mr. Wilson" as a tired professional pug. He presented himself to the press as an obliging, nice chap, always ready to pose for the cameramen on Major Drummond-Moray's lawn.

There are snags to the role of a decent man in a dirty world. The new Prime Minister proved this at his first evening village meeting. On Saturday night at Glen Lyon he had told a questioner he would be "surprised if there was any delay" in starting four Scottish hydroelectric schemes—one of them sited in West Perthshire. His young Labour opponent, Andrew Forrester, jeered that Sir Alec was admirably qualified to succeed a Prime Minister who was "just not told what was going on." The four schemes, Mr. Forrester brutally pointed out, had already been held up for periods varying from three months to four years.

In spite of the gaffe, the story had a happy ending. The Scottish Hydroelectric Board applied for its schemes to go forward within hours of Sir Alec's statement. Official obstacles melted away, and the Kinross electorate received a useful demonstration of the advantages that might accrue from having a Prime Minister as their member of Parliament. In case the point had not been driven home, Sir Alec gave it a few more bangs at his whistle-stop meetings. The constituents of the Prime Minister, he smilingly pointed out, could at least count on their grievances being dealt with promptly. This line of thought offended visiting Labour M.P.s, who complained about the undemocratic loading of this by-election contest. This showed itself perhaps most clearly in the affair of the highland railway lines threatened by Dr. Beeching's ax. Certainly Sir Alec's pledge to his constituents during the campaign that adequate alternative methods of transport would be provided before any railway line was closed was more than anyone could have hoped to extract from a Prime Minister in any other circumstances, or indeed from any other Conservative candidate in any circumstances at all. In the end the new Prime Minister had to pay heavily for this particular pledge by being forced on the floor of the House of Commons to extend it to England and Wales as well.

Only two other specters, one from the past and one from the future, rose to trouble Sir Alec while he was still on the hustings. The one from the past was far the more romantic. It was "the Red Duchess of Atholl." From the moment of his appointment Sir Alec had been attacked by some sections of the Labour Party as "a man of Munich," and the fact that the seat he was now fighting for had been represented for fifteen years by "the Red Duchess" provided an opportunity for ramming the charge home. This remarkable lady had been M.P. for Kinross and West Perthshire from 1923 to 1938, when she resigned the seat (she had already resigned the Conservative whip) and unsuccessfully fought the ensuing by-election on the Chamberlain Government's appeasement of dictators both in Spain and at Munich.

As Chamberlain's P.P.S. at the time, Sir Alec had been sent up to speak for the Duchess's Conservative opponent, and at

Auchterarder in December 1938 he committed himself to the observation: "The Munich settlement was undoubtedly a gain to European peace. The Prime Minister's reception in Germany proved to the dictators the great difficulty they would experience in getting their people to agree to war."

But, despite the Labour Party's vigorous use of this quotation, Sir Alec twenty-five years afterward remained quite unrepentant. He continued to defend the Munich settlement, if on rather different grounds, and he proudly told a by-election press conference that he could not recall a single occasion on which he had voted against his own party in Parliament. This record distinguished him sharply both from his immediate predecessor, Harold Macmillan, and from Winston Churchill, who had written to that self-same "Red Duchess" in the aftermath of Munich, "Your defeat at this moment would be relished by the enemies of Britain and of freedom in every part of the world." But so far as the by-election was concerned, Munich was the ghost that refused to walk. Labour M.P.s had rather better luck—though not much— with another exhumed quotation in which Sir Alec as a young man had suggested that unemployed Scottish miners should be apprenticed to domestic service in the south of England.

The specter from the future was much more mundane. It was known as "Winter Keep"—the title given to the Government's new form of subsidy for marginal farmers. It had already come under heavy criticism, and Sir Alec's most formidable opponent, the Liberal candidate, Duncan Millar, used its potential damaging effect on Scottish agriculture as his main campaign plank. The uncomprehending, Sassenach journalists, who had to hear the topic debated at every meeting, took to ordering "gin and winter keep" in the bars afterward.

For it was clear, at least to outside observers, that none of these issues would influence the result of the by-election.

What mattered was the impression that Home made personally on this backward and feudal Conservative seat; the new Prime Minister seemed more and more deliberately to be using his lairdly charm and probity to demonstrate a reversal of the political tide. It was here, among his own sort of people, that he set the style of his leadership.

A lower-middle-class shop girl, voting for the first time, explained in one innocent phrase why she would back the Conservative cause. "Tradition," she said offhandedly, and tossed her head. On this, his home ground, the Prime Minister could and did get away with anything, even technical breaches of the electoral law. He bought two electors drinks in Auchterarder to their glad surprise, and two months later in the House of Commons he had to listen to George Wigg making heavy jokes about it. The tone of the Tory campaign was set on the first day when the nation's new leader stopped off at a hotel in Amulree to meet a roomful of ghillies and shepherds. "I just wanted him to meet my glenfolk," explained the proprietor's wife, who again had carefully supplied them all with drinks; in the lounge of that same hotel one of Perthshire's numerous Old Etonians could be heard accosting the new Premier with the casual comment "Hello, Alec—long time no see."

The contest was less a race than a procession; at noon on November 8 the new Prime Minister—an M.P. at last—was able to walk out of Perth town hall with a broad smile and a 9,328 majority. He had collected three times as many votes as even his nearest runner-up, and in the exultation of the moment the Conservative Party's new leader felt justified in announcing that everything, even the loss the previous day of the much more crucial seat at Luton, could now be forgotten. At Kinross the Government had turned over a new leaf and begun a new chapter.

As three out of four later by-elections that year were to demonstrate, it had done no such thing. But the Kinross by-election was nevertheless important and valuable to the Conservative Party. First, the fortnight's virtually unopposed publicity transformed Sir Alec from a nebulous, unknown quantity into being a national leader; and secondly its impressive-looking result—though, in fact, less good statistically than it appeared in the headlines—provided the three-week-old Premier with a reassuring boost of confidence. When the Luton result was announced Sir Alec had commented gloomily that the electorate was obviously bored with the Conservative Party "and after twelve years in office there is nothing much that we can do about it." His own result next day suggested there was. Could not his own personality shake the electorate out of its lethargy?

Sir Alec returned to London a hero. His first public engagement took place on the evening of the next day, Saturday, November 9, when he made a silent but well-publicized appearance at the British Legion festival of remembrance in the Albert Hall. In the best British sporting tradition he leaned out of his box and shook hands with Harold Wilson, who was sitting in the box next door. Two days later to a fanfare of party loyalty he was formally gazetted leader of the Conservative Party at a mass meeting of M.P.s, peers and prospective candidates in Church House, Westminster. To this gathering every Conservative M.P. was summoned by two-line whip in order that even the humblest back-bencher should be able to say he had played his part in a meeting held (as the notice put it) "to elect a successor to the Right Honorable Harold Macmillan as Leader of the Conservative Party." One or two recalcitrant Butlerites resented this fiction so much that they refused to turn up; yet Butler himself placed the new leader's name in nomination. It was the third time he had performed this galling task. Having been chosen by acclamation, the party's new leader treated his followers to a stirring message about "spoiling for a real tough political fight," a fight which, he urged his audience, must from now on never be out of their minds.

It was very much in Sir Alec's. That same night he converted the Prime Minister's annual speech at the Lord Mayor's banquet into the equivalent of a party political broadcast. Received with understandable rapture by the potentates of the City, he held out to them and to the whole nation (both television channels put out his broadcast, the BBC even offering a fulsome running commentary that was not accorded to Wilson the following year) the prospect of peace and plenty, provided it would make "one per cent more effort." On foreign affairs he appeared at some pains to demonstrate his "expertise." He included a long passage about being "over the watershed of danger" with Russia, and went out of his way to pass the torch of Britain's prestige in the world to his former rival and now his colleague, Rab Butler. The listening Butler appeared on the screen looking enigmatic.

The Lord Mayor's banquet was only a prologue to the main drama next day. Never before in British political history had a Prime Minister been introduced to the House of Commons as a new member; and there was not an inch of empty space on the Commons' green leather benches when on the afternoon of Tuesday, November 12, Sir Alec stood fidgeting nervously at the bar of the House awaiting the summons from the Speaker: "Members desirous of taking their seats." At first there was anticlimax: Sir Alec was not the only member due to be introduced that afternoon. Standing alongside him was William Howie, who had won Luton for Labour for the first time since 1945. Since the certificate of his election had reached the Speaker before a similar document from the Returning Officer at Kinross, it was Howie who first advanced up the chamber. He was greeted with loud Labour cheers but they were soon to be dwarfed entirely by one of the most extraordinary scenes of enthusiasm that the Commons chamber can ever have witnessed. As Sir Alec began his ceremonial march up the length of green carpet toward the Speaker's chair the entire Government side of the House rose to its feet, cheering, waving and in a few cases apparently even singing. If hero worship alone could make a hero, Sir Alec would have become one that afternoon in the space of two or three minutes.

But Sir Alec had more to do that afternoon than simply make a formal entry into the House. He also had to perform the Prime Minister's traditional duty of making the first major Government speech in the debate on the address. For any new Prime Minister there could hardly have been a more difficult challenge; for one who had only just come into the Commons an hour earlier after an interval of more than twelve years, and who, moreover, had never made a speech from the Commons front bench in his life before, it was clearly a brutal task. The ordeal was made worse by the fact that the new Prime Minister had latterly come to receive in the newspapers a build-up almost as extravagant as the original demolition job. The Butlerite *Daily Express*, which had called Home's selection "a bad, bad, bad decision," now wrote of him as a kind of political Tarzan. That very morning's headlines chanted "Sir Alec's Great Call: Wealth and Peace."

In the House of Commons Sir Alec tried to repeat very much the same speech that he had made the evening before at the Mansion House; but he got a very different reaction. Thrown by his lack of knowledge of parliamentary procedure, punctured by frequent Opposition interruptions even on one occasion pulled down by his own Chief Whip, his whole performance brought his own supporters down to earth with a bump. Whatever qualities the new leader might subsequently show, it was plain from the very first moment that he would never emerge as a Demosthenes of parliamentary debate. "I must not," he remarked at one point, "take up too much of the House's time." A delighted Opposition taunted "Go on! Go on!"

In British politics the orthodox doctrine has always been that a party leader has to establish his dominance first in the House of Commons, and that only then can he hope to make an impression in the country. When Sir Alec had finished that first speech there were glum faces on the Government side of the House. But Sir Alec himself remained remarkably cheerful. Having dismissed his performance as "Beta Minus," he apparently gave it no more thought. Of course he knew, as no one else knew at the time, that he did not propose to spend much time in the House. Perhaps the most astonishing comment on his twelve-month premiership was that he made only four major speeches to his parliamentary colleagues; he had made up his mind on the day he succeeded Macmillan that his whole effort was to be concentrated on making a direct appeal to the country.

Wilson would later describe this as Home's greatest mistake: "He should have allowed me to go on and on making speeches, probably boring people in the process, while he gave the impression of getting on briskly and crisply with the actual job of governing the country. But as it was he made himself into a national candidate much too early—all those speeches and tours; it was almost as if he was the Leader of the Opposition trying to get into power, not the man already supposed to be doing the job."

At the beginning Wilson feared that the emergence of a new Tory leader might damage the Labour Party's chances. In the week the new session of Parliament opened, he summed up the threat involved with characteristic shrewdness: "The real danger of this chap coming in is that, taken together with everything that happened last month, it could easily persuade people that they've already had their general election. That's why I have to keep hammering away on the

theme of 'the same old gang,' and fortunately it obviously
is. It's not just that Home himself, like Macmillan, is obviously out of touch—what does he know about old-age pensioners or the 11-plus? It's also that he's kept far too many of
the old crowd of Ministers; it would be much more difficult
for us if a whole lot of fresh faces were sitting in the Cabinet."

Later on a number of leading Conservatives were to accept
the force of Wilson's point. Why, they asked, had Home not
seized the opportunity in October to form a Tory Cabinet
somehow entirely dissociated from the familiar faces of the
previous twelve years? The criticism was unfair. The Conservatives might have rallied the ranks and recovered with
astonishing rapidity from the bitter struggle over the succession; but there was one legacy that the new leader at least
could not dodge. Butler's threatened veto had meant that
Home had had to ask each one of his colleagues in turn if
they would be prepared to serve with him; and once he had
done that—and indeed procured pledges from them—he
could hardly turn around and say their services were not required after all.

Having once been reduced to soliciting pledges, he could
never expect to occupy the dominant position that a Prime
Minister usually holds today in twentieth-century British
politics. Butler's abortive revolt had not only ossified the
Cabinet; it also reduced the status of the Prime Minister. As
the months went by the new Prime Minister was to
strengthen his position first with the party in the country and
eventually with the Parliamentary Party at Westminster; he
was never able to arm himself with a Premier's normal
power basis—an unquestioned dominance over his Cabinet
colleagues. All of them were in a position to know (and remember) too much of the method by which he had come to
power, a method which, as Iain Macleod was later to explain,
had shown scant respect for the views or preferences of the
new Prime Minister's own Cabinet colleagues.

But if "No Change" was necessarily the order of the day at home, it was soon to be dramatically and unexpectedly overturned abroad. His second week as a member of the House of Commons had been a busy one for Sir Alec. Although he had chosen not to exercise a Prime Minister's normal prerogative of replying to the debate on the address (badly disappointing Harold Wilson by his decision), he had that week delivered his first party political broadcast as Prime Minister and appeared twice at the dispatch box on Tuesday and Thursday to answer Prime Minister's Questions. Perhaps exhausted by all this endeavor, Sir Alec drove down on the evening of Friday, November 22, to Sussex to spend a restful weekend with his old friend from the Coronation days of 1953, the Duke of Norfolk. It was to prove no rest, for it was there, in Arundel Castle, shortly after seven o'clock, that Britain's month-old Prime Minister heard the news of the assassination of President Kennedy in Dallas.

Like everyone else in Britain—one of his ministerial colleagues, Quintin Hogg,* wept openly that night at a by-election meeting in Marylebone—Home was crushed by the news. But at such moments there can be no privacy for Prime Ministers. Sir Alec left Arundel Castle at once and by eleven o'clock that same night was broadcasting a memorial tribute to the nation. Speaking immediately after him in the same program was Harold Wilson, having rushed dramatically from a large public meeting in East Flint to a BBC studio in Manchester. Wilson's behavior that night, both at the BBC and before a later interview at Granada, made a lasting impression on those who witnessed it. It was almost as if he could not accept what every news bulletin was now announcing to the world. "It can't have happened," he said time and again. At one point while receiving a phone call from Down-

* The former Lord Hailsham, who had renounced his peerage on November 20, with the characteristic comment "Lord Hailsham is dead. God bless Quintin Hogg."

ing Street, he pressed his head hopelessly against the wall. He
recalled how he had seen and talked to Kennedy only a few
months earlier in Washington and how he had thought to
himself that here at least—whatever might happen elsewhere
—was one constant force that could stir a nation out of
lethargy and inspire the rest of the world. In the main Wilson's reaction was numbed emotional shock; but subcon-
sciously he must also have been aware that the death of the
forty-six-year-old President had kicked one of the main props
from under Labour's appeal. From the moment of his election in 1960 President Kennedy had represented, if
obliquely, a challenge to everything that was stuffy, traditional and out of date in Britain. Now the Siegfried across the
Atlantic was dead; and the young of all the West were without a hero.

On the night the news broke Eldon Griffiths, one of the
Prime Minister's two speech writers, claimed on television
that the President's death must leave Sir Alec the dominant
figure in the Atlantic Alliance. This view was too optimistic
even for many Tories, some of whom in weeks to come were
to wonder privately whether the party had really been wise to
let go of Harold Macmillan. Certainly the former Prime Minister would have had the stature to tower if only temporarily
over the Western Alliance; few bar Eldon Griffiths expected
the same from Home.

Indeed that night Sir Alec's own performance on the
memorial program for the President badly disappointed some
of his own followers. Because of the pre-election atmosphere,
the BBC invited all three party leaders to take part, and
where both Wilson and Grimond came over as genuine,
human personalities, Sir Alec seemed stilted and formal. But
it was not the official BBC program that in the end brought
British domestic politics into the tragedy in Dallas. Just before the BBC program went out at 11 P.M. the London ITV
company, Associated-Rediffusion, mounted a program of its

own which included an interview with George Brown. For the Labour Party that interview was to have a sequel as unfortunate as anything in the whole pre-election period.

For the moment, however, all attention was naturally focused on the United States. It was announced that both the Prime Minister and the Leader of the Opposition would fly to Washington for the President's funeral. After some struggle Wilson had succeeded in joining Sir Alec and the Duke of Edinburgh on a plane of the Queen's Flight due to leave London Airport for Washington that Sunday afternoon. Jo Grimond, the Leader of the Liberal Party, flew at his own expense. No funeral of the head of a foreign power had ever attracted the presence of all three British party leaders; yet that week in November, as grief and shock spread throughout the country, it did not even seem remarkable.

The House of Commons was bereft of its leading spokesmen when it met on Monday, November 25, to pay to the dead President the same exceptional tribute which it had paid to Hugh Gaitskell—that of adjourning in his memory. But even this did not seem to matter; the gap caused by their absence was more than filled by Harold Macmillan, making his first appearance in the House since his illness. With a speech of grace, style and pathos he reminded everyone on both sides of the House just what a vacuum he himself had left in British political life. The tall, languid, if now stooped, figure who had virtually been howled down when he last appeared in the chamber in July had the comfort of discovering once again that he could still control the Commons with the melancholy droop of an eyelid.

At first the shock of Dallas brought almost a truce into domestic British politics. It was not to last for long. On the morning of Saturday, November 23, Harold Wilson received at his home in Hampstead Garden Suburb a telephone call which was to worry him in America. It came from the ever-watchful Labour back-bencher, George Wigg, who wanted,

first, to know whether the party leader had seen George
Brown on television the previous night. As Wilson had not,
Wigg explained exactly what he had thought of Brown's performance. It was not, in Wigg's view, a matter that could be
left where it stood; some action would have to be taken. The
public would expect it.

In the mass of world news Brown's broadcast had attracted
very little notice, though the *Daily Express* that morning ran
a passage from it on page two. In the light of cold print this
did not appear to read any too coherently. Probably, apart
from George Wigg, the only people seriously alarmed by
what had happened at that stage were those who had actually
been with Brown at Associate-Rediffusion's London studios.
There had taken place what Brown himself later described as
"a verbal argument . . . a strong discussion." It seems that
Brown, having been summarily summoned out of a Mayor's
dinner in Shoreditch, was somewhat taken aback to find that
his companions in the broadcast were not British politicians
but an American columnist (John Crosby) and a Hollywood
film star (Eli Wallach). Nor were matters improved when
Eli Wallach mistook the deputy leader of the Labour Party
for a television interviewer and announced that the producer
would have to find another one if he was to go on. Eventually
all ruffled feelings were smoothed down and the only substantial complaints received by the television company that
night were that Brown had spoken about the dead President,
and indeed his wife, in overfamiliar terms.

Not until Brown returned from a lecture tour in Germany
almost a week later was there any sign that the incident
would blow up into a major political row. Brown had been
encouraged to carry on with this trip by the Labour Chief
Whip, Herbert Bowden, even though it meant that he as
well as Wilson would be away from the House when the Commons met for the Kennedy memorial tributes. His absence
from this occasion contributed to the extraordinary subse-

quent furor. (In the lobbies of the House of Commons rumors multiplied that he had been firmly ordered to keep away from the Commons, and though very few Labour M.P.s had actually seen his broadcast, lurid accounts of it began passing from mouth to mouth. By the time Wilson returned from the United States on Tuesday, November 26—a day earlier than Home and Grimond*—he found the Parliamentary Labour Party in a state of something approaching uproar.

In Germany Brown himself had no knowledge of any of this. Although none too happy about his own showing the previous Friday night, he returned to London on Thursday, November 28, fairly confident that the whole affair should have blown over. He was soon to learn his mistake. In his own room he found a pile of indignant letters protesting against the tastelessness of his performance and, worse than that, in Wilson's room upstairs he found, a few moments later, a badly worried party leader and an even more anxious Opposition Chief Whip. Both insisted that the broadcast had caused a good deal of disquiet in the party, and Bowden at least seemed to suggest that something would have to be done about it. At first Brown misunderstood and thought that he was being asked for his resignation. Wilson immediately made it clear that there was no question of that, and it was left for Brown and Bowden to work something out together that might soothe any indignant party feelings. They agreed that Brown should make a personal statement at the party meeting that evening—an arrangement which Wilson later approved as the best answer in the circumstances.

In the event it proved the worst solution possible. Not only did it allow every newspaper in the country to make a polit-

---

* Home and Grimond were diverted by fog from London to Manchester and all stayed the night at the Duke of Devonshire's Chatsworth Castle in Derbyshire. Pointing out a big fourposter bed, a Home aide remarked to Grimond: "You could get the whole Parliamentary Liberal Party in there."

ical bonfire out of what had been, at worst, a personal indiscretion; it also gave the Conservatives the very thing they had been looking for ever since the Profumo crisis—a chance to publicize splits in the opposite party. For the first time Wilson began to face criticism of his leadership from within the ranks of the Parliamentary Labour Party.

This criticism was not confined to his clumsy handling of the Brown affair. It owed a good deal to the easy passage that the new Government was having in the House of Commons. When Harold Wilson had announced in his speech in the debate on the address "We shall play the ball and not the man," the Labour benches had given a loyal cheer. They did not want to bully the new Prime Minister before he had found his feet. But as weeks went by and not just Home himself but individual departmental Ministers as well emerged unscathed from debate after debate, the back-benchers began to inquire what had gone wrong.

In fact the tactic of giving the Government what almost amounted to a clear run was a deliberate decision of Wilson's. It had been his view all along that the new Government would be bound to enjoy "a honeymoon period," and that any efforts of the Opposition to disrupt it would almost certainly boomerang on those who made them. In all his own performances he thus tended to concentrate on killing the new Prime Minister with kindness. But as the Government quietly began to appropriate to itself more and more of the Labour Party's own policy proposals a mood of bewilderment seized the Labour ranks.

By the time the House broke up for the Christmas recess Sir Alec had good reason to feel pleased with his first nine weeks in the premiership. True, the pendulum as yet showed little sign of swinging back to the Tories; of the four by-elections held after his own at Kinross only one—in the East Anglian seat of Sudbury and Woodbridge—had shown a swing low enough to contain any hint of a possible fourth

Conservative election victory. But at least no one was any longer treating that prospect as a total absurdity. On the Sunday before Christmas the new Premier's former harshest press critic, the *Sunday Times*, went so far as to liken Home's position to that of Harry S. Truman in 1948. "Sir Alec," it remarked in a tone of surprise, "does have some of President Truman's advantages. His ability is not intellectual in character: sometimes for better and sometimes for worse he discusses national issues in uncomplicated terms much as the ordinary elector probably discusses them himself." As a tribute to Home it may have been curiously left-handed, but as an analogy it was for Wilson actively sinister. For the next nine months one name he never liked having mentioned was that of Governor Dewey—the man who, fifteen years earlier, had fallen off the wedding cake in America.

6. The Road Show

I will give away his secret. Whenever things became
most tense, he would go away on his own for half an hour
and arrange a vast bowl of flowers.
     R. A. BUTLER, *looking back on Sir Alec Douglas-Home as Prime
Minister, December 9, 1964*

AT the beginning of 1964 the great question became
"When?" Somehow the mere fact of having it posed transformed the atmosphere of Westminster. The Tories, who
before Christmas had been gradually growing in confidence,
suddenly gave way to anxiety; it was almost as if a single date
—January 1, 1964—had compelled them to come to terms
with the fact that this was bound to be Election Year. Was
there enough time for the cause to be saved? Had their own
wounds healed sufficiently for them to be in a fit condition
to go into battle?

The year could hardly have opened less helpfully for Home
and his Government. No sooner had Parliament reassembled on January 14 than two events combined to rip off the
bandages in which the Conservative Party had successfully
wrapped itself since October. Sir Alec had in part owed his
placid passage in the first two months of his premiership to
the fact that his Government had simply ticked over; even his
more thrusting, dynamic Cabinet ministers had recognized
the wisdom of allowing the Conservative Party to convalesce
after its various nervous shocks. But by January at least one
"modernizing" Minister was already restive. Edward Heath,
disappointed in his hope of getting the Foreign Office when
Home originally formed his Cabinet, had been rewarded instead with a glittering new title, that of Secretary of State for
Industry, Trade and Regional Development. So far, however,

140

the job had proved to be grand-sounding and nothing else. If Heath was to make his mark as a Minister of drive and energy, it was essential for him to get some major innovation onto the statute book under his name. Having warned the new Prime Minister on the day he was appointed that he would regard the modernization of Britain as the first change of his department, Heath had looked around for an issue to demonstrate that the Government in general, and he in particular, meant business. By the beginning of January he was sure he had found it in three initials that in the next five months were to reverberate day after day in newspaper headlines—RPM.

Resale Price Maintenance—the system whereby a manufacturer can enforce by law the prices at which his goods shall be sold—had long attracted political criticism; indeed one of Harold Wilson's last acts as president of the Board of Trade in 1951 had been to produce a blistering white paper attacking all such price-fixing arrangements. But for thirteen years after that the problem of actually doing something about abolishing RPM had defeated both major parties. It was the tiger that nobody wanted to ride, for the very good reason that arrayed behind the system of fixed prices stood a whole army of small retailers and lesser manufacturers all convinced that RPM afforded them a protection without which they would go to the wall.

When the Cabinet, after a series of worried meetings, finally agreed on January 15 to allow Heath to place his proposals for the abolition of RPM before the House of Commons they knew very well that some strong outside cohorts would be raised in protest against the decision. But no one seems to have anticipated the degree of opposition within the Conservative Party at Westminster, opposition that was eventually to bring the Government within one vote of defeat on the bill's committee stage. The widespread Tory antagonism to the measure owed a good deal to the way in

which the matter was handled. Many of the more traditional
Conservative back-benchers found it hard to forgive Heath
for introducing a major departure from policy without the
slightest warning, still less with any attempt at consultation.
The only important political effect of the whole RPM controversy—which was to drag on for five months without in the
event playing any important part in the election at all—was
the flood of resentment and suspicion that it once again let
loose on the Tory benches in the Commons. More than any
other single action Heath's announcement that January afternoon was responsible for delaying until well on into the
summer any visible recovery of morale among the Conservative members at Westminster.

The second blow which fell on Home that first week of the
new parliamentary sitting was superficially much more dramatic, though its long-term effects were much less lasting. For
almost three months nothing of the hidden story behind
Home's accession to the premiership had come out in public.
Then, on the last Sunday of the Christmas recess, Randolph
Churchill published a book, *The Fight for the Tory Leadership*, purporting to give a definitive account of everything
that had occurred at Blackpool and afterward. Its publication
did not come as a shock to members of the Cabinet, most of
whom had known about it for some time and a few of whom
had been treated to late-night readings by the author. In the
week or so before the book's publication review copies of it
were eagerly sought in political circles, and for a short period
this blue paperback came near to enjoying something of the
status of *Fanny Hill*. But if most people were simply curious,
one man was coldly furious.

A month after he left the Government Iain Macleod had
taken over the editorship of the *Spectator*. But even the quick
change from party potentate into professional journalist had
not tempted him to break his bargain with Home to say
nothing whatever about the circumstances in which he and

Enoch Powell had withdrawn from the new Government. Those who had looked for dramatic political revelations in the *Spectator* under its new "rogue elephant" editor had gone totally unrewarded. As a political journalist Macleod had proved himself discreet, even reticent, to a tactical fault; he had upheld Baldwin's motto, "sealed lips." Now, however, the publication of Churchill's book changed his whole mood. Recognizing instantly the source of most of Churchill's material, he resolved that this was a version of events which could not possibly be allowed to stand unchallenged on the historical record. In his own paper on Friday, January 17, he wrote a 4,500-word review of Churchill's book, branding it at the very beginning as "Harold Macmillan's trailer for the screenplay of his own memoirs." (Although Macleod was not aware of it, Macmillan had gone to the length of correcting Churchill's galley proofs.)

Macleod's article was perhaps the frankest ever written by any politician about events in which he himself had had a personal involvement. He told the whole story of Blackpool as he had seen it through his own eyes, complete with names times and places. But what excited Fleet Street was not merely that the Tories' traditional tight security barrier had, for once, been broken; it was far more that Macleod's whole thesis amounted, in effect, to a challenge to Home's title to be leader of the party. If the former chairman of the party and leader of the House of Commons had any doubts about the impact he would make they must have vanished with the next morning's headlines. Almost without exception they concentrated on such phrases as "The Big Fix," "How Macmillan Kept Butler Out," "Charge Against Etonian 'Magic Circle.'"

Not unnaturally the Labour Party was elated by this uncovenanted bonus. "There they were," ran one exultant comment, "thinking all their scars were about to heal, and then this fellow comes along and tears all the scabs off so that the whole process has to start all over again." Some shrewd Labour politicians even became convinced of the probability of an early election, believing that the Tories, in Dunkirk fashion, would choose to cut their losses and bring the troops back home in order to prepare for the election after next.

"Some of the Cabinet think like that too," said Harold Wilson on January 28, "but not Home. He's coming back from the States on February 14 and if he can come back with one line in the communiqué about peace talks or a better world he may have a March 19 election. But I think he wants to stay on till October. He thinks he's only got to get himself known and he'll make it." At this time Wilson was also highly critical of Home's handling of government. "This RPM is just another example of lack of political judgment. Attlee would never have taken a decision like that, and anyway there'd have been a Herbert Morrison to stop him. Even Macmillan wouldn't have done it. But their Herbert Morrison, Rab Butler, is sulking on one side. He's going to have the salt rubbed in his wounds when he goes to Washington with Home, but as number two . . ."

Laughingly, Wilson said: "You might say that Alec is an amateur who can't control his professionals. Wilson is a professional who can't control his amateurs." Even at this stage he was obsessed, and not entirely pleased, by Home's reputation as amateur. He was still smarting, for instance, at Home's reference to the "14th Mr. Wilson." He would keep reverting to this remark, and always with some new justification: "Of course everybody is the fourteenth somebody. Therefore people will identify with me." He admitted, even in January, that Home was "going down well with the Tory women" and would later admit that he went down well with women in general. One musing remark, in particular, showed how deeply Wilson was worried by Alec the Amateur: "I was given a book on my eighth birthday called *Test Match Surprise* by Jack Hobbs. It was about a cricketing peer, Lord

Ravensdale, if I remember rightly, who gets attacked by the press but goes on to make 51 in the second innings, and to take 5 for 50." No doubt the memory of this birthday present was still fresh in boy Harold's memory when he posed, at the age of eight, in front of 10 Downing Street. Forty years later he was beginning to dread a general-election surprise from another cricketing peer.

In January both party leaders began big provincial tours. Home wanted to make himself known to Conservative Party workers throughout the country and to restore their confidences after the dark days of 1963. He planned a series of fourteen big speeches, often accompanied by visits to local industries. This trip would be not only influential but instructive. The more Home saw of Britain and British life, the better equipped he would be to debate on domestic policies. Wilson's tour was less extensive. He was to give six policy speeches to put the party's views on the record. Some of these speeches appeared later that year in *The New Britain*, a Penguin book. Deliberately, he declined to tour regional industries because this had been Gaitskell's custom, and Wilson wanted to play the whole campaign in the opposite way to Gaitskell. Both party leaders regarded the other's tour as a blunder. In Home's view, the Wilson stomp emphasized Labour's dependence on its "one-man band." In Wilson's view, Home should have stayed in London to get on with the job of government, leaving the propaganda to better speakers. Probably both were right in their mutual criticism. But the tours went ahead, and helped to mold the whole year's campaign in the form of a Presidential combat between two leaders.

Wilson started off first—at the Town Hall, Birmingham, on January 19. This speech on the New Britain portrayed in Wilson's own words "the kind of society we wish to see in Britain and the steps that will have to be taken to create it. We want the youth of Britain to storm the new frontiers of knowledge, to bring back to Britain that surging adventurous self-confidence and sturdy self-respect which 1964 can mean. A chance for change. A chance to sweep away the grouse-moor conception of Tory leadership and refit Britain with a new image, a new confidence." He called for a return of "brashness and saltiness, and political irreverence, our energy, determination, and merchant-adventuring spirit which gave us our influence in the world" . . . "We want a Britain . . . where every . . . pub is its own Parliament-in-miniature." These last two passages—one oddly imperialistic and the other just laughable—never reappeared in any of Wilson's speeches. It was rumored that they had come from the pen of Lord Willis, the Labour TV writer and Life Peer.

Sir Alec Douglas-Home's visit to Swansea next day was an almost unqualified disaster. In the first place, all the arrangements went wrong. When Home was invited six weeks before, the local Conservative organization had arranged a half-day visit to the Steel Company of Wales at nearby Port Talbot. But the works were now closed by a labor dispute, and when Home arrived in Swansea he was taken instead for a look at some factories and a model crane. "But the afternoon was supposed to be spent at Port Talbot," a Swansea Conservative official complained over a lunchtime beer, "and they wouldn't let him near the place with a strike on. So what do you do when you've got a spare Prime Minister on your hands? Only one thing, of course. Send the b—— down to the docks." And this was what they did. A motorcade of eight cars, three of them empty apart from the driver, moved into Swansea dockland. Twice Sir Alec got out of the car, looked bleakly around and got straight back in again. There was nobody to meet him or cheer. "He's not taking a very long look," somebody said to Lord Brecon, the Minister of State for Welsh Affairs. "Yes," Lord Brecon agreed, "but what is there to look at?"

That evening in Swansea, Sir Alec delivered perhaps the

worst speech ever made by a British Prime Minister. The text, as it appeared in the press release and later in Home's collected speeches, *Peaceful Change,* was an adequate attack on Wilson's speech of the previous day. Indeed the newspapers next morning called it "scathing," "flaying" and "scorching." But in truth Sir Alec was no such thing. He rose to his feet with a ghastly smile. His tongue flickered in and out in an effort to dry his parched lips. He reminded one P. G. Wodehouse fan of an aging Bertie Wooster who had been roped in to recite Christopher Robin poems to the annual village concert. From the very first it was clear that he had not mastered his text. Scarcely one sentence corresponded to what appeared in the press release, and often he was quite incomprehensible. Quite apart from the verbless, senseless sentences there were constant dropped negatives, garbled statistics and pure howlers. "It's only two months, I think, since I became Prime Minister of this Government," he said, almost exactly three months after kissing the Queen's hands. The number of students at the local university had risen "from 800 to 300." The river Mersey emerged as "Muzzy." The name Trawsfynydd—more understandably—was simply left out. His gibes at the Labour Party were suffocated by the manner of telling: "We—ur—they prate of automation." He even managed to misquote Wilson's speech so that "landlord and peasant mentality" came out as "landlord and peasant neutrality." A sympathetic, embarrassed audience simply did not know when to cheer.

Afterward, the exhausted Sir Alec visited the local Conservative Club. Here his reception was rapturous. The matrons whose hard work keeps local organizations active were delighted with Home and queued up for the honor of shaking his hand. "Thank you, thank you," he said over and over again as he walked among them, "you were a splendid audience." The journalists and Conservative Central Office were less impressed by Sir Alec. His apparent inability to read from a text prompted the joke, later published by a Conservative newspaper, that the reporters on Home's tour were clubbing together to buy him the other half of his half-moon glasses. Conservative Central Office made two decisions. If his speeches were going to be written by others, they must not contain complex tongue-twisting phrases. For example, Home was tripped up by the characterization of Wilson as "a slick salesman of synthetic science." Secondly, Home must be given adequate time to rehearse his text.

Five days after Sir Alec's disaster, Wilson spoke in the same Swansea hall. There could not have been a more striking contrast. This was to be his comprehensive and detailed plan for the economic regeneration of Britain. It was long, highly technical and, to noneconomists, heavy. Yet by his very power and authority on a subject he really understands, Wilson kept his audience in a state of constant excitement. "I went on twenty minutes too long," he said afterward, "but if I hadn't, people would have said I was deliberately leaving bits out. The audience was being tortured, but then there's a masochistic streak in the Welsh. They're used to listening to those sermons. Swansea was the best place to give that speech." In truth, for all his mock modesty, he was delighted with his reception: "It was like 1945 all over again. In fact more, because in 1945 people were very quiet. Do you know they could have filled that hall three times over? One local party had ordered three double-decker buses before discovering that it had been allotted only fifty tickets." He was particularly pleased that the local steelworkers had not protested at his plea for a return to work at Port Talbot. "There wasn't even a rotten egg," he said afterward. "I'm sure this means that the people there don't want the strike to go on."

The Sunday newspapers did Wilson proud on his Swansea speech; even the Tory editorial writers congratulated him on his full and detailed explanation of Labour economic policies. And on Monday, Home too showed a sudden improvement when speaking at Bury, in Lancashire. He began with an awkward joke about having had George Hirst, a Yorkshireman, as his cricket coach, and he stumbled a bit through the official statement on housing. But the recent troubles in Cyprus, East Africa and Malaysia gave him a chance to speak on a subject he knows much better. "A few weeks ago," he exclaimed in great indignation, "I heard the Opposition liken our troops to a stage army. Well, all the world is now its stage and they are acting very well on it." Most politicians hesitate to make party capital out of the fighting forces, but Home's apparent sincerity enthralled the audience.

Home got a better reception at Bury than Wilson did at Leeds that Saturday, February 8. This had been Hugh Gaitskell's territory from the time he won a Leeds seat in 1945 to his death just over a year before. The three established Leeds M.P.s on the platform beside Wilson—Denis Healey, Charles Pannell and Alice Bacon—were all Gaitskell admirers and had struggled to stop Wilson getting the leadership of the party. The applause was more subdued than at Birmingham and Swansea, and there were some sour comments on Wilson among the audience. It was noted with disapproval that he did not once praise or even mention his dead predecessor. But if he had, as Wilson well knew, he might have been accused of hypocrisy. This was the last occasion when rancor about the past poisoned the new harmony of the Labour Party.

Meanwhile Home made a quick visit to Iceland, Canada and the United States. When he got to Washington on February 12, President Johnson remarked to a crony: "I can see what's in it for him. But what's in it for me?" It was a shrewd question. The British Prime Minister had always believed that he could win the next election on foreign affairs and defense issues. He understands them and he is well received abroad. Indeed on this visit he astonished statesmen and journalists with a sharp and straightforward talk. Questioned in Canada on the current situation in Panama, he crisply replied: "Panama is a matter for the United States. We are interested in communications all over the world being kept open and I think the United States is perfectly well able to deal with the situation. I rather wish they had allowed us to deal with the Egyptian situation as we wanted to." Even anti-Suez Canadians and Americans were impressed by this bulldog bite.

But how could he bring home to the British his fine command of world affairs? The crafty Macmillan had managed this before the 1959 election. He had visited the U.S.S.R. and was widely, even hilariously, publicized in a white Russian fur hat. He had backed this by a stupendous TV talk on foreign affairs with the American interviewer Ed Murrow. But Home had none of Macmillan's cunning. It was no use his claiming in speeches that it was Britain's possession of the bomb that brought about the nuclear test ban treaty. He needed President Johnson to praise him, and praise him publicly, to convince the British public. But what was in it for Johnson? Considerably less than nothing.

Ever since the Nassau talks of December 1962 the United States Government had resisted British pressure for a more independent nuclear strike force. Indeed Kennedy and Johnson were marginally better inclined to the defense ideas of the Labour Opposition. Both Presidents believed that the credit for nuclear test bans belonged primarily to the U.S.A. and the U.S.S.R. Why should Britain steal this credit from them? Furthermore, there was one immediate reason why Johnson did not wish to do Home a favor. He had been having much trouble from Congress because of his moderate Cuba policies. In order to block the demand for military action he was obliged to show that the U.S.A. was doing everything short of force to overthrow Castro's regime. In the very week of Home's visit, the news broke that Leyland's,

a British firm, had made a contract to send a fleet of buses
to Cuba. The British Government, in accordance with its
traditional policies, refused to join in an economic blockade.
Therefore the Prime Minister came back from Washington
on St. Valentine's day with private messages of good will
but no political Valentine's card to show the British public.

A March election was now ruled out. The polls showed
the Conservatives trailing by six to eight points. The Parliamentary Party was still divided on RPM. And although
Home declared on TV the following Monday that "the economy has seldom been stronger," the next morning's trade
figures showed a disastrous gap. Yet the Young Tories gave
Home a hero's welcome when he spoke to their annual meeting in London on February 15. Last year they had booed a
reference to Macmillan. This year they were solid behind the
new leader. If their loudest cheer of all went to Edward
Heath, even this reflected well on Home because Heath was
reputed to be his favorite Minister.

The old Tories loved him; the women Tories loved him;
the young Tories loved him. Unfortunately for Sir Alec
Douglas-Home he had not yet won the love of the country
in general. Everywhere he went he talked of getting to know
people and letting them get to know him. Yet when he actually visited homes or factories he appeared aloof. In his
own old-world constituency of Kinross and West Perthshire,
he could chat with the locals about cattle, the weather and
winter keep. On industrial Clydeside, only fifty miles away,
he walked around in a daze of bored incomprehension during a day visit in February. At Lithgows's shipyards the cleri-
cal staff lined up to clap, and Home smiled. At Rootes car
factory the men booed, and Home smiled. Here at Rootes,
just to please the photographers, he stopped to speak with
some of the workers. Most politicians would have had the
curiosity to ask how people liked this new factory, in a new
town formed from Glasgow overspill. Indeed the experiment

was so famous that it had even been mentioned several times in Home's speeches. Yet the question Home chose to ask of these workers was: "How long have you been working here?" It was a strange question to ask in a brand-new factory.

Some of Home's own jokes were amusing. In Newcastle, for instance, he began his speech by saying that "For some hundreds of years my family visited the northeast of England from time to time. The last plunder I carried away was a wife from Durham. But you can't do that twice." He generally fluffed the jokes which had been added by speech-writers, Eldon Griffiths and Nigel Lawson. At Newcastle, again, there was a joke reference to a current Beatles hit. Home was supposed to say, "I am too modest to claim that the country loves us, but *you know that can't be bad.*" However, he stumbled and said "You know, er, that can't be too bad," so that the audience simply stared at him in bewilderment.

The more Home impressed his own side, the less he impressed the general public. For instance, he chose, on March 6, to speak to the Unionist Party in Belfast. Electorally this was quite pointless. The six counties of Northern Ireland are overwhelmingly Tory, simply because the Unionist Party is identified with Protestantism. He was speaking not just to the converted but to the fanatical. Not surprisingly the crowd in the Ulster Hall, blazoned with slogans like "We Are the Queensmen" and "Safeguard the Ulster Bridgehead," gave Home a loyal welcome. He in his turn accepted the gift of an Ulster tie, emblazoned with the traditional Red Hand of the North, which he promptly exchanged for his own in front of the TV cameras. This ceremony was watched with delight that evening by Harold Wilson, who realized that it would lose Home thousands of Roman Catholic votes in Merseyside and Clydeside.

On March 13, Home began his first whistle-stop tour in Devon and Cornwall, an area of potential Liberal threat.

At these open-air public meetings he faced severe heckling and found it not to his liking. "I know your problems," he said in Camborne, and was promptly quashed by the obvious answer: "Then why don't you do something about them?" For all his expressed wish to meet people, he did everything possible to avoid them. When running half an hour ahead of schedule between Penzance and Camborne, he drove the whole distance at 12 m.p.h. rather than stop at intervals to meet and chat with the farmers. Yet once again Home managed to charm the ladies at each of his whistle-stop meetings. With a coy reference to the birth of his first grandson, he would begin each speech: "I apologize for not bringing my wife, but I think the ladies present will agree that I've got a very good excuse."

The two party leaders spent so much of their time and energy on the road that they seldom came into actual conflict. But in March they clashed with a vengeance. Wilson had gone to the United States to accept an honorary degree from Bridgeport University, Connecticut. He also took the opportunity for a meeting with President Johnson* but it was not this conversation that made the headlines back home. A few days before Wilson had whiled away a train journey by talking about the United Nations with Harold Hutchinson, political correspondent of the *Daily Herald*. He suggested, for instance, that British ships, just like British troops, might contribute at times to the UN force. Three days later Hutchinson filed this as a background piece. Late on the evening of Monday, March 2, a Reuters correspondent telephoned Wilson in Washington to say that another news agency claimed he wanted to put the British Navy under UN control. Would he deny this? He would and did, and a few

---

* The serious aspect of this meeting on March 2 was slightly frustrated by the presence of Wilson's wife, son and assistant, David Ennals, who had come in to shake hands with the President and stayed throughout the fifty-minute interview.

minutes later both UP and Reuters issued a denial. But
Tuesday's *Evening Standard* carried the big headline "ROYAL
UN NAVY STARTS A ROW," and other newspapers on Tuesday
and Wednesday carried headlines or stories implying the
same thing.

When Wilson arrived back from America on Wednesday
morning he found himself in a predicament. He could not
report the *Evening Standard* to the Press Council since the
Daily Mirror, a Labour newspaper, had also carried a headline suggesting that he wanted to put the Navy under UN
control. He did not want to withdraw the idea, which he
considered sensible. But he knew that the public had a
particularly jealous love for the Navy. Indeed so has Wilson
himself.* All the statements and denials he made before
leaving the U.S.A. and on coming back to Britain failed to
clarify his exact shade of meaning on what control the UN
should have. But not for the first or last time, it was Home
who solved the problem for him.

On Thursday morning, the day after Wilson's return,
Home was speaking at the meeting of the Central Council
of the Conservative Party's National Union in London. He
was clearly in a fighting mood. He first of all made a reference
to TV confrontation which infuriated the Labour Party. He
was willing to face Wilson, but "when I want to I shall send
for him, and not the other way round. After this rather
autocratic promise he turned to the Royal Navy: "Mr.
Wilson goes to the United States and makes a great speech
on behalf of the Socialist Party, suggesting that they are going
to take some new initiative by putting the British Navy at
the disposal of the United Nations. He calculated he will get
the headlines and make a great impression, and no one will

---

* It led him into one of his rare moments of discomfiture during the election campaign. "Why," he asked from a public platform on September 29, "do
I emphasize the importance of the Royal Navy?"—only to be rewarded with
the crushing shout, "Because you're in Chatham, you bloody fool!"

question it. And someone has questioned it. He has had to come back and say it meant nothing at all."

Home had blundered. Whatever Wilson said to Harold Hutchinson in a train, he never referred to the Navy in any speech, "great" or small. Home made his second mistake in the House of Commons that afternoon when he gave Wilson an opening on the naval affair in question time. Immediately Wilson denied that he had ever made a speech on the subject and Home was forced to concede: "If the right honorable gentleman says he did not say these things in a speech and I have insinuated that he did, of course I withdraw it, naturally. That's the thing to do. But we still have to have explained these extraordinary headlines which come to us." At a mass meeting that evening, Home made a further —and this time unreserved—public apology. He had been generally humiliated, and for no real reason. His charge against Wilson was quite fair. He had spoiled it by referring to a speech.

By early April the two leaders had finished their much publicized speaking tours; and without doubt Wilson had come off best. He had established himself in the public mind as a serious, even too serious, reformer with a fluent knowledge of economics, housing, industry and education.* His speeches and broadcasts were invariably sound and professional. He got his emphasis right. He knew his lines. He was not troubled by hecklers. At open-air meetings and small informal chats he could be witty and gay, as when he challenged Home to "come out from behind his thistle." On these occasions he also revealed a knowledge of ordinary people. When, for instance, in March, he went round some

---

* A speech on foreign affairs, promised to Edinburgh that spring, was never given. During the campaign he was supposed to speak on foreign affairs at Middlesbrough. This too was changed to a speech on home issues. Throughout 1964 he made only one speech on foreign affairs—at Bridgeport University, Connecticut.

slums in the Jamaica Road district of Edinburgh, he spoke
to the unfortunate tenants with sympathy and a knowledge
of their difficulties.

But if Wilson was good, Home had improved almost beyond measure. His speeches were still poor, but no longer
disastrous. The strain still showed through during the first
few minutes. His knuckles would clench and turn white. His
great grin would recede almost to ear level, and his tongue
flicker in and out in the old reptilian fashion. But more and
more frequently in these speeches he would acquire a burst
of confidence after the first twenty minutes, and his nervousness would give way to passion. The bomb, Wilson, De
Gaulle, the United Nations—the very thought of these seemed
to send a rush of blood to his head and he would find the
words tumbling helter-skelter out in attack. In these moments of anger his head would shake; he would wring his
hands and start to stammer with indignation: "But-um, I
doubt-um if Mr. Wilson-um . . ." This passion communicated itself to the audience. In contrast to Wilson, Sir Alec
at public meetings almost invariably roused peoples' emotions—whether love, anger, sympathy or pure derision.

Compared to him Wilson seemed rather a cold fish. He
scarcely ever seemed nervous. He could put an edge of sarcasm into his voice but never anger. He never flushed or
blanched; his voice never cracked with emotion, as Brown's
did. Unlike Harold Macmillan, he never wept tears of emotion, one from each eye. His appeal was always aimed at the
intellect or to the colder emotions like pride and ambition.
By tradition in British politics, the women vote Right and
the men vote Left. The personalities of Sir Alec and Wilson
tended to intensify this division. The women were taken by
Home's boyish charm and aristocratic dash. The men identified with Wilson's professionalism, common sense and tough-
ness. Not since Cromwell and Charles I themselves have any
opposed politicians in Britain so perfectly illustrated the

twin trends of Roundhead and Cavalier, of Parliamentarian and Royalist.

The comparison went even further than that. By the beginning of April 1964 Parliament had sat for longer than almost any in peace since the days of Charles I. The Conservative Party was torn apart between those who wanted a quick election in May or June and those who wanted to stick it out to the statutory limit that autumn. At almost every meeting in March, Sir Alec had teased his audiences by talking about "when the election comes in June [long pause] or October." By April the joke was wearing thin, and so were the nerves of the Cabinet. The younger members, supported by the Chief Whip, Martin Redmayne, were almost unanimous for a spring election. The Chancellor of the Exchequer, Reginald Maudling, argued that Britain was facing serious economic difficulties which demanded serious remedies. He believed that the Government should either introduce stringent and unpopular fiscal controls, or go to the polls. He preferred the second course. The older members of the Cabinet, and in particular Selwyn Lloyd and Butler, argued that the Government would be bound to lose a spring election but that the country might be won round after a fine summer.

Sir Alec belonged to neither camp and had never had any strong prejudices for or against an autumn election. "He's the sort of man," Macleod once observed, "who gets up in the morning, rubs the window and looks out to see what sort of a day it is." If he had had his way, Home would have gone on into late April, watching the skies each day for a sign of Conservative weather. But the approach of the Greater London Council elections on April 9 obliged him to make up his mind fast. This was the first poll of the greatly enlarged authority which had been set up by the Conservative Government in place of the old London County Council. It extended deep into the suburban, middle-class commuter lands of Surrey, Kent, Essex and Middlesex. Although there were good local-government arguments for this new authority, it had been opposed by the Labour Party for political reasons. The new territories, it was argued, would give the Tories a permanent control over the government of London.

As early as February it became clear from canvass returns and local party reports that the G.L.C. was not so obviously Tory as the Labour Party had feared. Indeed the Labour Party had quite good hopes of gaining a majority. By April this hope had turned into solid confidence. Both Wilson and Brown conducted strenuous speaking tours through the marginal boroughs of G.L.C. just to show the importance they gave to the result. Soon both parties were drawn into regarding the G.L.C. poll as a trial run for the general election. A Labour win would fill the party with fighting spirit. The Tories, if they lost, would feel in no heart for a general election only a few weeks afterward.

This problem soon affected Sir Alec's thinking. If he announced a spring general election before April 9, only to see the Tories crushed in the G.L.C., he would be forced to go into action with a depressed army. If he announced an autumn election before April 9, he would risk getting an anti-Conservative protest vote in the G.L.C. poll. Yet if he did not announce the election date until after the G.L.C. results, he could quite fairly be accused of hesitation and dithering. By delaying the poll announcement until the beginning of April he had been boxed. He was forced to choose an autumn election and forced to announce it on April 9. This he did, at 6 P.M.

As Lord Poole had prophesied in Conservative Central Office, Labour won the G.L.C. by 64 to 36, capturing even such affluent boroughs as Bexley and Enfield. Paradoxically this result helped Sir Alec Douglas-Home in his own party. It proved that an early general election would have been suicidal. Earlier in the year Wilson had remarked that some of the Tories seemed to be suffering from a death wish, or boredom with office. Nobody could lay this charge against Home. Speaking to the authors over a drink in the Gothic, paneled Prime Minister's room at the House of Commons a fortnight after the G.L.C. elections, he sounded more cheerful and confident than at any time since becoming Premier. "I'm getting myself known in the country at last," he said; "there are splendid crowds and faces at every window. . . . I shall be very glad to see you after the general election—in this same room." There was no doubt that he meant it.

7. The Adman Cometh

We really must plus up the integrity image.
Labour advertising adviser at a Transport House meeting

NEWS, just like claret, has good and bad years. The legendary vintage summer of 1963 is still recalled with delight by anybody owning shares in newspaper publishing companies. The summer of 1964 was almost totally barren. The scandalmongers were inconsolable. The *Sunday Mirror's* vain attempt to repeat the Profumo uproar by outrageous hints concerning a peer of the realm resulted in brisk legal action and compensation. There were a few weeks of saucy pictures and jokes concerning topless bikinis, but nothing comparable to the antics of Christine Keeler or Mandy Rice-Davies. There was not even a Great Train Robbery, although one of the robbers, Charles Wilson, escaped from prison in Birmingham. "Brown Sees Cell from Which Wilson Escaped," said one of the headlines, and Charles, throughout August, got rather more coverage than Harold. The actual events of politics can be listed in one paragraph—and then dismissed. They had little bearing on the autumn general election.

On May Day Harold Wilson stood on a coal lorry in Hyde Park to tell a rally of 3,000 people his views on Cyprus: "Britain should now make three proposals to the United Nations. First, we should offer to put in the heaviest tanks we have got, and ask UN contingents to do the same. . . ." A London Labour M.P. who was standing on one side reported afterward: "When he mentioned heavy tanks I was so surprised I nearly fell off the lorry." On May 12 Wilson gave his general support to the Government's policies on Aden. This time, surprise developed into a tiny mutiny, and Ian

Mikardo said later, in public, that Labour leaders should not underestimate the "growing rumble of criticism" in the constituencies. On other matters Wilson was able to please his left wing. He denounced the sale of frigates to Spain and he rubbed home the charge of waste against the Government for the handing of missile contracts to the Ferranti electronics company. The first of these controversies, despite the attention given to it by the press, failed to excite the public; but the shout of "Ferranti" was to become a favorite Labour heckle throughout the general-election campaign if only because, by British tradition, the subjects of scandal often have Italianate names: Marconi, Profumo, Ferranti.

There were four by-elections in May and two in June, and the Conservatives were pleasantly surprised by losing only one of the four seats they were defending. Lord Beaverbrook died and earned a surprisingly warm obituary from Harold Wilson: "He was a great controversialist, passionate and intent on fighting for the causes in which he believed. Whatever disagreements we, or any other party, had with him, everyone of us respected him for his deep loyalty to the Commonwealth ideal."

The only real news was the weather. From the beginning of June to the end of the summer the temperature hovered in the seventies and eighties. The British seaside towns had their best season in history, and by August almost everyone in the country seemed to have a suntan. This in itself was helpful to the Conservatives. Good weather brings good temper and therefore contentment. Nobody, stretched out on a beach, wants to bother with trade gaps or the shortage of colleges of advanced technology. Those people who did study the newspapers found that Home was getting the headlines. The troubles in Cyprus, South Vietnam, Malaysia and Aden gave him an opportunity to show his considerable knowledge of foreign affairs. And it was just in this field that the Labour Party was weakest. Even in June 1963, when the polls

showed Labour 20 per cent ahead, a majority of the population still believed that the Tories were better suited to
handle foreign policy.

The summer of 1964 was a time of truce for the two political leaders. Both men took characteristic holidays. The
Wilsons went to their bungalow on the Scilly Isles for three
weeks of walking and boating. The Homes went up to Scotland to fish, hunt butterflies and—from August 12 on—shoot
grouse.* The truce applied only to the main protagonists.
Throughout that summer the two party organizations were
busy preparing for the battle in October. The real events
of the summer took place in Smith Square, near the Houses
of Parliament, where Transport House and Conservative
Central Office stand, uncomfortably, face to face.

Transport House, as its name implies, belongs to the
Transport and General Workers' Union; hence the post-
election joke that Wilson was so kind toward landlords that
he had made his own landlord, Frank Cousins, the Minister
of Technology. Joking apart, Transport House has always
suffered from the T & GWU spirit that rules the building.
Physically it is cumbrous, cramped and old-fashioned. Psychologically it is handicapped by an air of conservatism,
doing things by the book and sometimes by sheer laziness.
Although the Labour Party is never so poor as it pretends,
it continued to pay meager salaries to its officials. Even the
all important head of the research department received only
£1,650 a year as compared with the £5,000 paid to his opposite number in the Tory Party. Here again Labour was
making the same mistake as most of the trade unions. Although Wilson had encouraged many changes at Transport
House, the ultimate power rested with Len Williams, the
general secretary of the party. When the job became vacant

---

* It was a terrible season for grouse, Home reported: "A washout. An absolute washout. They've got some terrible disease. Only yesterday my keeper
found two of them with wings fluttering on the ground."

after the retirement of Morgan Phillips at the beginning of 1962, there had been a sharp division within the National Executive Committee, which decides new appointments. Nine members, mainly elected by the constituency parties, wanted to replace Phillips by Peter Shore, head of the research department. The trade-union members of the N.E.C. favored Len Williams, then national agent, on the good trade union principle of "Buggins's turn." The trade union members of the N.E.C., who are politically on the Right, are always strong enough to vote down the constituency party members who, for the most part, represent the left wing.

For all his admiration of Kennedy, Wilson never acquired a team of advisers comparable to Kennedy's. The Labour Party traditionally forms a campaign committee to work out both the strategy and tactics of the election. At the beginning of 1963 the N.E.C. agreed to form it once more, but with one important difference. The members of the committee were not specially chosen but were simply the chairmen of all the subcommittees. This was a hint that Wilson and his close colleagues would pay far less attention this time to the advice of the campaign committee. And in fact it had little influence on the party's three precampaign problems of advertising, publicity and policy.

The Labour Party's traditional horror of advertising had, if anything, been increased by the Conservatives' embracing of it from 1957 onward. At the previous election Hugh Gaitskell had rejected all offers of help from professional advertising men on the grounds that he did not wish to copy the Tories' "use of Colman Prentis and Varley."* But in the early Sixties, opinion within the party had shifted. Advertising men were called in for talks, and a satirical night club put on an act in which a bumbling Labour alderman asked how he could introduce phallic symbolism into his election

* The advertising agency that has handled the Conservative account since 1948.

address. In February 1962 there was a meeting in the House of Commons committee rooms of all the people who had written in from the advertising trade with offers of help. The meeting was chaired by Alice Bacon, attended as well by Len Williams, George Brown and the newly appointed director of publicity, John Harris—and was, from all accounts, totally fruitless. That summer the embryonic publicity group did a dummy run of advertisements for a rich Norfolk Labour party, and, just before Christmas, held an important meeting at a pub, The Pavïour's Arms, near Transport House. On this occasion John Harris and Percy Clark of Transport House talked with most of the advertising people who were to become the advertising group: Miss Ros Allen, David Kingsley and Brian Murphy. On the basis of research done by Mark Abrams' research organization, they decided that most of the party's publicity should be aimed at the "target voter" and especially in the marginal constituencies. (This was the policy used so successfully by the Conservatives in 1959.)

Everyone in the group disagreed with everyone else on the means of advertising, but they were all agreed on the aims. They wanted to rid the Labour Party of its old, Puritan image and to make people think that, under a Labour Government things would *happen*. They also wanted a symbol which could become Labour's trade-mark. The second was easy to find. As early as January 1963 the advertising group agreed on the "thumbs-up" sign, which seemed optimistic and lively. The idea had come from watching the compere of the TV show "Sunday Night" at the London Palladium," and several of the advertising advisers wanted to borrow the show's slogan as well. Just as the compere talked of "swinging" and "dodgy," so the party would say "Tories Dodgy—Labour Swinging." But the majority of the group thought that the point would be lost on some of the public.

Everybody agreed that the word "go" was necessary to the

slogan. It implied dynamism and action; it was short and pithy. "Labour's on the Go" was the first slogan suggested and it met with approval from the group. But Percy Clark said that in his part of the world (Cheshire) it might sound as though Labour had diarrhea. And another north-country-man, Harold Wilson himself, said that the slogan reminded him of "Labour's on the po." Because of these scatological echoes the slogan was dropped. The advertising group finally hit on "Let's Go with Labour, and we'll get things done," not so much by inspiration as by hard work and a process of elimination. Both Wilson and Brown approved the slogan, which was extensively used during the year and a half before polling. In May 1963 they took space in the national news-papers for "Let's Go with Labour" ads showing Wilson's face, the thumbs-up sign and a little bold-type text under-neath. The copy dealing with pensions, education and the cost of living was written entirely by two of the outside ad-vertising advisers, Brian Murphy and Ros Allen.

It was Ros Allen who contributed most to the controversial and eventually unused advertisement designed to attract women voters. Transport House had wanted something re-lated to consumer protection, but the advertising group realized that this was too heavy a subject for most women voters. They decided on something more emotional in ap-peal. After innumerable discussions the ad emerged. It showed a women taking a baby out of its bath and the cap-tion read: "Like Mother-Love . . . there are some things a man cannot understand." The implication was that while the woman was happy with her husband and adored her child, she was bothered by certain feminine worries—like the rising cost of living. Although she didn't know much about politics—rather a man's business—she was going to vote La-bour next time. The advertising group were so pleased with this that they planned to place it in the *Sunday Mirror*, which had the largest number of women target readers. However,

Wilson and Brown were shown the ad and immediately said it made them feel sick.

One other ad was scrapped but for different reasons. It showed a delectable girl with tongue peeping saucily from between her lips, and the men on the advertising group were captivated. But Mark Abrams had it "researched" for reactions, and it was found that most women thought the girl in the ad looked like a "tart," "husband stealer" or "loose woman." So much for the Labour Party's one timorous venture into eroticism.

Wilson's views on advertising were more modern than Gaitskell's. His views on broadcasting were even more conservative. It was made clear from the start that politicians rather than TV experts would decide on the important broadcasts. The man that Transport House chose as its broadcasting officer in 1962, Clive Bradley, had never before worked with TV and his experiences were confined to overseas BBC sound broadcasting. Soon after Bradley's appointment, Wilson told him that the election broadcasts of 1959 had been too slick. They had given the impression of snide destructive criticism. He, Brown and Bowden all believed that as little film as possible should be used in the broadcast on the grounds that any points made by film could be better made by the politicians themselves. This view was contrary to the experience of most TV propagandists and particularly of the Conservatives.

In spite of Wilson's bias against film, the Labour Party in 1963 hired Mithras Films, an independent company, to film their annual Scarborough Conference and to shoot a number of strips for political broadcasts. Little of this was used. Throughout 1964 a broadcasting advisory committee, chaired by Anthony Wedgwood Benn, met occasionally in the House of Commons. It included several M.P.s, a TV interviewer, George Ffitch, and reporter James Cameron. The activities of this committee can best be judged from the brief minutes of the fifty-fourth meeting on June 18, 1964. "There was a long discussion of the themes of the election broadcast in the light of the changing political situation," but only two views were attributed. "Mr. Christopher Mayhew spoke of the major parties' programs seeming dangerously similar, and he emphasized the importance of getting across the distinguishing fact that the Labour Party had both the sense of purpose and the capacity to carry our their program. . . . Lord Willis hoped that the program would reflect the need for more cultural, athletic and leisure facilities, and that they would show that life under a Labour Government would be enjoyable."

The Labour Party gave several political broadcasts during 1964 which were extensively analyzed by Mark Abrams' researchers. They discovered, for instance, that while Labour supporters most enjoyed Mayhew's bitter attack on the Tories on August 26 the "target" voters considered it too bitchy so this brutal style was dropped. Whatever advice the broadcasting committee gave, the Labour leaders themselves were obsessed by the idea that they were not themselves as well known to the public as their Conservative counterparts. This feeling reinforced the prejudice against film and in favor of straight talk from politicians. By the end of August, Wilson had decided upon the style if not the exact subjects of the forthcoming campaign broadcasts.

Yet even by the end of August, the Labour Party still had not worked out its policies in the manifesto. This was not because of any particular argument over what these policies should be. Issues were never really important in the election, whatever the politicians said at the time, but it was important so to phrase the manifesto as to avoid offending certain interests. It was Harold Wilson, for instance, who in 1964 rewrote the whole section about the delicate issue of defense. Otherwise Peter Shore, the head of the research department, prepared most of the manifesto, with help on the opening and closing paragraphs from Hugh Cudlipp, the *Mirror* group executive. Considering that they had taken almost six weeks to write the document, it was curiously rough even by August.

Only Wilson, Brown, Crossman, Shore and Len Williams had seen the manifesto when, on September 8, it was shown to the N.E.C. and the "shadow" Cabinet. Both bodies were allowed only half an hour to read it before the meeting was opened for criticism. The N.E.C. was full of criticisms and had soon covered the manuscript with their corrections, cuts and question marks. But by the end of the evening it went off to the printers. Only afterward did the Labour Party notice the strange gaps and inconsistencies in the document. Agriculture was left out altogether. Its policies on pensions and land prices were obscure. Some of the plans for education were virtually meaningless: "secondary education will be reorganized on comprehensive lines. Within the new system, grammar school education will be extended." Many candidates were to be tied in knots while trying to unravel the logic of those two sentences. Indeed Dick Crossman was not the only senior Labour man who thought the whole manifesto "absolutely flat."

There were differences of opinion at Transport House but no real splits as at Central Office across the square. There the party machine was at total odds with much of the leadership. For one thing, the machine was far more powerful than at Transport House. The nominal chairman of the Conservative Party was Lord Blakenham, formerly John Hare. A mild, bushy-mustached gentleman with the air of a kind-hearted colonel, he had, as Minister of Labour, got on well with the trade-union leaders, earning the left-handed compliment from one of them: "He's a good deal richer and a great deal less stupid than he looks." His surprise appointment to the party chairmanship in October 1963 was largely the result of Selwyn Lloyd's point-blank refusal to take on the job. But

once installed in the chairman's office, Blakenham brought to
his task all the typical caution and thoroughness of the born
army staff officer.

The political flair in the Central Office—as in the previous
three general elections—continued to be provided by Lord
Poole. A former M.P. and a thrusting city tycoon, Poole had
been in the course of ten years by turns treasurer, chairman,
deputy chairman and joint chairman of the Conservative
Party before, in October 1963, accepting, at the special request of the new Premier, the more modest office of vice-
chairman. Quick-minded, overbearing and one of the cleverest men in politics, Poole had never been a particularly
popular figure, especially among Conservatives in Parliament;
he was remembered—resentfully—for his eager championing
of the Hailsham cause in the Tory leadership struggle. But his
gifts as an organizer and a strategist are commonly acknowledged, not least by his political opponents. In a *bravura* moment Poole himself once announced that he was "the poor
man's Bobby Kennedy"; but probably a better analogy came
from Harold Wilson, who called him "the Tory Weygand."
He is the man the Conservatives always bring back whenever
the party is faced with disaster. It was he who, after Suez,
provided Macmillan's electoral salvation by winning the
party over to massive pre-election advertising, and he justly
takes credit for the successful slogan "Life's better under the
Conservatives—Don't let Labour ruin it." His looks belong
to the Cavalry Club, but his heart is in Madison Avenue. It
has been unkindly said of the Conservative strategy in 1963–
64 that "Poole told Blakenham what to do, who passed it on
to Home, who made a botch of it." Certainly throughout the
summer of 1964 Poole's views on important questions both
of policy and organization usually carried the day.

The real clash in the Conservative Party came between
Central Office and the younger, more adventurous part of
the Treasury bench. The first great battle was fought over

whether to have a spring election. Central Office was over-whelmingly in favor of putting it off until October, but the junior members of the Cabinet nearly all wanted it in June. "It was always Alec's instinct to go in June, you know," one of them was to explain later. "But being the sort of chap he is, he found it impossible to go against his responsible advisers—in this case the organization men. They simply told us that if we went in June we'd lose. It seemed to me a pretty facile argument—after all, the important point was that we couldn't do any more governing. The delay ossified everything."

The Central Office view on a June election was bluntly expressed by Poole: "A lot of Ministers got unduly influenced by civil servants who told them the Government couldn't be properly carried on. It was bloody silly; if civil servants don't want to do the job, then you sack them and get some others who can. I made Blakenham bang the table and say he'd walk out if Home had an election in June. People never want advice; they want to be told what to do: that's one of the great secrets of life."

Some people refused to be told what to do, even by Poole. Although Central Office got its way on leaving the election until October, it was overruled on when to hold the by-elections. Central Office wanted to put off the by-elections altogether. "What was the point," they argued, of electing four men to Parliament for only a few weeks?" But the younger element in the Cabinet was determined to hold these elections in order to rally confidence among party workers and to avoid the charge of political cowardice. They argued that the timing of by-elections was a matter for the Parliamentary Party and not for functionaries who, in Sir Edward Boyle's phrase, were "getting too big for their boots anyway." The surprisingly favorable results in three of the four by-elections seemed to support the Ministers' view.

In the Conservative Party, by contrast to Labour, it was

the party machine, not the leadership, that controlled propaganda. In January 1964 Central Office had worked out the main themes of the advertising required from their agency, Colman, Prentis and Varley. They would use Home's face in some posters, although not to nearly such an extent as Macmillan's in 1959; they would play down complicated issues like defense and play up the 1959 theme of prosperity. Most of the newspaper advertisements and posters showed happy families and slogans like "It's Your Standard of Living—Keep it" and "Conservatives give prosperity—Don't chuck it away." It was only a slight variation on the theme of 1959.

There was no Conservative grumbling about the advertisements. But many were critical of the TV broadcasts. The most notorious was the "soap opera" film put out on August 19. It began by showing a housewife saying goodbye to her husband on his way to work on the day of their wedding anniversary. No present. She leaned on her vacuum cleaner and sulked. A Conservative canvasser called. No thanks, she said, we're Labour here. Just then the husband rang to say that her present was down in a showroom—a car. A Labour canvasser called—a pompous duffel-coated intellectual who prated about Harold Wilson's views on international liquidity. She thought back to the days of the Labour Government —coupons, queues, shortages—and compared this with the affluence of her home—washing machine, refrigerator and now a car. By the end of the film she has come to realize that whatever her husband's prejudice, Labour had nothing to offer her.

This broadcast created a sensation. Although the *Daily Telegraph* political correspondent said: "I have never seen any party make more telling use of ten minutes on the television screen." *The Times, Daily Mail* and the intellectual Sunday newspapers were outraged. Reams of angry letters arrived for the correspondence columns. But Lord Poole was quite unrepentant: "It was my idea entirely. In any election

you've got to have a bloody good bit of rough stuff, and
preferably you want it just before the campaign starts. After
all, if you don't parade the circus down the street no one will
buy a ticket for the night. In 1959 we had Charlie Hill; in
1964 we hadn't got him, so we put on this instead. I had it
all done in February, and not by C.P.V. I asked around and
found a sort of man who makes television commercials. He
did it, I liked it and then I held it up my sleeve until it was
the right moment to use it."

Many Tories disliked the broadcast. "I thought it was
pretty awful," said R. A. Butler, while Maudling thought
"they gave up the soap-opera stuff because they were frightened of the reaction it got." He himself had appeared in a
curious form of party political broadcast: "Did you see that
awful thing they made me do—with all that pop music? It
was ghastly! They showed me one thing during the summer
and at the end I just said 'Where's the Fairy Snowman?' It
was all you could say."

Throughout the summer, leading Conservatives would
refer to the Central Office people as "they." And never were
"they" more blamed than over the question of land prices.
The high cost of urban land and the immense sums made
from speculation were perhaps the only issues that really
came to life in the general election. It was the burden of
almost every Wilson speech and a cause of considerable embarrassment to the Conservatives. The Labour Party, always
shy of its historical commitment to outright land nationalization, had as long ago as the summer of 1961 perceived that
conditions had been created by the free market in which a
variation of this old doctrine could be presented with impu-
nity. Unashamedly it proclaimed the need for the nationalization of urban building land. There were many, including the
Housing Minister, Sir Keith Joseph, inside the Conservative
Party who wanted the same thing, or at the very least a tax
on development. But no such proposals were found in the

Conservative manifesto. Afterward it was almost impossible to discover a Conservative who would take responsibility for this omission.

The truth probably was that the party's high command had simply left the whole thing too late. Had a land-betterment tax been introduced in the 1963 budget, or even had the tax catchment area for capital gains made on land speculation been increased from three years to ten, Conservative candidates would have had at least some breast plate against the damning recital of the vast profits made during the past thirteen years on the tiniest parcels of building land. But by the time the electoral threat was seen, any attempted answer to it might well have done more harm than good. A sudden change of policy during the summer of 1964 would inevitably have been presented by the Labour Party as "a deathbed repentance," and might easily have appeared to the uncommitted public as an example of guilty conscience in action.

Nevertheless the issue of what to do about land prices was far and away the most contentious one that arose in the Tory camp during the summer. In favor of grasping the nettle were former Housing Ministers like Duncan Sandys and Henry Brooke, together with the Chancellor of the Exchequer, Reggie Maudling, the leader of the House of Lords, Lord Carrington, and of course Sir Keith Joseph himself. Within the Central Office Lord Poole shared their view, but it was flatly rejected not merely by Lord Blakenham but also, much more surprisingly, by Sir Michael Fraser, the head of the Conservative research department. Far from being in any sense a "class" argument, the lineup both within the Cabinet and outside was in fact dictated by doctrinal considerations. To the purists—very conscious of the fact that one of Harold Macmillan's most popular actions as Housing Minister had been to abolish development charges as long ago as 1954— the mere idea of restoring government interference with the play of the free market was anathema; to the "revisionists,"

certain that in the future government planning would have
to take priority over the principle of free enterprise, the
notion that the availability of land could somehow be
equated with the production of steel appeared totally absurd.
"Look, you've only got a certain amount of land in this country," one of them explained in a moment of exasperation.
"It's impossible to increase it whatever you do. I'm not just
in favor of development charges or a betterment tax. I'd like
to see all land owned by the community; considering the population we've got and the space we have to live in, it's the
only rational answer."

Probably only one man could have resolved the argument
—the Prime Minister himself. But, though partially persuaded of the need to do something, he found it difficult to
make up his mind what. "As we don't know the answer," he
remarked at the end of one of the last discussions of the subject, "wouldn't it be more honest for us to say so?" And that,
in effect, was what the Tory manifesto did. The section on
the Supply of Land included one of the most flaccid political
statements of all time: "In considering any further measure
to tax land transactions, the test must be that it should not
adversely affect the price or the supply of land." As a statement of the position its honesty was beyond doubt, but so
was its vulnerability.

The Tory land-prices controversy was virtually the only
issue that arose during the summer in either party that involved considerations of doctrine and principle. Attention
was concentrated in both major camps on questions of tactics
and strategy. Yet if there were no shifts in policy there was,
in the case of the Labour Party, a decisive change of posture.

During the short campaign for the leadership of the Labour Party, the press, and to some extent his own colleagues,
regarded Wilson as the candidate of the Left. At the same
time, the opinion polls showed him to be much more popular than Brown with the middle classes. Once elected, Wilson

took the point and made it the main basis of his strategy. Throughout 1964 he worked to increase the middle-class appeal of the party. It was shown, for example, in the advertisements, where not only style but also the content were fixed on a middle-class target. In 1959 one of the main advertisements read, "Labour will never forget the old folk," over a picture of an aged couple. There were no old folk in 1964. Both the advertisements and the published propaganda made their appeal to efficiency rather than sentiment. At Scarborough in October 1963 Wilson had purposefully replaced the old grievances of the industrial revolution with the new challenge of the scientific age to come. As *The Times* was to remark of the manifesto, the emphasis was on social engineering rather than ethical purpose. Quite deliberately Labour toned down the old indignation about poverty. Quite deliberately it concerned itself with business efficiency, technology and modernization. This new emphasis appeared in Labour's approach to housing and land prices—the overriding issues of the year. Instead of concentrating on the evil of ancient slums it bothered more with high rents and the heavy mortgage rates for house buyers. This was a clear appeal to the more prosperous working-class voters, because most of the people in ancient slums still paid low rents. The section on land and housing in the 1964 manifesto showed the same shift of emphasis. Its appeal was less to council-house tenants and more to intending buyers of houses. "Labour will introduce a policy of lower interest rates for housing. . . . This policy of specially favorable rates will apply both to intending owner-occupiers and to local authorities building houses to let. We should like this policy to apply to all owner-occupiers, but unless interest rates generally fall, it would be too expensive. We will, however, review the problem and see whether, and in what form, help could be extended to hard-pressed existing owner-occupiers." To the diehard left wing—one of whom was heard to remark, "It's

the most naked bribe in the whole history of British politics"
—even such qualified promises were a rank heresy. They
seemed to betray Labour's old belief in publicly owned
housing. It was an admission that the prosperous artisan and
lower middle class were now able and anxious to buy their
own homes.

The Conservatives were shifting in the opposite direction.
The back-room strategists of Central Office were quick to see
that Home made little appeal to the rising, ambitious, lower
middle classes. But they took comfort from his aristocratic
appeal to women and even to the more old-fashioned working-class voters. They therefore set out to woo both these
sections of the community. More social reforms (jokingly
known as Beveridge Mark II) and concessions to the trade
unions were written into the manifesto. TV broadcasts, like
the "soap opera," were framed to appeal to the great mass of
the nation that left school at fifteen.

These almost unconscious policies bore fruit at the general
election. For instance Iain Macleod (Enfield) reported a
swing to Conservatism in former Labour wards and a drift
away in the more expensive new housing estates. Solidly
working-class seats in the Black Country resisted the swing
to Labour, while solidly middle-class Hampstead almost
elected a Labour M.P.

Nineteen sixty-four marked a revolutionary if almost unnoticed change in the relationship between the two parties.
The old difference of class mattered less. And a new difference, of color, for the first time mattered at all. The grimy
borough of Smethwick has since taken almost the whole
blame for the introduction of racial prejudice into British
politics. In fact at least two other constituencies, Eton and
Slough and Birmingham, Perry Bar, were lost to the Conservatives on the same issue. It is probable, though not prov-
able, that a few—two, for example, in Lewiston—marginal
Tory seats were held because of the antiblack vote.

This book has no claim to being a work of sociology, and there is no space to try and explain the cause or even influence of the color question. The Conservatives had passed the Immigration Act and the Labour Party was known as the champion of racial equality. To this extent the antiblack voter tended to prefer the Conservatives. But no reputable Tory said anything that was overtly racialistic, nor did Central Office condone racialist propaganda by local party workers. The hatemongers of Smethwick, Perry Bar and Eton and Slough were sly and anonymous. Stickers appeared saying "If you want a nigger neighbor vote Liberal or Labour"; some Conservative canvassers hinted that immigration brought leprosy and sexual vice. But none of these things could be definitely attributed to any one candidate. Indeed the Conservative political education officer sent to observe Peter Griffiths at Smethwick found nothing to criticize in the conduct of his campaign, although deeply disliking its implications.

Neither party yet appreciated the significance of the color question in the coming election. There had been no serious race riots in Britain for more than six years; there was scarcely a mutter of trouble in 1964. Race, to the average newspaper reader, was something that mattered in Mississippi or Salisbury, Southern Rhodesia. It was not something that bothered Wilson or Home as the summer drew to a close in September, and they buttoned their coats for the start of the great election campaign.

8. To See the Queen

As Conservatives we are against change. We resist it for
as long as we can. But when it has to come we make it decent.

> CAPTAIN CHARLES WATERHOUSE, *the former Conservative M.P. and*
> *Suez Group leader, at the Tory rally held in Nottingham on*
> *September 12, 1964*

THE Labour Party election campaign started on Saturday afternoon, September 12, in the Empire Pool, Wembley, to the sound of the Grimethorpe Colliery Institute Band. This was the traditional rally to rouse in the party workers a spirit of victory. The organizers this year had not been content with the brass band, the Welsh male-voice choir and the big set speeches. There was the Humphrey Lyttleton jazz group, readings by actress Vanessa Redgrave in a maternity smock, Pakistani dancers representing a freed subcontinent, and African drummers to symbolize aid to the underdeveloped countries. The hit of the day was a comic Socialist monologue by Harry Corbett, one half of the TV serial "Steptoe and Son." The 10,000-strong audience whooped with delight as Corbett explained to Dad over the telephone: "No, they're not going to nationalize you. Look, I've had a look at the manifesto* and you're not in it."

Harold and Mary Wilson sat through all these performances in the gallery on the left of the hall. Five pounds lighter as a result of his climbing exertions on holiday, he was wearing a smart lightweight suit, a new lighter shade of television make-up to blend with his Scilly Isles' suntan, and a green tie, in contrast to the red affected by Brown and Greenwood nearby. He smiled good-naturedly throughout the show and

---

* The manifesto, published the previous day, proposed the nationalization of steel, road transport and urban building land.

began his speech in good vaudeville style, with a laugh at the Tory advertisements: "I congratulate the Conservative Administration on having invented the garden swing, and we are asked to believe that no one ever had a piggy-back ride until the Conservatives came into office. *Keep It,* says the poster—and I make this pledge in answer to the scare campaign being mounted day by day that we have no intention of abolishing garden swings, piggy-back rides, or even sitting on the grass, but do be careful about seeing that the grass does not belong to somebody's private game reserve."

The serious speech that followed was to remain the theme of his whole campaign. "On the one hand, you have a tired Administration which has no longer anything to offer the country, no objectives, no horizons, no heights to conquer: a party which has no more vision of the future than a desire to keep things as they are, to preserve the status quo, to conserve. . . . On the other hand, we in the Labour Party think Britain can do better. We do not feel that what we have so far achieved is good enough." He went on to admit, as he had to, that the country was more prosperous than it had been five years ago. But he insisted that this was the result not of Government policies but of the British people's hard work. He then attacked the Conservative "Stop-Go-Stop" economic policies and went on to his always successful passage on land prices and housing.

It was an effective performance, but by no means that of a rabble-rouser. "There's no headline in it," said the *Sunday Express* reporter. Worse, there was no new phrase or slogan that might have echoed throughout the campaign. There are all kinds of excuses for Wilson's platform speeches: his flat monotone voice, his academic manner, his need for the stimulus of debate. But it was quite clear from this very first speech of the campaign that he lacked the basic material of a good orator: a good text. The audience at Wembly gave Wilson a loyal cheer, but it was not as loud as the one they gave George Brown, whose far more flamboyant oratory ended the evening, nor nearly as enthusiastic as the one given to Nye Bevan, whose photo was flashed on the screen during one of the readings.

Some of the more reflective delegates left the Empire Pool in a state of despondency. The campaign had not opened up with the fanfare necessary to arouse the electorate. Three months of sunshine had lulled the country into a state of happy self-satisfaction which could be helpful only to the party in power. The public-opinion polls confirmed the general sense that Labour's lead was melting. On August 27 the *Daily Mail* N.O.P. had showed the Conservatives ahead by 0.9 er cent, the first time that Labour had lost the lead to the Conservatives since December 1961. Although the *Daily Telegraph* Gallup Poll came to the rescue next day with a Labour lead of six points, the trend back to the Tories was under way. Even Wilson was not too happy. "I wasn't exactly excited by it or pleased," he said of the N.O.P. poll, "but Gallup would still give us a majority of 80." He comforted himself with elaborate statistical theories on random and sample polls. The slip in popularity prompted a grumbling discontent within the Labour leadership. Many of them were worried by the danger of concentrating the Labour case on the personality of Wilson. "It's one hell of a gamble," one leading Opposition spokesman said on September 3. "It's not just other people he won't have on posters. He won't have policy ideas either. I've tried twice to reason with him. But I've now given it up. Anyway I'm not the proper person to do it, could be misinterpreted. He's even eased Dick Crossman out; he wanted to write the manifesto and wasn't allowed to."

The Conservatives too had a big start-of-campaign rally on Saturday, September 12. Sir Alec himself addressed a crowd of the loyal in Friends House in Euston Road. His speech was transmitted by land-line hookup to twelve sim-

ilar meetings all over the country, where the voice of the
leader was planned to introduce a subsidiary speech by one
of his Cabinet Ministers. "Saturday's going to be a very
odd affair," said R. A. Butler, who was chosen to speak at
Manchester. "I suppose we'll just sit there while the loud-
speaker performs for three or four minutes, then the audience will break into frenetic applause, and I'll have to get
up." It happened exactly that way, although thanks to a
poor set speech even by Home's standards, the applause was
rather less than frenetic. After the bit of the speech which
was relayed, Sir Alec warmed to his audience and denounced
the Labour Party manifesto as a "menu without prices."
This phrase—not Sir Alec's own but produced by one of his
scriptwriters, George Christ*—not only made the headlines
next day; it was also used by Conservative speakers throughout the campaign, so that the Labour Party was obliged to
quote and refute it. Right from the start Home, or his
speechwriters, scored over Wilson in bringing out memorable slogans.

On Monday, September 14, both party leaders went north.
Sir Alec left Kent by special plane for Scotland, where he
was due next day to meet the Queen and tell her the date
of the election. Wilson left for Huyton to be adopted formally as the Labour candidate. It was obvious that Home's
trip would attract more publicity; yet even Wilson must
have been disturbed at the lack of interest shown to a party
leader on the threshold of a general-election campaign.
when the 2:25 Liverpool train drew out of Euston station,
he appeared at the corridor window and waved to a crowd
—of the stationmaster and two TV cameramen. There was
not one representative of a daily newspaper on the train.

Harold Wilson loves train journeys. "There's nothing better than making a speech on a Saturday and traveling back

* A former lobby correspondent of the *Daily Telegraph*, who had migrated,
appropriately, to become editor of the *Conservative Weekly Newsletter*.

the next day. You can read all the Sunday papers and sleep.
I always sleep well on trains. Once coming back from Scotland I slept eleven hours." He can also relax. As soon as the
2:25 drew out of Euston, he lit a big cigar, put his feet up
on the seat opposite and opened Bruce Catton's book on the
Civil War, *A Stillness at Appomattox.* "I read the previous
one and enjoyed it very much," he said; then, as if to answer
the thought that this was no time to read books, he went on:
"I've got nothing much else to do at the moment. I've shut
up shop for the present. If anyone, a Canadian or anyone,
wants to come and see me, I'm not available. But things are
very quiet at the moment. There's a lull. Not like last week,
which was very hectic, starting with Blackpool [the T.U.C.
conference]. And the weekend was very hectic, as you can
imagine. Things won't really hot up until the day after dissolution, September 26."

The Wilson entourage on the train consisted of Michael
Pentreath, an able press officer and former journalist, and
Mrs. Wilson, who sat in the window seat on the same side
as her husband, legs curled up beneath her. Occasionally she
read from her book, *A Prologue of Love,* but more often
stared out of the window. Often she asked questions about
what she saw in the countryside, and almost invariably Wilson knew the answers. "Why don't they use the canals more?"
she asked, or, near Bedford, "Do they really use straw for
making bricks?" She was eager to talk of the family: "Did
you know that Giles had got his 'A' level?" "Yes," Wilson replied, "he just scraped through. He isn't the brightest scholar
in the family. We'd all been helping him during those weeks.
I was even helping with Virgil. I don't like it [Virgil] much.
I prefer Livy and Caesar—the straight stuff."

The train dawdled between Bedford and Stafford, and the
leader of the Labour Party dozed off to sleep. The book fell
on his lap, the pipe (which had replaced the cigar) went out,
and Michael Pentreath drew the side curtain in case some

passer-by or photographer should chance to see Wilson with closed eyes and slightly agape mouth. He slept for only a few minutes, picked up a newsaper and started to talk about politics.

"Home says Labour has done nothing to reduce restrictive practices. Who does he think he is?" He read a bit more. "I see in his whistle-stop tour of Kent he hasn't allowed himself much time anywhere. It's just a short speech and away. All whistle and no stop." Here Wilson smiled to himself. He was obviously pleased with this joke at Home's expense and later used it constantly in his speeches. "And I hear he isn't getting more than two hundred or two hundred and fifty each time. He'd do better to take a hall in the evening and speak to two thousand people—and the television. Look how short a time he's staying in Dover! . . . Of course he's shy. He doesn't like meeting people."

He looked at the Vicky cartoon showing all three political leaders lined up for the start of a race. "Vicky doesn't know much about cross-country running. In the first place I wouldn't have my pipe in my mouth. In the second place, my hands are in the wrong place." But his thoughts kept wandering back to deeper issues: "We had a comeback last week with the T.U.C. and the party political broadcast which everyone seemed to agree was the best we ever had. Good swift teamwork. . . . He'll have the initiative this week, what with Balmoral. . . . I shall wait a few days until after the Tory manifesto before issuing an open challenge to Home on land prices and the Common Market. If I make an attack on land prices and [Sir Keith] Joseph retaliates, I won't go after Joseph. Michael [Stewart] must go after Joseph. This manifesto will be all a lot of platitudes. I've heard it's going to be called 'Prosperity and Purpose.' If he uses the 'purpose' I'm going to send him a letter asking if he wants a free copy of my book, *Purpose in Politics.*

"A year and a month ago I said: there are three things the

Tories will fight this election on—nationalization, which doesn't worry me; the deterrent, which I knew would die out; and the cost, which did worry me. We've got a perfectly good answer but it's a sophisticated answer, difficult to explain." Clearly the "menu without prices" shaft had gone home. But Wilson rightly guessed where he could hit back at the Tory weak spot. He went on: "I'm not going to reply to him [on prices] this evening. I'm going to go on the land prices, which they haven't said anything about and I don't think they'll have anything about it in the manifesto." He was pretty well right.

Wilson went back to his book for a bit. Then a thought occurred to him and he began to talk about the anxieties of the campaign. "I feel more relaxed now the campaign has started. But it was a horrid fortnight before, when the Tories were making all the running. 'Tories present their Battle Plans,' said the *Standard*—when they hadn't even got any." He was quite clearly, though not admittedly, worried by the poll figures. Once again he discussed the figures favorable to himself: "The really interesting thing was the answers on 'who do you think would make the better Prime Minister?' Previously they'd always asked, 'How do you think Home and Wilson are doing as party leaders?' I think it's the important question because people who don't want Home as Prime Minister aren't really going to vote Tory, are they? I mean we're getting round to the Presidential system here." What about the reaction to his plans for the "first hundred days" of office? Would he use that phrase again after the hostile comment? He gave a wry smile. "No. I was thinking of Kennedy, but other people thought of Napoleon. Then of course Home said that I wanted to solve all the problems of Britain in a hundred days. He's not very accurate, that man."

When the train left Stafford, the Wilson party went through to the restaurant car for high tea. Nobody greeted him, or even stared at him, although later in the meal a man shyly dropped a good-luck message beside Wilson's plate. They had ordered lamb chops. "If Rich* were here he'd be telling us we were eating too many calories," said Wilson, who promptly took a second helping of sauté potatoes. He ate the chop with gusto. "I could do with the same all over again"—and although he had asked for Worcester sauce, he was brought a bottle of H.P. "It's the *Sunday Times* that's responsible," Wilson said, referring to his wife's famous remark to that newspaper: "If Harold has a fault, it is that he will drown everything with H.P. Sauce." After Wilson had smothered his chop with the sticky brown liquid, Michael Pentreath started to study the label, with its long guarantee written in English and French and its antiquated illustration: "I never realized before," Pentreath mused, "that H.P. stood for Houses of Parliament." Clearly this thought had occurred to Wilson. "Aye," he said, "and they haven't changed the label in thirty years, to my knowledge. When I was studying French at school, I used to stare at that label. . . ." Here he leaned back in his chair, half closed his eyes and began to recite the words: *"Cette sauce de haute qualité est un mélange de fruits orientaux, d'épices et de vinaigre de malt."*

The train stopped at Crewe and Harold Wilson leaped from his chair to buy a newspaper on the platform. "Don't get left behind," Mrs. Wilson called anxiously, but he was out of earshot already. He came back within two minutes and started to pore over the coverage given to Home's whistle-stop tour. He was enraged by the remark of Home's: "The Socialists say you're a soft and flabby lot." He derisively imitated Home's upper-class pronunciation "sawft." "Nobody would have said that. It's not the sort of phrase we'd use. It's a typical public-school phrase. We'll get someone to write

* Alfred Richman, a *Sun* journalist who was sometimes seconded to Wilson as personal assistant.

a letter to *The Times* about that, asking him to substantiate the charge. Somebody very respectable, who would never use such an expression. Noel-Baker, for example."*

While he talked about Home, Mrs. Wilson had a look through the same newspaper. "Oh dear," she exclaimed, "it says there's going to be rain for a month, after that lovely summer." Her husband did not seem depressed by this item of news. He grinned from ear to ear. "Oh well," he said cheerfully, "we've got to have equal representation in the weather." Back in the compartment, the conversation changed to the evening's meeting in Huyton. "It seems funny to be doing a speech in my constituency," Wilson said. "I'll be doing the usual patter: economic, social and how the country's lagging behind."

He was suddenly in his most cheerful, self-deprecating mood. He mentioned the program for last Saturday's Wembley rally which had carried a long introductory extract from Bevan's famous last speech made at the Labour Party conference of 1959. "Did you notice they left out Nye's bit about a 'vulgar society'? I left it in when I last quoted that speech, and it was used against me. Perhaps I should cut it out, but I hate to cut quotes."

The train drew toward Liverpool, and the little group of campaigners began to get their things ready. "Do I have to wear a hat?" asked Mrs. Wilson plaintively as she fitted a red hat on her head. "Red doesn't suit me." Her husband was kind but firm: "Yes, you'll have to do that, otherwise they'll think you're a Tory because of the blue suit. Anyway the constituency's split asunder by Everton and Liverpool supporters, so if you wear red and blue you've got both their colors. Though, mind you, there's a long tradition of Labour leaders' wives wearing blue. Dora did and Vi always did." "Yes," said Mrs. Wilson sadly, thinking of Lady Attlee's

* The letter appeared in *The Times* of September 21 over the signature of the venerable ex-Cabinet Minister, Chuter Ede.

recent death, "Vi always looked very good in blue." Then Wilson, who almost always wears a green tie, added: "Nye always wore a blue tie, very clumsily knotted, a real mess. . . ." Any further thoughts on dress were checked by the train's arrival in Liverpool.

The Huyton agent and half a dozen journalists were at the station to meet Wilson. He went almost immediately to his constituency, which lies to the east of Liverpool. It is here, in Huyton, that Wilson seems most at home; and the people of Huyton venerate him, as they showed on October 15 by returning him with a majority of almost 20,000. Yet Huyton was once considered a marginal seat.

The consituency included the old village of Huyton itself with the new estates sprawling around it, the ancestral home of the Earls of Derby, several factories, hundreds of acres of rolling farmland, and the whole new town of Kirkby. This last bustling community—known throughout Merseyside as Dodge City—houses thousands of Irish families from the old slums of central Liverpool. The birth rate is said to be the highest outside Red China, and the crime rate is one of the highest in Britain. It has fine skyscraper flats and bright new schools; but the telephone boxes are constantly smashed, litter lies thick on the grass verges and there are frequent fights in the streets. A Kirkby urchin went up to a cluster of journalists in the election campaign and suggested: "If you want a good headline: "Hooliganism Is Disgusting in Kirkby." It is also a boisterous, thriving community with all the Beatle-exuberance of Liverpool and some of the planned civic pride of a new town.

Here in his Huyton constituency Harold Wilson is king. Although Yorkshire-born, he went to school on Merseyside, and his flat West Riding voice has nasal Merseyside undertones. He has sat for a constituency in this area since he won nearby Ormskirk in 1945; indeed Kirkby itself was both in the old Ormskirk and in the new Huyton division formed in

1950. Not surprisingly, Wilson knows scores of his constituents by name and often answers questions put to him from an audience by saying: "I'm glad you asked that, George."

After the private adoption meeting that Monday, September 14, Wilson went to a public meeting in a Huyton school. He had prophesied an attendance of only 100, but more than 250 crammed into the tiny hall. They included many young men with Beatle haircuts and leather jackets, many surprisingly pretty young women—a type seldom seen at Labour Party meetings. The introductory speaker, Councillor Gordon, gave Wilson a typically north-country greeting. "Many of us have been browsing over books about Harold Wilson that have come out in these last three or four weeks. In fact I've heard it said that writing about Harold Wilson is a major industry. But the fourth one, out this week, doesn't even begin to describe him. The author obviously hasn't got one foot on the ground. He didn't know Harold Wilson as we know him. . . ." He ended his praise for Wilson's work in the constituency by making a small presentation. Referring to the time at the recent T.U.C. conference when Wilson's pipe had caught light in his coat pocket, Councillor Gordon said: "We hope, Harold, that you won't burn that indicative finger"—here he wagged his finger Wilson-wise in the air—"and I have here a little Dickens character—it's actually a pipe damper—and I hope that you, Harold, will use it and won't burn your finger."

It was a matey, almost a family occasion, and Wilson spoke to his audience like an uncle, or at the very least like a friendly family doctor. He first of all denied the rumor—never seriously believed—that he had tried to get a safer constituency. If Huyton would do him the honor of selecting him once again, he would be proud—and so on. In fact he knows as well as anyone that because of the ever-increasing overspill from Liverpool slums, Huyton is bound to become more and more a safe Labour seat. He went on to say how glad he always felt to get back to his constituency, which brings "a breath of cold refreshing air to the hothouse which Westminster sometimes is." His talk that evening was devoted to the details of life in the constituency. For instance: "Seven or eight years ago I was taking one of my surgeries, when a youngish lady—widowed—said could I get her her postwar credits. . . . I raised it with Heathcoat Amory—his politics were as misguided as the rest of them but he had a touch of humanity—and as a result tens of thousands of people were enabled to draw their postwar credits on hardship grounds." Then he talked about education and "the number of parents who came to see me about this, parents who were happily settled here but seriously considered leaving their homes in Huyton to go to Kirkby to send their children to one of the fine comprehensive schools there. . . . I'll give you another one. One of the most extraordinary of all the problems I've had to deal with, the problem of old-age pensioners' bus fares. . . . Everyone of us knows what it means to somebody who has been moved out of the center of Liverpool, what it means if they want to visit a son or daughter the other end of Liverpool." Naturally he did his best to take personal credit for every reform, but there was no doubt of the understanding concern he felt for all these everyday problems of his constituents. They in turn listened fascinated. There was not a cough, not a shuffle of feet as Wilson talked on in a quiet, casual voice or when he finally answered questions. These too were mostly specific local problems. A woman, for instance, asked about playground facilities for children: "If they play football, they're in the wrong place, and if they sit on the wall with their transistors, they're annoying somebody. Whatever they do, somebody's chasing them." A sympathetic Wilson said that he understood how she felt but that childrens' playgrounds could not take top priority among all the things in Britain that needed doing.

This evening speech in Huyton showed Wilson at his superlative best: warm, knowledgeable, in touch with the country. He had not bothered to make a prepared speech simply because he knew that nothing he said was likely to get in the newspapers, still less appear on television. Yet the impression he made was far better than all his rehearsed set speeches and contrived TV appearances. In the same way, he is far more popular in his constituency than in the country at large. They talk of him as sincere, yet the country at large calls him clever; they call him friendly, yet the country at large calls him cold.

As Wilson had rightly prophesied, the limelight was turned on Home during these first few days of the campaign proper. While Wilson chatted to his constituents, Sir Alec was off to see the Queen at her summer home at Balmoral. As a Scot, a former 14th Earl, and the father of a royal lady-in-waiting, Home has long been on close terms with the royal family and well understands how to exploit the public's royal romanticism. During the struggle for the leadership of the party, several Home supporters claimed that "the Queen is for Alec." Throughout the following year Alec was eager to prove that he in turn was for the Queen. "In no circumstances," ran the peroration of one of his favorite speeches, "will I take the decision about the future of Britain out of the hands of the Queen's Ministers and the Queen's Parliament." Where any other politician would simply have said "Britain's Ministers and Parliament," Home was anxious to flaunt his loyalty. All British politicians protest that the Queen should be kept out of politics, but none of them mind dropping the hint that she is on their side.*

Home made the most of his flight up to Scotland to tell the Queen the date of the poll. At the end of his Monday

* The Queen's actual views are not known. The heir to the throne, Prince Charles, was seen wearing a Scottish Nationalist rosette during the mock elections at Gordonstoun school.

whistle-stop tour of Kent, he was to have gone by Golden
Arrow train to London and then on by scheduled flight to
Aberdeen. But the tour ran late through the hopfields of
Kent, and Sir Alec ordered a special plane from the Queen's
Flight to await him at Lympne Airport in eastern Kent. He
drove there from Dover at 6 P.M., changing jackets in the
back of the car, and boarded the scarlet-and-black Heron
plane at 6:30 P.M. Three and a half hours later he alighted
at Dyce Airport, near Aberdeen, then drove up the Dee
Valley between rugged hills topped by the cairns put up by
Queen Victoria in memory of Prince Albert. Late that night
he was greeted by the Queen; but the official reception
waited until ten o'clock next morning.

The announcement of October 15 as polling day was a
nonevent. Every newspaper in the land had forecast as much
for many weeks. The logic of survival had forced Home to
hold the election that autumn instead of spring; the only
viable date in the autumn was October 15. But the ritual
request to the Queen for dissolution, the Heron flight to the
Highlands and all the concomitant newspaper stories added
a note of grandeur and gallantry to Home's simple acceptance
of the inevitable.

9. Quiz Game

This is not a Presidential election. It is the
British general election.
> SIR ALEC DOUGLAS HOME *at his Lanarkshire home, Castlemains,*
> *September 19, 1964*

SIR Alec Douglas-Home returned from Balmoral to Downing Street at 4:30 P.M. on Tuesday, only to be embroiled in a
comic misunderstanding. The house was littered with cables
and cameras and TV men from both BBC and ITV. This
much he had expected. At 4:45 P.M. the ITV team, producer
Jeremy Isaacs and reporter George Ffitch, arrived at Number Ten to be told that Sir Alec's recording planned for 5:30
would take place ten minutes earlier. Then Ffitch, with the
BBC's Robin Day, were led to an improvised make-up room
on the same floor. Soon after 5 P.M., while Isaacs was talking
with Paul Fox of the BBC, another BBC producer, Anthony
Craxton, burst in looking highly worried. Apparently George
Ffitch had said to Sir Alec: "Well, Prime Minister, I think
I'd better give you an outline of what I'm going to ask. I
thought first of all I'd put to you what are the real issues in
this election."

The Prime Minister frowned: "Oh, I'm not doing anything like that. I'm not going to talk politics. I agreed to go
on to discuss the constitutional significance of October 15,
and that's all." Ffitch was thunder-struck, as well he might
have been. No viewer in Britain could have any conceivable
interest in the constitutional significance of why Home had
chosen October 15. "But, Prime Minister . . ." he protested.
It was no good. "No, I'm not doing it," said Sir Alec, who

then sat down in a make-up chair, folded his arms in a petulant gesture and added: "I'm on strike."

At this point Isaacs and Fox were brought into the discussion. They insisted that they had agreed on the nature of the interview with John Groves, the Prime Minister's public-relations adviser. The embarrassed Groves agreed that he had consented but blamed Conservative Central Office for suggesting that the questions asked should touch on the issues in the campaign. Here Home interrupted crossly: "But I don't know what the issues of the election are." He turned to Frank Pearson,* his Parliamentary Private Secretary and constant shadow: "Well, what are the issues?" At this point Isaacs and Fox withdrew, saying, "Prime Minister, perhaps we'd better leave you for a few minutes."

A few minutes later the Prime Minister himself came in. He had agreed to talk about the issues and promptly sat down on the sofa in front of the camera. It was on this very sofa at almost the same stage of the election campaign in 1959 that President Eisenhower had conducted a famous, almost notorious, TV chat with Harold Macmillan. Although this meeting between Prime Minister and President had been billed as a nonpolitical broadcast, Harold Macmillan had lost no opportunity to turn it to his advantage. He praised the success of his own recent visit to Russia and claimed that "the old British pound sterling" was in good shape. Now Home sat on the same sofa and, in some opinions, pulled off as good a TV trick. "He knew he was going to do it [the political broadcast] all the time," said Jeremy Isaacs afterward. "It's just that he's a player who wants to be thought a gentleman, a player who wants to be considered an amateur. The man's a professional in-fighter. He knew what the whole thing was about from the start."

The other two party leaders were given the opportunity to

---

* The Conservative Member for Clitheroe, who brought to his job of being P.P.S. to a Tory Prime Minister the appropriate qualification of having once been A.D.C. to a Viceroy of India.

appear after Sir Alec. Although Grimond, in Manchester, went to the BBC TV studios to make the recording, Wilson, in Liverpool, insisted on facing the cameras in a banqueting room at the Adelphi Hotel. It was a big mistake. The lighting was bad. The background was flat. Jeremy Isaacs, who was producing all three interviews for ITV, said afterward: "It was entirely Wilson's fault if he looked bad. I begged Bradley to bring him back to London. I said I'd give him a studio with a House of Commons background, but he refused to cancel an appointment with the editor of the *Liverpool Daily Post*. And then of course the cameras we'd hired from Granada packed up and so we had to use the BBC ones that they'd almost started dismantling." He was equally critical of Wilson's performance: "He threw away chance after chance. He just wouldn't give crisp answers, and when he tries—for instance 'a powerhouse instead of a monastery'— they're no good as catch-phrases."

At this early stage in the campaign it was not TV but an old-fashioned public speech by that old-fashioned orator Quintin Hogg that set the electorate fizzing. The Secretary of State for Education and Science was addressing a meeting in Birmingham when he suddenly veered away from his set speech to make an attack on Harold Wilson: "Mr. Wilson is reported as saying that he wanted to carry out his plan as a military operation. Those of us who have had experience of military operations do not want military operations in our own country in time of peace. The demand for a military operation is the theme song of the dictator from time immemorial. The characteristic of military operations is the disregard of human happiness and rights. . . . Therefore to Mr. Wilson, who knows nothing whatever about military operations from first hand, I would say: 'Chuck it, Smith.' " The *Daily Mail*, which led its front page with this story, rubbed home Hogg's point with a solemn note in brackets: "[According to the current *Who's Who*, Mr. Hogg was com-

missioned in the Rifle Brigade during the war and was
wounded in the Western Desert. Mr. Wilson is listed as having been Director of Economics and Statistics, Ministry of
Fuel and Power 1943–44.]" The imputation was taken even
further by Julian Amery, speaking in Preston on October 2:
"I don't want to criticize his [Wilson's] war record. I'm sure
he did good national work in an office somewhere in London"—a remark that helps to explain why Amery is one of the
less liked men on either side of the House of Commons.

There was no mention of Hogg's speech at the press conference held next morning at Church House to launch the
Conservative manifesto. Butler, Maudling and Blakenham
sat on the platform with Sir Alec, who was looking trim and
confident. He had clearly done his homework on the contents
of the manifesto, for he answered question on rates and housing with firmness if not with certainty. He was less good on
the subject of computers and made the interesting Freudian
slip "anyone who has installed an imputer . . ." But it was
symptomatic of Home's increased confidence that the first
question he passed to one of his colleagues—Butler—concerned the M.L.F., on which Home himself is well qualified
to speak. It was not an inspiring performance but it took the
lead story of the two London evening newspapers. It might
have taken the lead the next day had it not been for a clever
counterstroke by Harold Wilson.

He chose this moment to ask for a TV confrontation. The
subject, of course, had been aired for nearly a year, and the
public was led to believe that Home had all along shied away
from the challenge. This belief does not fit the facts. At the
beginning of the year Wilson said publicly that he would like
a confrontation but that it could not be made to extend to
other leaders besides himself and Home. "It would be uncon-
stitutional for us to put Gordon Walker up as shadow
Foreign Secretary or Jim Callaghan as shadow Chancellor. I
haven't appointed them yet." Privately he spoke rather differ-

ently of the whole confrontation issue: "I was none too keen on the broadcasts. The Tories might well have done worse than suggest a confrontation between Home and myself, then Callaghan and Maudling and then, if Macleod had still been in the Government, him and Brown. Besides, some small thing might have gone wrong. I might have got hiccups from smoking a dusty pipe."

Both parties felt disappointed so far by the impact made by their leaders. On September 22 at Conservative Central Office Lord Blakenham hardly sounded a model of confidence: "I think he's making ground, don't you? But of course he hasn't got over to the country. He's splendid with the party workers. Their confidence in him has percolated up to the House of Commons but he just hasn't really come across to the bulk of the electorate. Still, there's time yet, and he'll be getting lots of exposure in the next week or two." Across Smith Square at Transport House, Dick Crossman was equally discouraged by Wilson's lack of appeal to the women voters: "Can't do anything with him. Just hasn't got the appeal. Have to wheel in other people who come across to women."

A few days later, on Saturday, September 19, Wilson proved the critics wrong by a masterly whistle-stop tour of marginal London constituencies. In verve, charm and perhaps even in vote-winning, this was his best day of the campaign. He started with a meeting in a cul de sac near St. Pancras Station. Some three hundred people, including many students from nearby Bloomsbury, listened with rapture to his six-point denunciation of Conservative housing policy: "Finally I make no apology for dealing with a subject that is of great interest to everyone here—housing. Thirteen years of Tory rule have left Britain with a million families without homes of their own, at least a million slums, and two and a half million other houses lacking such elemetary amenities as fixed baths, piped hot water or indoor sanitation." This and the ten-minute exposition of Labour proposals was to be Wilson's stock speech throughout the election. It became such an instinctive reaction to any audience that when, on October 16, Wilson spent longer than was expected at Buckingham Palace, a disgruntled journalist was heard to remark: "He's giving the Queen the housing speech."

But in its heyday, in mid-September, the housing speech sounded fierce, fresh and exciting. The audience warmed to it and especially to the denunciation of property profiteers and the Rent Act. The audience at Holborn clearly loved Wilson. There were one or two of those strange hecklers who always attend outdoor meetings—"Prostitution is an honorable profession" yelled one—but no real opposition. At every stop on his tour, Wilson allowed fifteen minutes for his speech and fifteen minutes for questions. "When you've got the microphone in your hand, you're on top," he explained, "and it's easy to answer questions at public meetings because you can first repeat the question and this gives you time to think of the answer." Again, the pause for questions showed up his style in a better light than Home's. "This is a whistle-stop tour with a difference," he said over and over again. "We've all been reading about some others; they are all whistle and no stop." Again, he knew that his own particular style thrives on questions and heckling.

Many questions dealt with immigration. "What about the blacks? What about the Immigration Act? You're bringing the blacks over!" Sometimes the hecklers and questions almost drowned out the microphone, but Wilson with great skill and patience answered the questions and generally won over the crowd to his point of view. He said over and over again that the real color problem in British cities is caused by bad housing and social conditions; that the Labour Party is opposed to bad colored landlords but also to bad white landlords; that anybody opposed to colored people as such is repeating fascist slogans and should be ashamed of himself.

The biggest impression of all was made by one argument in particular. "There are a lot of people in this country, possibly including some of this audience, who are alive today because of what has been done within the National Health Service by colored doctors and nurses."

After three meetings the Wilson party stopped for lunch in the upstairs restaurant of the Alexandra public house by Clapham Common, within 200 yards of the headquarters of the British Trotskyist Party and also of the home of the other Wilson, Charles the train robber. The restaurant is lined with portraits of former Prime Ministers and the landlord tactfully placed Wilson under the picture of Lord Attlee. One of the regular drinkers there was so impressed by the sense of history that he actually tugged Wilson's sleeve and addressed him as "P.M."

Although Wilson had been annoyed when a photographer caught him drinking a pint of beer—he hates to be shown eating or drinking—he was clearly in high good humor as he wandered around the restaurant afterward talking to journalists and well-wishers. Throughout the afternoon's tour he was so relaxed that the organizers of the campaign found it difficult to prevent him answering questions long after the scheduled time of departure. "Why aren't the Communists allowed time on TV?" yelled a Communist, to which Wilson replied that he had seen Hugh McDiarmid, the Communist opposing Home, talking on TV the previous night. "Rubbish," yelled the Communist, to which Mr. Wilson blandly said, "Yes, he may have been talking rubbish, but he was on TV last night." He managed to make light even of immigration. "What about Gordon Walker at Smethwick?" asked one persistent racialist at Clapham. "What about Mr. Gordon Walker?" Wilson replied. "As far as I know he has always lived in this country."* As a Labour Party supporter told the

* Oddly enough Gordon Walker spent the first five years of his childhood in what is now Pakistan, like so many of his former Smethwick constituents.

man from the *Sunday Telegraph*: "It's a pity that he does not come across on television like this."

And so it proved next week when the three leaders appeared on consecutive nights to face the BBC's "Election Forum." A fortnight before, on a special election "Gallery" program, the BBC had asked viewers to send postcards with questions which they would like one of the leaders to answer. The cards were to be marked Lab, Con or Lib, according to who was expected to answer, or Gen for General if the question could be put to all three. About 19,000 postcards arrived at the BBC, of which only 1,200 were marked Lib, and the rest divided equally between the two big parties. The BBC staff sorted out the postcards before they were given to the three interviewers. "They thought it was going to be grass-roots democracy," said a BBC man who had worked on the program, "but they didn't realize all the special interests. Practically all the questions came from old-age pensioners." A fair number were sent by party propagandists hoping to get a tricky question put to the opposing leader. The BBC made no pretense of choosing the questions at random. They were chosen and allocated to the three interviewers so that if the politician evaded one difficult question, the next would deal with a related subject.

The BBC set its heart on these programs as the nearest possible thing to actual confrontation. They were held at the new Studio 4—of "Z Car" fame—in Television Center, at a special new table alleged to have cost £800. The politician was made to sit on a dais slightly above his questioners, and each session began at 9:30 P.M. to a roll of drums.

The first to appear, on Tuesday, September 22, was Jo Grimond. He was in his usual relaxed state and traded good-natured insults with his interviewers, Ian Trethowan, Robin Day and Kenneth Harris. "After the election," said Day, a former Liberal candidate, to his former leader, "you can always go out and govern Malawi." But Grimond's relaxation had a considerable TV skill. Of all the three leaders, a BBC man recalls, he took far the most care and time with his make-up. "For instance, he knows that he has to have a bit of black above the eyes." He gave, as always on TV, a sparkling and impressive performance. The interviewers appeared to be treating him rough. They asked 24 questions with 13 supplementaries, while Wilson was asked 27 question but got only 4 supplementaries. This was not, however, discrimination. Apparently there had been so few postcards marked "Lib," and of those so few that were usable, that supplementary questions were necessary to fill out time, though Grimond appeared for only twenty minutes, compared to half an hour each for Wilson and Home. Moreover Grimond always keeps his answers crisp and short. It was not a flawless performance—he fluffed the immigration question and did not know the cost of abolishing prescription charges—but it probably swelled the surge toward Liberalism which continued, almost unnoticed, throughout the campaign.

Jo Grimond had come alone to the studio. The following evening Wilson arrived in time for dinner with John Harris, his chief of publicity, and Clive Bradley, his broadcasting officer. Since the program was unscripted nobody quite understood what these two were supposed to be doing, and Bradley caused much irritation by demanding to check the BBC's equipment from the lighting to Wilson's chair. Wilson himself was very nervous, although he came out with a joke about keeping the chair warm for Home the following evening. After his inquisition he asked rather ruefully why the three interviewers had been less tough to him than to Grimond. This may be partly explained by his greater eminence and his sharp ways with a hostile questioner. Even more, he himself slowed down the pace of the program with long and ponderous answers. Although the set gave him a wise and handsome look he came out with no good phrases such as his hero, F. D. Roosevelt, used in his fireside chats. Instead the audience heard the least attractive Wilsonisms: "Quite frankly," "I'll be absolutely honest about this," and the familiar boasts of his past success at negotiating with the Russians. It was not one of Wilson's best performances. Talking with TV technicians afterward, he seemed to imply that he did not hope to win many votes by TV but was very concerned not to lose them by making a rash statement or slip.

The BBC team was impressed by Sir Alec's broadcast the following night. Indeed most of them reckoned it far more successful than Wilson's. He had been rather nervous, of course, crossing and recrossing his legs, but without the old irritating flick of the tongue on dry lips. Before the program began he had been quite jovial. While doing the voice-level tests, Robin Day said: "Sir Alec, our first question comes from a lady in Curzon Street who wants you to know that if you lose the election it won't be because of your smile, which she finds much more warm and attractive than Mr. Wilson's. What have you got to say about that?" Sir Alec's reply was delightful: "I think she must be the only lady in Curzon Street that I don't know."

He laughed a good deal during the questioning but did not come out with any jokes. "Don't you think a command of economics is essential to a political leader?" came the first question. "A leader ought to have common sense," was the reply. "What about a TV debate with Mr. Wilson?" "A British election should not be a confrontation of personalities. I saw the Nixon–Kennedy confrontation. That cured me forever. The British election is fought on politics which are carefully considered over a period by the whole electorate." He was questioned about the statement attributed to Peter Griffiths, the Conservative candidate for Smethwick: "Smethwick rejects the idea of being a multiracial society." After saying "We must keep all racial prejudice of any kind out of our minds," Home refused to repudiate Griffith's statement because he had not seen it in full.

"How did I do?" asked Home nervously when the thirty-minute ordeal by question was over. The BBC team assured him that he had done better than Wilson. Highly delighted, Home stayed for half an hour of chitchat with everyone from producers down to electricians. Among 7,700,000 viewers was Harold Wilson, who saw the program at home in Hampstead. As soon as it was finished he got on the telephone to friends. His verdict was: "Much better than I expected, but he left himself open on pensions." When flustered, Home had referred to pensions as "donations." He was to regret this bitterly, as Wilson rasped out the derogatory word in speech after speech during the campaign. And Wilson noticed another Home slip of the tongue which was to serve as valuable ammunition. "We are now building 400,000 houses next year." This confusion of tenses raised a laugh from Glasgow to Hammersmith and from Bristol to Newcastle. In fact Wilson relied so heavily on this rare occasion when he himself saw Home speak that one can only suppose that his staff did not provide him with equally funny quotations. Perhaps it was just the fact of seeing Home personally that provided the laugh. "I saw Sir Alec on television the other night [pause for laughter]. Yes, I did [pause]. I've got a TV set too, you know [laugh]. He's not my favorite program, mind you [loud laughter]." This long gag got funnier as the campaign wore on and Wilson's timing grew ever slicker.

A few hours after the TV forum, Sir Alec took the night sleeper from Euston to Gleneagles, the famous golfing hotel in his Perthshire constituency. From there he was driven to Culdees Castle, the pink mock-Gothic pile that was, as usual, his base in the constituency. It is conveniently near the town of Crieff, where the adoption meeting was to be held. This is the most Tory part even of Home's most Tory constituency. Here the landowners tend to wear kilts and drive Jaguars, while the farm laborers sometimes actually tug their forelocks as a sign of respect. Undoubtedly these are Home's "ain folk" and he speaks their language of grouse shooting, winter feed and the weather. "I always feel better as soon as I'm out of London," he once said, and in Scotland he quite visibly cheers up.

He made his Friday adoption speech in the cinema at Crieff, a hall of entertainment that seems to date back to the Buster Keaton age of movies. In the long low auditorium, smelling faintly of dust and old tickets, on a dais draped with a dingy Union Jack, he gave a lively address to a few hundred party workers, the press and the TV cameras. There was plenty in it to please the headline writers. He said that Socialist propaganda sounded like "an anthology of Gibbon, Marx, Dante's *Inferno* and Theodore White." He quoted George Brown: "The great thing the next Government will do is to introduce planning into every aspect of our life." He paused, swallowed and peered over his half-glasses: "Just think of that, brothers: every aspect of our life and all planned by George Brown." He made his usual references to the bomb, the cost of the Labour program and the need to help what he calls "the underdeveloping countries." Some of his speech caused surprise. He referred to the "Socialist Government" as though it had already gained power, and he said that if Labour carried out its plans for steel this would be "the first manufacturing industry to be nationalized." He was not apparently aware that Labour had nationalized steel before.

The Earl of Doncaster, thanking Sir Alec afterward, recalled the time when he himself had been a candidate and had made so bad a speech that he apologized afterward to the chairman. Apparently the chairman replied: "Don't worry, we've had some candidates here who couldn't even read." This joke, made to a Prime Minister who suffers notoriously from difficulty in reading prepared texts, rang a little embarrassingly even in Crieff. But it was typical of the tone of jolly amateurishness that pervades the Kinross and West

Perthshire party. There is an air of "Good heavens, what a joke to see all us chaps in politics" that is certainly appropriate to the place itself but puzzling to outsiders. Among the audience at Crieff was Allen Drury, the American author of *Advise and Consent* and an experienced reporter of the highly professional world of American politics. He was seen leaving the Home meeting with a distinctly mystified air.

10. Three Per Cent

At least when George drops a brick it's a golden brick.
    A Transport House official

FROM the start of the campaign many Conservatives were expecting to get a windfall from some Labour indiscretion. It might be an imprudent promise like Gaitskell's notorious pledge in 1959 to reduce taxes. It might be a tactless outburst from the volatile George Brown. On Saturday, September 26, it seemed to the overjoyed Tories that both these things had happened at the same time: a rash promise—from George Brown's lips.

The sensation broke, as so often in British politics, in a remote country hall in front of an audience that did not notice. The Labour deputy leader was speaking at Lea, a picture-postcard village in his constituency of Belper, in Derbyshire. The meeting was held in the dining room of the gray-stone village school and was attended by only eighteen villagers. The rest had preferred to visit the local flower show two hundred yards down the road. Perhaps Brown was tired at the end of a hectic three-day, ten-meetings-a-day tour. He had spoken for half an hour before asking for questions. There were two, one about pensions; the other, put by a young man whom nobody seemed to know, concerned mortgages. Would Mr. Brown be more specific about what Labour would do for people buying their houses? To which Brown replied: "I thought our policy on this subject had been stated fairly clearly. But what we propose to do is to have immediate discussions with building societies, local authorities and other interested parties about reducing the mortgage rate. We shall try to get it down immediately for new mortgages. We have something in mind to the order of three per cent though we are not committed to that figure."

The *Sunday Express* reporter Roy Assersohn used this reply in the story he telephoned to his newspaper and was surprised to find it treated with great excitement. He thought it would therefore be wise to check his note with Brown, who acknowledged its accuracy.

Shortly after midnight Wilson and his entourage were taking a late meal in the dining room of the Grand Hotel, Bristol, to the sound of a three-piece band, when Michael Pentreath, at a separate table, was called away to speak to a journalist. It was a "stringer" from the *Sunday Express* who told him what Brown had said and wanted to know if any specific figures for mortgage rates had been mentioned in Labour's manifesto. No, said Pentreath, who then returned to the dining room to alert both Wilson and Harris to what was happening. On the advice of Harris, Pentreath later told the *Sunday Express* reporter that Wilson was just going to bed and did not wish to comment.

The next morning's *Sunday Express* splashed the story on the front page of its later editions, which do not reach Bristol: "BROWN'S BOMBSHELL—3 P.C. HOME LOANS. If Labour win the election." The story began: "Mr. George Brown, Labour's deputy leader, made a sensational promise last night to intending house purchasers. He said that Labour was thinking of reducing new mortgages to around three per cent, compared with the six per cent now charged by most building societies." The report then went on: "In reply to a questioner who asked what Labour would do for house purchasers, he said: 'We propose to make arrangements with the building societies so that people can borrow money at less than the prevailing interest rate. We will then have the problem of what to do about existing mortgages but this we will have to look at more closely as it's a problem which was provided by the Tories. For the new mortgages we have something in mind to the order of three per cent, though we are not committed to that figure.' " There are many discrepancies between the *Sunday Express* and next day's *Daily Express* report of the exact words used by Brown to the questioner, even though Brown checked the note made by Assersohn. It seems that the *Sunday Express* elaborated its original story with a second telephone interview with Brown later that night.

But Brown did not accuse the *Express* newspapers of misreporting—rather of misrepresentation. Anybody who read just the headline and first two paragraphs of the *Sunday Express* report would assume that Labour had pledged itself to a 3-per cent mortgage rate. If he had said 4½ per cent, or even 4 per cent, there would scarcely have been any fuss. But a figure exactly half the existing 6 per cent sounded dangerously rash. It might also embitter existing occupiers who would see new buyers cashing in on a cheap rate subsidized by the public. The 3 per cent remark, however qualified, had all the ingredients of a political disaster.

By noon on Sunday the whole press was telephoning to everyone who could comment on mortgage rates, but above all to Wilson. At midday Brenda Dew, Wilson's second secretary, rang Transport House for a full report of the *Sunday Express* story, but Wilson, who was going on to speak at Plymouth that night, refused to make any comment until he had seen the transcript of what Brown had said. Meanwhile Len Williams held a quick conference with his advisers at Transport House, spoke to Wilson by phone, and then rang Brown in Derbyshire, asking him to say nothing except that the Labour Government would not be committed to any specific figure.

On Saturday night, when he heard the news, Wilson had turned angry. On Sunday he felt more worried than annoyed. Transport House wanted to play down the story and hinted to all newspaper inquiries that they were thinking of taking the *Sunday Express* to the Press Council. It was also decided to send a special press officer to help Brown to deal with the anticipated horde of reporters. Terry Burke, himself an ex-journalist, just caught the Belper train at St. Pancras, but the panic was quite unnecessary. Brown had adamantly refused to be drawn any further on mortgages; when the auxiliary press officer arrived, all the reporters had given up and gone home.

Moreover, it turned out that the 3 per cent scare was not after all so dangerous. The next morning's *Daily Express* led on it, but most of the press was more interested in the first flight of the TSR-2 and in the Warren Report on Kennedy's murder. Professional jealousy helps to explain this silence. The *Sunday Express* had a scoop with Brown's Saturday-night speech; any overemphasis of the story would therefore flatter the Beaverbrook newspapers. The battle of 3 per cent would be fought out in the press conferences, which, as never before in British politics, were aimed at setting the style and pace of the election campaign.

In the 1959 general election, Morgan Phillips, the then general secretary of the Labour Party, had taken morning press conferences at Transport House. This time Wilson wanted to take them himself. The new general secretary, Len Williams, shone as back-room organizer rather than as lively spokesman. Other possible spokesmen were ruled out for different reasons. Brown? He might bully the press or get angry. He was also too valuable as a whistle-stop speaker to spare for Transport House. Dick Crossman? Witty. But he might have been too clever and said something rash. Gordon Walker? An excellent choice. But even then it was clear that he needed to spend most of the campaign trying to save his Smethwick constituency. The only other possibility, Wedg-wood Benn, was much too junior in the party hierarchy. Be-sides, Wilson was eager to do them himself. He likes journalists and knows how to get on with them. He also believes that a good politician can test the political mood from a press conference. Moreover, like all politicians, he never gets tired of seeing his name in the newspapers.

Where Wilson went, there went the press conference. Whenever he was in London, it would be held in Transport House at 11:30. It was on the insistence of Percy Clark, the red-bearded and astute deputy director of publicity, that Labour held its conferences before, rather than after, the Tories. He realized that this would enable Wilson to take the offensive, while Maudling, whose conference started at 12:15, would have to spend much of his time replying to what Wilson had said. If the Labour Party got the time of its press conference right, it was not nearly so fortunate in the place. Transport Hall at the back of Transport House recalls everything that is drab, archaic and solemn in British socialism. It is a dark, drafty, basement room, decorated with six Doric columns and murals of naked but sexless pre-Raphaelite ladies. They are shown at the loom and the plow and so on, illustrating the motto *Labor Omnia Vincit. Absque Labore Nihil.* The doors rattle and squeak; mysterious workmen thump and crash in adjoining rooms. Sometimes one hears the noise of ping-pong.

The Labour Party had done its best to brighten this sepulcher of the Socialist past. A series of posters were hung behind the platform: "Let's Go with Labour for a New Britain" against a huge map of the British Isles.* Blue velvet was draped over the table to hide the shoes and socks of Wilson, John Harris and Len Williams. And even the upper slopes of that last, vast man were often half hidden in a fog of pipe or cigarette smoke.

The first Labour press conference, held on Friday, September 25, got off to a bad start. A little group of the "lobby" correspondents objected to the TV cameras, not only because of the whirring noise they made but because they, the corres-

* The map left out Northern Ireland, an unconquerable Tory stronghold.

pondents, did not want to appear on TV. The *Evening Standard's* Robert Carvel and *The Times's* David Wood were particularly adamant on the last point. "This involves an issue of principle for some of us," said Wood a few days later. With some papers the issue is one of commerce rather than principle. The proprietors do not want the public to see the press conference on TV before they read about it in the newspapers. Most of the lobby correspondents were merely jealous of having to share their traditional top talks with a whole lot of outside journalists. As the left-wing *Tribune* quite rightly sneered: "They wanted to hold the election off the record."

Wilson himself sometimes behaved as if these were lobby chats rather than mass, televised press conferences. His style, at first, was intimate, sarcastic and full of in-group jokes about what certain journalists had written. "It is not for me to intrude on Mr. Maudling's private grief . . . " "You yourself wrote, David, in February," etc. On Monday, with the 3 per cent dispute to be settled, he spent five minutes knocking down some of the stories about him in Sunday newspapers. No, there was no spy in Conservative Central Office.* There was no Hampstead telephone clique. When it came to serious issues, he continued in the ironic tone. Instead of giving a forthright, serious exposure of Britain's economic crisis, he quoted instead from the newspapers: ". . . but before various Ministers and other spokesmen of the Tory party, or for that matter leader-writers, suggest that this is a piece of my imagination on my part, I notice that I have the support of the City Editor of the *Daily Mail*," and he read out an article on the "massive" trading deficit. Through these early press conferences he would constantly quote from the

* There had been. For a year Transport House had received anonymous letters, postmarked Surrey, giving low-grade but accurate advance information on the program for Tory meetings and speakers at by-elections. However, this source of information dried up before the election campaign began.

Daily Telegraph, "a Tory newspaper," or *The Times*, "which I may remind you is not a Socialist newspaper." All this irony was enjoyable enough to those present but unlikely to get into the newspapers. For one reason it is very hard to report an ironic speech without having to point out that it was said "sarcastically," and sarcasm is a rude word in the view of the public. Secondly, no newspapers will want to quote what another newspaper wrote.

However, this very fact was useful to Wilson in avoiding dangerous questions on 3 per cent. It was a "rather typical *Sunday Express* stunt," he said, and did not believe that either the treatment or headlines were justified by what George had said. This was the line agreed upon at a meeting in Len Williams's office at ten o'clock that morning. George Brown had arrived after only a few hours' sleep and explained his position to a quiet but not hostile meeting. Everyone agreed that although Brown had been unwise to mention a figure at all, the fault lay with the *Express*. At this stage, Wilson still believed that the 3 per cent tag was damaging to the Labour Party. Later he came to think differently.

The subject was, of course, raised at the Conservative press conference at Central Office across Smith Square the same morning. These affairs were a very comic contrast. As soon as a journalist entered the hall he was met by a group of pretty young women offering handouts of Hogg speeches and other star attractions. He was asked, and obliged, to record his name and newspaper on a list, in order, so it was said, to prevent spies from Transport House.* The conference room was decorated in pastel green with wispy paintings of London scenes in light brown. The atmosphere was rather

---

* As a precaution this was totally ineffective. At least one Tory press conference was attended by Dr. Michael Young, acting head of the Labour Party's research department.

like that of a public-relations cocktail party in the King George V suite of a very expensive provincial hotel. The conferences were just as carefully organized.

Every morning Reginald Maudling would reach Central Office about 11:30. He went straight up to a first-floor room for a meeting. Those present normally included Lord Blakenham, party chairman; Lord Poole, one of the three vice-chairmen; Sir Michael Fraser, research department chief; Peter Goldman, director of the Conservative Political Center; George Hutchinson, director of publicity; Gerald O'Brien, the press officer; and sometimes Nigel Lawson, one of Home's own speechwriter-advisers. Together they talked over the morning's newspapers and tried to establish a line for the conference. At about noon, O'Brien would slip out to talk to one or two journalist friends who had been to the Labour press conference and could tell him what Wilson had said. Later, when the Conservatives grew more confident, they sent shorthand writers, including Lord Blakenham's daughter, to report on Wilson across the square.

On most days Maudling and Blakenham shared the platform in front of a photographic triptych of a school, a flyover and a house under construction. The conference would begin with a few introductory words from Blakenham and a few shouts of "Speak up! Can't hear!" from the back of the room. There was no complaint about Maudling, who handled all questions with quick, courteous fluency. The first Tory press conference fell on this Monday after the 3 per cent row, and Maudling played it brilliantly. The impression Brown gave was that interest rates for people buying new houses would go down to 3 or 4 per cent. "If this is their intention they should say so. If not, they should also say so."

As Chancellor of the Exchequer, Maudling's role was not an easy one. Harold Wilson had talked of a "trade crisis," and Maudling knew that the half-yearly balance-of-payments

figures to be published on Wednesday would substantiate
Wilson's accusations. At Monday's press conference he confessed that the economy was "facing a testing year" but af-
firmed that it was strong enough to support the Conservative
program outlined in the manifesto. He spoke of a need for
"effort and a vigorous new drive to expand our exports." He
denied emphatically that there was a crisis.

Although Maudling handled the subject well, the economy
was becoming a weak area in the Conservative line of battle.
For one thing, it had been Maudling himself who had tried
to persuade Home to hold an election in June because he,
Maudling, knew that the economy would stagnate by
autumn. Having warned of a crisis in private, it was hard
now to deny the crisis in public. It was he who insisted that
the Government, during the height of the campaign, should
reveal its heavy borrowing from the Central Banks. To make
matters worse Selwyn Lloyd, a former Chancellor, put his
foot in it during a speech on Tuesday, September 29. Attacking Wilson, he said that in 1951 "the Labour Government,
faced with another crisis, chucked in their hand and ran
away." This was a clear admission that Britain faced a crisis
now, and Wilson was able to make great play with it.

Meanwhile the 3 per cent argument had died down. The
Express newspapers led with it on Tuesday for the third consecutive day—"Brown Blitzed"—and indeed quoted some
bitter attacks from Conservative leaders. Sir Alec told the
Socialists that if they did not know the right mortgage figure
"they must stop bandying tempting ones about as illustra-
tions or examples." Sir Keith Joseph said that plans for cut-
price mortgages were "lunatic" and Macleod said that the
"bounds of Brother Brown's indiscretion will get wilder and
wilder yet." Unfortunately for the Tories, they did not. Indeed, Brown's part in the general-election campaign was so
exuberant and successful that he must claim a good part of

the credit for victory. His long speaking-stomp through Britain was, in entertainment value, the only performance worth watching in the campaign.

At 11 A.M. on Monday, September 28, Brown left Transport House in a large silver-and-black Daimler for a 2,000-mile tour of England. He began in southwest London and the dormitory belt of Kent, an area where tens of thousands of new house owners were particularly interested in mortgage rates. At Bexley Heath he immediately faced questions on 3 per cent, but decided to counterattack: "I am not going to spend the next three weeks denying the allegations of the *Daily Express*. I'm sure that the capacity of the *Express* for distortion is unlimited." The speeches are not the best part of a Brown tour. He prefers to get out among the crowd, kissing babies, sampling potato chips from a girl's plate, or simply slapping backs and shaking hands. Stopping at one point of the tour to chuck the chins of twin babies in a pram, he was surprised to see one of them burst into tears. But Brown, quick as you like, quipped, "Which twin is a Tory?" Almost alone among British politicians, he has something of the Lyndon Johnson mass magic, or charisma, in the fashionable phrase. He loves a crowd and wants to be loved back in return. In the cattle market at Dartford and the huge new L.C.C. housing estate at Nottingham, he captured the housewives and the schoolchildren and the well-to-do factory workers. In a big new shopping center, all cellophane wrappings and metal baskets on wheels, he looked like Lyndon Johnson wooing the Middle West. And at tea with party workers he suddenly turned into a jolly, somewhat hearty uncle who patted ladies on the back, called them "dear" and chuckled fruitily at their feeblest jokes. He surpassed himself at a Darby and Joan pensioners' afternoon party held in the Maldon Labour Hall. "I've just come in to say hello—no politics," he announced, but within a few minutes he jumped up to lead them all in community singing. He knew all the songs from "Roll out the Barrel" to "When Irish Eyes Are Smiling"—Brown is very proud of his Irish ancestry—and he sang them all in a powerful, rich tenor. As he sang, Mrs. Brown looked on with partial approval: "You know, if he does that when our daughters are here they hate it; it embarrasses them horribly. He can go too far, you know, when he gets warmed up to it. Still that ten minutes [of singing] has been more refreshing to him than an hour's sleep." And so thought the old-age pensioners, for they gave him a quite spontaneous chorus of "For He's a Jolly Good Fellow."

As his tour grew increasingly friendly, Brown went on to the offensive about mortgage rates. "We all owe a debt of gratitude to the *Sunday Express* distortion factory," he said at Ilford on Tuesday, "for setting the election alight." When a woman heckler at Rayleigh shouted, "No more clangers!" Brown proudly rejoined: "Now listen, dear. My latest clanger was to say that people should be allowed to buy houses at lower rates of interest than you can get them for at the moment. I stand by that." He called mortgages "the big issue of the election." And at Transport House the same morning, Wilson too had begun to scent electoral benefits from the mortgage dispute: "It is faintly amusing [pause]—I won't put it any higher [pause]—to see Conservative leaders being forced to make pronouncements about things they know nothing about in their own experience. . . . Some of them until this weekend would not have known the difference between a mortgage and the back end of a camel." As Wilson was often to point out to hecklers, he himself was paying out 6 per cent on his house. Even Maudling later came to believe that the mortgage dispute had helped Labour. "They'll have to live with it, of course, but there's no doubt they succeeded in turning it against us."

But Labour remained cautious, as was seen on the evening of Tuesday, September 29. At about 5:30, Lord Longford, the well-known Labour peer, rang up Transport House from Birmingham. He wanted to speak to a housing expert from the research department because he had undertaken to go on the BBC's "Ten o'clock" program to debate mortgages with Peter Goldman, director of the Conservative Political Center. The chairman of this debate, Lord Longford remarked, was to be Robert McKenzie. This telephone call created bewildered horror in Transport House. Throughout the campaign it had been customary for both the BBC and ITV to check with party headquarters when inviting speakers. In this case Longford had simply accepted the invitation without Transport House having been told by the BBC. Now the Labour Party was very embarrassed. Quite apart from their chronic prejudice against Robert McKenzie, who is thought to be anti-Labour, they feared that the expert Goldman would know far more of the intricacies of housing than Lord Longford. A Transport House publicity man put this point to Lord Longford over the telephone. Nonsense, said the distinguished Earl; he knew a lot about mortgage rates in his position as a director of the Alliance Building Company. This remark still further depressed Transport House. Only the day before Lewis Cohen, chairman of the Alliance and a well-known Socialist, had gone on record as saying: "I cannot think that my friend George Brown meant that the party is proposing a three per cent housing loan. It is just not possible." Nevertheless Longford insisted on keeping his word to the BBC.

Len Williams agreed to this. But when John Harris, who was on tour with Wilson in Kent, was telephoned, he insisted that Longford should not appear. One error alone was necessary for the whole 3 per cent row to blow up again. Then Wilson was brought into the argument. He too insisted that Longford should not appear. This placed Transport House in a nasty position. It could neither forbid Longford to go on the air nor risk flouting the orders of Wilson and Harris. At last Clive Bradley, the broadcasting officer, simply rang up the BBC and told them that Longford was not able to go on the program. When the producer of the program heard this, with only two hours to go before ten o'clock, he was understandably angry, and rang John Harris's deputy in person. The ingenious Percy Clark explained that since Longford was a senior peer and likely to be in the Cabinet, it was quite unsuitable for him to be paired with a back-room boy of Conservative Central Office. After telling the BBC, Clark promptly broke the news to Longford, who, being a good-natured man, did not protest too much.

There were some in the Labour Party at this time who thought that the whole campaign style was too cautious and timid. "My view is that we're being too defensive altogether," Brown had remarked the night before. "It's high time we really started fighting." Wilson's own confidant, Thomas Balogh, put the same point more vividly: "It's time we took the bloody gloves off." Certainly there was every reason for getting worried. The Gallup poll in the previous *Sunday Telegraph* showed the Tories ahead of Labour by half per cent, the first time they had gone ahead since July 1961. A further Gallup poll published on Wednesday purported to give five reasons for Labour's lost lead. These were:

1. The low political temperature.
2. Labour's failure to establish itself as a clear-cut alternative to the Conservatives.
3. The instability of the "protest" vote which had turned to Labour.
4. Labour's loss of working-class support greater than their gains from the middle classes, as revealed in early Gallup surveys.
5. Revived confidence in the economic situation.

The news on Tuesday, September 29, seemed particularly depressing for Labour. More than two hundred inspectors had gone on strike at the Hardy Spicer factory, in Birmingham, which produces 80 per cent of British motor manufacturers' propeller shafts. If Hardy Spicer were closed altogether by the strike, and kept closed, almost the whole of Britain's car industry would be brought to a standstill. This would certainly damage the Labour Party. Although the public is often sympathetic to strikes of low-paid workers such as the busmen, postmen and railwaymen, it tends to be bitter against strikers in highly paid industries. For instance, the dispute at the Steel Company of Wales, earlier in the year, was thought to have had this effect. Indeed Wilson attributed a bad Gallup result in January to this strike news on TV. "That Gallup result was almost entirely due to the Port Talbot strike. People have been seeing it on television almost every night and frankly some of the trade-union leaders haven't been making an altogether favorable impression." This was an understatement of the impression made by strikers saying they could not get by on only £30 a week. A strike at Hardy Spicers, with more well-paid strikers appearing on TV, would discredit the Labour Party by inference.

Wilson's morale was not high on the evening of Tuesday, September 29. It was soon to reach rock bottom. Throughout the campaign the Labour Party press department had arranged to collect the early editions of the newspapers so that if any important story was breaking, Wilson should know about it straight away. What appeared in one of them that night was drastic enough for Percy Clark to take the extreme step of driving to the Wilson home in Hampstead Garden Suburb. It was half past twelve when he arrived, but he noticed the light still burning in Wilson's bedroom. Without bothering to ring he pushed the next morning's *Daily Mail* through the letter box. From above, Wilson heard the clack and came down for the papers. "It's Tories to win by 80," said the *Daily Mail*'s second headline. And Wilson, who secretly set great store by the N.O.P., read the bitter news that the Tory lead had risen to 2.9 per cent.

11. Poor Dears

Harold has scored a boundary through the slips, but it was
a stroke he never should have played.
 FRED MULLEY, M.P., *one of Wilson's campaign advisers*

NEXT morning the Wilson's telephone rang at seven o'clock.
Since their new, ex-directory number had once belonged to a
car-hire firm, the Wilsons were used to peremptory requests,
at all times of day, for a silver Rolls Royce, or an MG to tour
Scotland. But this call came from the man who was perhaps
Wilson's closest adviser, Thomas Balogh. He wanted to know
if Wilson had seen the latest quarterly trade figures, due to
be published that day at noon. Yes, Wilson had read them the
night before and knew of the £290 million deficit. Now was
the time, Balogh argued, for Labour to pitch in with a
wholehearted attack on the Government's handling of the
economy.

On the face of it, it certainly seemed to present just the
opportunity that Labour needed. The Treasury was well
aware of the desperately serious balance-of-payments crisis;
earlier that year Maudling warned Cabinet colleagues of the
coming difficulties and the dangers of letting the problem
slide. He realized the atrocious financial situation that would
be faced by either party in power after October 15, and this
was just the consideration that made the Labour Party hold
back. "I think we're going to win this election," said James
Callaghan at this time, "and I'm going to be Chancellor of
the Exchequer." Because of this he was anxious that nothing
should be said during the actual campaign that would
weaken the pound for a Labour Government. He believed
that alarmist talk about the economy—even if true—would

threaten sterling and start a run on the country's gold reserves. And Wilson agreed with him.

For this reason Wilson had so far ignored the advice of Balogh, Crossman and others to accuse Home of deceiving the nation. It was not until Wednesday that he changed his mind—for two reasons: the N.O.P. polls made it clear that he was no longer certain of winning the general election,* while the trade figures were even worse than he feared. He was alarmed and infuriated by the possibility that the Conservatives might sneak back into power thanks to public ignorance of the economic dangers. His decision to act was the single most important moment of the campaign. It meant that Labour at last went into the attack, but it also created just those long-term difficulties that Callaghan had feared. The drain of British gold reserves really began from the time of the speech in which Wilson exposed the desperate plight of the economy.

Early that morning, Wilson, Balogh, Crossman and other advisers decided to write a statement on economic affairs to be slotted into that evening's speech at Norwich on agriculture. They worked on the draft of it throughout the day. Having once determined to go on the offensive, they were determined to do so as sharply as possible. "Harold didn't need much convincing that we needed to put the heat on," Crossman said the next day. "He was a bit shy, though, of attacking Home personally. He's a parliamentary performer and if he'd had his way he'd have talked about 'terminological inexactitudes.' He needed some persuading that what he was to say was 'I must tell you that the Prime Minister has lied to you and deceived the nation.' For a sophisticated man, he's curiously blind to the effect of the short, sharp sentence. Home is better at it than he is. The trouble is

* It was at this time that Ray Gunter, "shadow" Minister of Labor, told a friend, "You know *I'm* not going to be the next Minister of Labor." The friend, somewhat taken aback, asked who was. "Joe Godber" came the reply.

there's no one capable of composing them for him at Transport House. He must learn to talk in headlines."

This advice was good, and Wilson took it. A speech was prepared making the savage comparison of Home with John Bloom, the washing-machine magnate who had run into financial difficulties earlier in the year. It was a good speech and should have produced sensational coverage in the press next day—but for Wilson's one colossal blunder of the campaign.

With his head still full of economics that Wednesday morning, Wilson went to Transport Hall for the morning's press conference. When he stood up to make his opening statement, several journalists anticipated a comment on the trade figures. Instead, and almost casually, Wilson referred to another topic, the Hardy Spicer strike: "I am bound to say that some of us are getting a little suspicious about the fact that in every general election a dispute suddenly blows up in a firm whose production affects a large section of the motor-car industry. We are waiting daily and expectantly for news from British Oxygen where there were sudden disputes both in the 1959 and 1955 elections. In 1959 it was demonstrated conclusively afterwards that there was a political motivation to that particular dispute. This sort of thing, happening election after election, is a matter which cannot be left where it is. The Labour Government intends to hold a full inquiry with full powers, to get at the facts in any dispute which occurs in this general election." There was a stunned pause from the press. "My God," whispered a famous political correspondent to his neighbor, "he's done another bank rate."*

Although Maudling had already heard Wilson's charge before the Conservative press conference opened, he managed to give a show of complete surprise when the point was raised by a reporter. "I must say that's a rum one," he said

* A reference to Wilson's rash allegation in September 1957 that news of a forthcoming bank-rate increase had been leaked.

with a great grin. "Tory shop stewards going round sabotaging Mr. Wilson's election! Really!" It was the perfect tone of reply. In the light of Maudling's mockery, Wilson was made to look querulous and rattled. And of course other Conservatives pitched into the attack. "I have rarely heard such an irresponsible statement," said Godber, the Minister of Labour. "If it has any effect at all, it can only be to create divisions between the two sides of industry, to make the settlement of disputes more difficult and to impair our economy."

The Hardy Spicer remark brought delight to Sir Alec Douglas-Home, who spent most of Wednesday on a whistle-stop tour of northwest London. "He's warming up now," said an aide, who claimed that Sir Alec had even enjoyed the heckling. "He found it tremendously exhilarating, like being at the prow of a ship and being badly buffeted, but knowing that you are still moving in the right direction." And George Christ, another member of the entourage, said the next day: "I think we just have to sit back and let Wilson win it for us." The low-water mark of Wilson's campaign was appropriately the high-water mark of Home's confidence.

Apparently Wilson alone did not see the sensational nature of his charge against Hardy Spicer. Almost unquestionably it was a tactical mistake. It was essential that the fierce attack on Home at Norwich that evening receive the maximum publicity. But no speech on policy could hope to compete for space in the newspapers with allegations of plots by Tory shop stewards.

This was proved by Thursday morning's press. Only the *Daily Express,* whose political editor, Terence Lancaster, is a former Labour candidate, gave the Norwich speech the treatment it really deserved. "WILSON LETS FLY" ran the headline, and the speech was indeed strong stuff. Wilson accused the Prime Minister of "fatuous deception . . . twisted talk . . . crawling to the Americans." Home, he said, had been "deliberately misleading the British public for electioneering reasons, or living in a make-believe world into which the hard facts of economics and paying our way were not allowed to penetrate." He came out with the charge that was to resound through the rest of the campaign, that the country was borrowing at the rate of "more than a million pounds a day."

"The real trouble with Harold is that he's obsessed by 1959," said a senior colleague that Thursday; "he's determined to do everything the opposite way. He wouldn't do whistle stops* because Gaitskell had done them. He'll have to do some now, though. You can't keep having pictures of him all by himself on a platform while Home keeps getting photographed surrounded by people. Harold wouldn't have a strategy—just thought he could cruise to victory making nice speeches. . . . He actually wanted us to appear like amateurs in contrast to slick Tory professionalism. 'We'd be efficient,' he said, 'in everything, but let's deliberately have an unprofessionalism in our propaganda.' I had to tell him that was the hardest thing for any professional to achieve, something that the best of them had broken their hearts trying to achieve for years. . . ."

The same colleague criticized Wilson's determination to take the press conference each morning: "He doesn't even have time to read the morning newspapers. Of course mistakes get made. But it was all Harold's idea to do it this way. It was convenient. It meant that he didn't upset Len [Williams] and Sara [Barker]. He thought he was the Labour Party's sole asset, and the fact is he's not. Even people like Callaghan are quite good with the public. I think he may have got the point now—at least he's keeping out of the broadcasts. George is doing Friday, and Crossman, Stewart, Kenneth Robinson and Shirley Williams on Monday."

* Wilson admitted after the election that he should have made more whistle-stop tours.

On the 8:20 train from Norwich to London, Wilson had plenty of worries. If the Hardy Spicer dispute was not quickly settled, the whole motor-car industry might be brought to a standstill, and he could be accused of having interfered. Some light relief was caused by A. P. Herbert, a comic writer and former M.P., who greeted the Wilsons at Liverpool Street. But the rest of Wilson's reception committee was not in the mood for jolly chats. The party intellectuals, Dick Crossman, bareheaded and clutching a sheaf of papers, with Tommy Balogh in Homburg hat and dark overcoat, were waiting to brief him on the economy. They all got into the waiting gray Humber Hawk—Balogh in front, Crossman wedged between Harold and Mary Wilson—for twenty-four minutes of urgent talk on the way to the press conference at Transport House. They decided to play up the plight of the economy and to play down the Hardy Spicer affair.

When Wilson appeared at the conference he was wearing a red carnation instead of the usual red (and tired) rosebud, and was carrying in his hand a pale-pink cutting from the *Financial Times*—no doubt given him in the car by Balogh—reporting that the UN Economic Commission for Europe had said that the U.K. was the only country in Western Europe whose exports had tended to slow down that year.*

Several reporters questioned Wilson on Hardy Spicer, but he would not be drawn. He said that the day before he had not even known the name of the Hardy Spicer chairman. As for his comments on British Oxygen, he had relied on memory. The implication of this was that Wednesday morning's comments had not been based on any special evidence collected by Transport House. This gave Maudling an easy opening for reply: "If he does intend to accuse people of improper activities at this time he must bring forward evi-

---

* At the Conservative press conference the same morning, Maudling used the same E.C.E. report to argue that British exports would rise in the coming months.

dence and not just drop hints around in this rather casual fashion." Did Maudling think that Wilson was rattled? The Chancellor beamed in his friendly way: "A question about his state of mind is one for him rather than me, but it takes a worried man to sing a foolish song."

A worried man, maybe, but also a very lucky man. Just when the Tories felt that they had Wilson battered and crushed against the ropes, he was saved by the bell. The man responsible for his deliverance was Herbert Hill, chairman of Hardy Spicer. He is a good-natured, rather patrician man who was astonished and rather bewildered at finding himself the center of so much attention. Later he was to regret not having had a public-relations man to deal with the press, but that Thursday he felt quite confident about speaking to reporters in his Mayfair offices. To everybody's amazement he started to say some very odd things about the strikers: "They are people who are not of very high intelligence. If they were, they would understand the issues involved here economically. I feel very much that they are 'poor dears' and am very sad for them. They are our workers for whom we strive and whose welfare we seek to promote. They are a lot of misguided people."

Poor dears. The words were to haunt the Conservative Party throughout the campaign. The whole propaganda value of Hardy Spicer was lost. The rights and wrongs of Wilson's accusations were now quite forgotten in the hilarity and indignation which greeted those two words. It was useless or worse for Tory speakers to come to the aid of a maligned businessman if they were at the same time to be branded with his haughty and patronizing attitude to the workers. Later that evening Herbert Hill made things still worse for the Tories by issuing a writ against Wilson alleging slander. Now the Labour Party could duck all questions on Hardy Spicer and even British Oxygen by arguing that the case was *sub judice*. Wilson's proverbial luck was with him still. A reporter who visited Wilson late on Thursday afternoon said: "It was the only time I've ever seen Wilson really laughing. He just couldn't stop all through the interview."

The Tories were correspondingly glum. The Hardy Spicer remark was "an uncovenanted benefit," said Maudling later, "so we couldn't really complain if it went sour on us. I suspect it ended in a draw. But what really annoyed me about it was that it was the only time when we really got Wilson rattled. I'll never know why he did it—quite out of character for him to make a mistake like that."

The night brought Wilson further good news. At Euston, just after midnight, he was lying asleep in a first-class berth of the night train to Liverpool when two men from Transport House knocked on the door and brought in a first-edition *Daily Mail* with the result of a special N.O.P. poll on the marginal Tory seat at Coventry South. "It's 2.9 at Coventry South," one of them whispered. The leader of the Labour Party, in light-blue pajamas, grunted and stirred. "To us," added the man from Transport House. At which Wilson promptly sat up in bed and reached for the newspaper.

Wilson was going to Liverpool to hand in his nomination papers as candidate for Huyton. At 7:30 on Liverpool Lime Street Station, he took a quick, eager glance at the newspapers. All of them, as he had hoped, expressed the general revulsion against Herbert Hill's remarks. But the Labour Party still did not feel itself off the hook; although Wilson was eager to follow up his advantage by constant ridicule of the "poor dears" speech, more cautious voices feared the risks of legal trouble. In particular Arnold Goodman, the party's unofficial legal adviser, wanted to play things safe.

Early on Friday morning Wilson drove out to the Huyton Labour Party headquarters before handing in his nomination papers at ten. When he arrived, Arthur Smith, his agent, told him that it was all arranged that he would hand in his papers with the Tory candidate, an "anti-revisionist" Communist, and "Screaming Lord Sutch," the independent.* Wilson was horrified at this, realizing that it would give the other two candidates free publicity, and instructed Smith to inform the Returning Officer that he would prefer to come along later in the morning. He then returned to the Adelphi and found that he was in time for the last part of the regular ten-o'clock conversation on the "Telstar" telephone with Transport House.

Later that morning he went along to the Huyton Urban District Council Offices to hand in his nomination papers. As he emerged from the building and walked toward his car "Screaming Lord Sutch" approached Wilson and extended his hand. Wilson shook it brusquely and walked on. He was not amused. After all, he himself had long been trying to win the Beatle vote.

Because of the disruption caused by the fracas that morning, Wilson was half an hour behind schedule and nearly missed catching the train from Preston to Glasgow, where he was due to speak that evening. It was typical of the haphazard organization of the Labour Party that while Home and even Grimond toured by helicopter or plane, Wilson and party should have to drive at breakneck speed from Huyton to Preston to catch a train. Fortunately the train was twenty minutes late, and they had enough time to take a snack before joining it. Once inside, there was still trouble. Although it was not quite true, as Wilson said the following day, that "we didn't have a speech in mind until half an hour before Glasgow," it certainly wasn't prepared until halfway through the journey. The process of writing the speech was revealed to anybody who wanted to go and stare from the corridor. One of the two compartments was set aside for

* An antlered pop singer who wanted votes for teen-agers and knighthoods for the Beatles to mark their good work for Britain. In the end there was a hitch in his nomination papers and the Returning Officer disallowed his candidature.

Wilson, who sat by the window facing the engine, with John
Allen beside him, Mrs. Wilson in the corridor corner and
John Harris on the opposite seat. As Wilson wrote in long-
hand on a pad, with a packet of Castella cigars beside him,
Allen busied himself on research. He had Hansard on one
side and the digest of statistics on the other. In the next
compartment, secretaries and typists bashed out the speech
as the manuscript appeared.

The tension in the Wilson compartments was increased by
the arrival of a BBC TV team who wanted to film the speech-
writing. They wanted, for instance, to film Wilson calling
on one of his aides for some statistics. Both Allen and Harris
wanted to appear in the film, and Harris actually took the
digest of statistics from Allen's seat so that he would be holding it when Wilson took his cue from the TV producer. In
spite of these distractions, Harold Wilson managed to write
his 67-minute speech in only an hour and a half.

He was in tiptop form when he walked onto the platform
at Green's Playhouse, Glasgow, that evening. After the usual
peroration on housing and getting the British economy going,
he started to get heckled by a few people around the hall. By
encouraging them, and using them as feeds for his own quick
wit, Wilson provided the audience with fifteen minutes of
pure music-hall farce. He chose one particular woman heckler
as his butt; indeed he often referred to her in the intervals
between her interruptions. "Now, dear, you want to hear
about Ferranti . . . Now listen to this—it's right up your
street, this one." The more he got heckled, the better his
jokes became, and best of all was his mockery of individual
Tories. He would mention the name Home, or Brooke, or
Selwyn Lloyd, and then pause, with a mock solemn expression as the audience burst into laughter. He is a master of the
"have I said something funny?" style of comedy; and at Glasgow this Friday, after one of the most trying days of the
campaign, he was at his best. The climax came when he was

talking about the money spent on Blue Streak, and a heckler, very unwisely, shouted "Groundnuts." Wilson stopped in mid-sentence and turned with a look of mock severity to the right-hand side of the hall from which the shout had come. He paused, and the whole audience seemed to hold its breath, waiting for Wilson's retort to this old accusation. It was masterly. After a stare at the heckler, Wilson turned back to face the mass of the audience, leaned in a confidential manner on the raised lectern in front of him and said: "There's an aging Young Conservative." There was a great roar of laughter, but Wilson had not finished. When there was silence once more, Wilson paused, then said in the same pitying, quiet way: "His only contribution to the Blue Streak argument is to shout groundnuts." Then suddenly turning again to the heckler, he shouted: "Where have you been, Rip van Winkle?" For fifteen minutes he amused, moved and even bewitched his audience with the instinctive genius found only in great politicians and actors. It was extraordinary not just in itself but as a contrast to his usual dullness. Afterward, characteristically, Wilson said it had been an unsuccessful speech: "It was the heckling and the reaction that made it," he said.

On the same night that Wilson roused Glasgow to laughter, George Brown made one of the best political TV broadcasts of the campaign. It had been planned that Brown should open and close the program besides acting as link man for the other performers—William Ross, Lady Megan Lloyd George, Tony Wedgwood Benn and two company directors. All these, backed by some film, would explain the need for planning in society. The businessmen would say how this would help industry, while Ross and Lady Megan would speak of planning for Scotland and Wales. But as soon as the quarterly trade figures were released on Wednesday, Brown decided that the program should become first and foremost an attack on the Tory handling of the economic situation. Brown's script was prepared jointly by Thomas Balogh and Oliver Walston, the young Cambridge graduate son of a Labour life peer, who had worked as Brown's personal assistant for the past year. "Now there's no point in beating about the bush any longer," the broadcast began, and it was phrased throughout in similar brisk language. The technicalities of the balance-of-payments crisis were reduced to simple questions of buying houses, washing machines and groceries. At the end Brown was worried that he had appeared too rough and growling on the program and feared he would get bad notices on this account. But the broadcast went down well with the press, and apparently with the viewers, because a particularly high proportion of them kept on the sound as they watched. However, the audience-measurement survey explained, this may have meant only that a particularly high proportion of Tory viewers were listening for a Brown gaffe.

By Saturday, October 4, both parties were waiting anxiously for the Gallup poll figures to be published in the *Sunday Telegraph*. Neither side, of course, would admit to any anxiety about the figures. But even their public pronouncements were cautious. At the Conservative press conference, R. A. Butler made an appearance for the first and only time in the campaign. He warned of a "strong undercurrent for Labour," and of the need "to make our people fight even stronger." Later Lord Blakenham added: "We have always known this campaign would be a close and hard-fought battle." And Wilson in Glasgow, although claiming a "very remarkable change in the election atmosphere," seemed preoccupied, unhappy and more than usually caustic. He even confessed in public what he had often admitted in private— that the Tories were getting the women's vote: "I think there has always been marginally a point that a greater number of men than women vote Labour."

Butler later admitted having advance information of the Gallup figures before he made his Saturday-morning remarks.

But Wilson certainly did not know. In the words of one of his aides, he "sweated out the day" in anticipation. From Glasgow he went by train to Edinburgh, where he gave an afternoon speech in the Assembly Hall, and then by train on to Newcastle. The reception at Edinburgh was less than ecstatic; indeed, one lady walked out complaining, "He'll never be a gentleman like Lord Home," and at least two of the journalists sneaked off from the hall to a news cinema. But Wilson thought this the best speech of his campaign.

The Newcastle meeting was due to begin at 7:30, but Wilson, his party and the journalists were still in the Station Hotel ten minutes later. Everyone was determined to hear the Gallup poll results, but the *Sunday Telegraph* was maintaining maximum security. They refused to tell their own reporter at Newcastle even after the first edition came off the presses. Ironically it was the representative of the *Sunday Times,* David Leitch, who first heard the figure and rushed up to Wilson's suite to break the good news: a 4½ per cent lead over the Tories. As soon as he heard the figures, Wilson came down to the hall of the hotel and talked to reporters. He said his usual piece about not paying any attention to polls, but a triumphant and ineradicable smile gave the lie to what he was saying. So did his eagerness to hear the result of the Mark Abrams constituency surveys which were due to appear in the *Observer.*

That evening's speech was exuberant. He ridiculed Home and the "unique authority he commands in economic matters." He mocked Selwyn Lloyd—"the first act of Sir Alec . . . was to reinter that political corpse"—and rejected "the groveling defeatism" of the Tory Party. He made his by now obligatory references to Sir Alec Douglas-Home's election-forum broadcast, to the "patrician, arrogant way in which he referred to increases in pensions as donations" and to his boast "we are now building 400,000 houses next year."

With less than a fortnight to go before polling day, few

observers appreciated the recovery of the Liberal Party. True, the N.O.P. polls during the next week showed their support mounting to 9 per cent of the electorate, and it was guessed that they might increase their representation in Parliament. It still seemed inconceivable that they could live up to their boast of three million votes. More than two and a half years had passed since the extraordinary March of 1962 when Eric Lubbock, an unknown Liberal councillor, won the Tory stronghold of Orpington by 8,000 votes in a by-election; when an N.O.P. poll showed the Liberals leading both Labour and Tories, to become for a day the party with the greatest support in Britain. The Liberals had not gained a by-election since. They had done as badly in 1964 as they did well in 1962. The Liberals had made their comeback in the belief that the Labour Party was finished. "But why does Mr. Wyatt* want an election alliance?" wrote Jo Grimond in February 1962. "Because he sees no other way of keeping up the remotest pretense that the Labour Party is intact and at the same time holding onto the least theoretical prospect of power. Of course, and not for the first time, Mr. Wyatt has spoken out of turn. He is threatened with expulsion. But after a fourth election defeat there will be plenty of Labour men singing his tune, and doubtless his praises too."

Grimond had always banked on another Labour defeat which would allow the Liberal Party to emerge as the alternative left-wing opposition. Unfortunately for his plans the Labour Party staged a recovery while the Conservatives fell on dark days. Moreover, whatever its claims as a left-wing party, the Liberals seemed to get most votes in extreme Tory constituencies like seaside resorts and rich suburbs. It was apparent even to Grimond that his party was winning that portion of the right wing in the country which found the Tories too radical; the Liberal workers were generally radically minded

* Woodrow Wyatt, right-wing Labour M.P., who in January 1962 advocated a Liberal-Labour pact and was to repeat this demand again after the election.

leftists, but the Liberal voters tended to come from the right. Early in 1964 the Liberal Party had really begun to lost heart. The Labour Party was confident and united under Harold Wilson. The dissident Tories were coming to heel behind Home. At the Greater London Council elections that spring, the Liberals failed to get a single seat, and they were scarcely more successful in the rest of the country.

Their comeback in September was a surprise. It was caused above all by the changed relative strength of the two big parties. The Conservatives, helped by a fine summer, were regaining confidence. The Labour Party seemed to have lost its drive. On August 27 Mark Bonham-Carter, the party's foreign-affairs spokesman, prophesied that the Tories would win the election. He announced this after consultation with Grimond the previous evening. The second cause of strength was Jo Grimond himself. A dull and ineffective parliamentarian, he always flowers in general-election campaigns. His TV appearances were rated the best of all three leaders, and he was given good support by the other two Liberal election broadcasts. The leather-suited actress, Honor Blackman, proved a persuasive—if scarcely eloquent—Liberal speaker. Indeed she was even more useful to Grimond in politics than to Sean Connery's James Bond in the *Goldfinger* film that was showing throughout provincial cinemas during the campaign. Another top Liberal, Frank Byers, got excellent coverage from his handling of the party morning press conferences. Both the big parties affected to ignore the Liberal challenge. It was a mistake that would cost them both dear.

12. Enter Mr. Hogg

I think I broke the nose of one of them. I had my jacket
ripped off my back. Other stewards came to my assistance and
we hurled all four of them out of the hall.

> *Steward at Macmillan's Doncaster meeting on Monday, October 12*

THE British take their elections calmly. They do not mob
party leaders at railway stations. They seldom talk politics in
the pub and they do not like to reveal their political preferences to strangers. Yet England, extraordinarily, is occasionally the victim of sudden storms of electoral rage and violence.
One of these storms swept the country on Tuesday, October
6, only nine days before the polls. There had been signs of
approaching violence during the previous few days. An egg
struck Sir Alec Douglas-Home's back at Ashton-under-Lyne
the previous Friday, and hecklers had given Hogg the slow
handclap on Monday. But these were traditional greetings
and caused little offense.*

The rumpus on Tuesday broke out all over the country.
It was worst for Harold Wilson, who had to face a crowd of
more than 10,000 in the Rag Market, a huge hall near the
Bull Ring in Birmingham. He came in, feeling tired and
drenched with sweat after a meeting in Coventry where the
TV lights were uncomfortably close to the platform. As soon
as he climbed onto the platform it became clear from the
uproar that several hundred Conservative hecklers were dis-
tributed around the hall. When he started to speak they
chanted "Facts, facts, facts," and Wilson yelled back, "I'll
give you facts." An elderly woman screamed, "What about

---

* Sir Alec thought at the time that someone was patting him on the back.

immigration?" The Conservatives roared, and angry stewards rushed around the hall looking for people to throw out. But Wilson was not worried: "I will make my speech," he bellowed, and then, with a favorite gibe at Sir Alec, went on: "I may inform you it *is* my own speech. I wrote it myself, and I can read it, and I understand what it means when I have read it."

The hecklers gave a booming cheer to every reference made to a Conservative. "Macmillan?" Wilson asked. Then, after a tiny pause, he added: "You were in a bit of a hurry to get rid of him last year, and now you are wishing to heaven you hadn't." Later he gave them a mock warning: "Any more trouble out of you lot and I'll mention Henry Brooke." By the end of the speech the heckling had died down to a few sporadic shouts. It had been a tough opposition and Wilson had handled it well. But he added grimly afterward: "Heaven help Sir Alec when he gets here!" (Home was to speak in the Rag Market two days later.)

Sir Alec was having trouble enough that same day. Speaking on the steps of Leeds Town Hall early that evening, he was drowned out by scores of youngsters shouting, "Out, out, out . . . Go home, Home . . . We want Wilson!" Even the journalists huddled under the platform could scarcely hear what he was saying. A local Conservative official said that the hecklers were Communists, but the largest banner in the crowd, in the thick of the noisiest group, bore the legend "Leeds University Labour Club." Tense, angry and shaken, Home battled on with his speech. Not till the end did his temper flare when he let slip an unfortunate remark: "The Labour Party must be very hard up if they have to hire these people. . . ." Afterward he turned to his campaign ADC, Lord Oakshott, and said: "Do we have time for a drink?" This was a sign of the state which heckling had caused in the abstemious Prime Minister. "Yes, for a quick one. You need it after that," said Oakshott. Perhaps Home already realized that his last remark was a gaffe. The implication that Labour had paid hecklers was obviously fatuous and could be made to sound like bad sportsmanship.*

By the time Home had got to Bradford the telephone exchange was jammed with Conservative calls to Central Office. And next morning Lord Blakenham had to tell a press conference that Sir Alec's words on heckling "should not be taken too seriously." A reporter answered, "This election is about *words*. Which words of the Prime Minister's *are* we to take seriously?"

In the fury about the heckling at Leeds, few commentators bothered with Home's second speech the same evening—at Bradford. It was, however, one of the few really important speeches of the campaign. On a platform under the Bradford coat of arms (*Labor Omnia Vinit*—Labour Conquers All) Sir Alec turned to the delicate subject of immigration: "What had been a trickle of immigrants from the Commonwealth was developing into a flood. We saw that if it was not brought under control it would create very serious social and economic problems—problems of employment, housing and education, for instance. So we brought in legislation. The Socialists, aided by the Liberals, opposed it all along the line. . . . But for the Immigration Act there would now be an additional three hundred thousand immigrants with their families—an influx of nearly a million people, an influx which it would have been quite impossible to control."

This was the first time in the campaign that Home had

---

* As a matter of fact the Labour Party did sometimes organize hecklers, but only to heckle Wilson. At the meeting at Middlesbrough, on October 4, Charles Shopland, the secretary of the local party, had arranged for "hecklers" to be stationed throughout the hall to shout "Spanish frigates" and "What about groundnuts?" It was known that Wilson's replies to these two shouts always brought a good response from the crowd. If Wilson knew of this fake heckling—he smiled rather quizzically when the question was raised—he certainly did not encourage the shouting down of Home and other Conservative speakers. He always believed that the more people heard Home, the fewer were likely to vote for him.

mentioned immigration. The Conservative Central Office had advised him to make the statement first here at Bradford rather than two days later, at Birmingham. Otherwise he might be accused of trying to cash in on racial prejudice in the West Midlands.

The heckling of Home and Wilson made a few lively paragraphs in the newspapers. The heckling of Quintin Hogg in Plymouth that same evening provoked a reply which will surely find a place, however grubby and small, in the British political history books. The Secretary of State for Education had been talking about ideals in public life: "Mr. Wilson has said that Mr. Macmillan debauched the standards of public life . . ." when a young man in the crowd bellowed, "What about Profumo?" Then, in the words of the unexcitable *Times* next morning:

Mr. Hogg snatched his glasses from his face and retorted: "If you can tell me there are no adulterers on the front bench of the Labour Party you can talk to me about Profumo." At this point other hecklers stood up and joined in the shouting, bellowing, "Profumo, Profumo." Mr. Hogg shouted: "If you cannot tell me that, you had better not dabble your fingers in filth. If you cannot tell me that, you had better keep your mouths shut because that sort of filth should be kept out of public life. So let us have no more filth of that kind."

It took several minutes before the noise subsided and Mr. Hogg was able to resume the theme of his speech. At Plymouth station before he left on the midnight sleeper for London, Mr. Hogg said: "I do not regret one word I said. I have always thought these things should be kept out of politics. But I thought it was necessary to give a salutary lesson to the foolish young man who chose to taunt me with the Profumo affair. Everyone knows that these sort of things are not the monopoly of any one party."

In normal times, Hogg's outburst would not have caused much excitement. But these, for Britain, were not quite normal times. In the last two years an unprecedented number of rumors had been in circulation about men in public life. One of these rumors, concerning Profumo, had proved true. Later Lord Denning investigated further rumors concerning the private life of other politicians on both Front Benches. He found no justification for any of these stories. However, a number of vague, spiteful and unsubstantiated rumors continued to spread, with variations, throughout the country in bars, bridge parties and business lunches. The explosive scandals of summer 1963 had created a kind of moral fallout that hung like a fog over the land.

In this murky, rumorous atmosphere, Hogg's entirely innocent statement acquired a significance that he certainly did not intend. Both politicians and press responded with unwonted anxiety. The news of the Hogg remarks reached the Rag Market, Birmingham, at 10 P.M. while Wilson was still on the platform. The director of publicity, John Harris, who had heard of it from a London newspaper, burst in on a group of journalists under the platform. "Quintin Hogg's gone mad!" he said, and then gave an accurate summary of what had been said to the heckler. One reporter turned to a colleague and said: "Well, that's the lead in all the papers tomorrow morning." It was a plausible prophecy, but it failed to come true.

When Wilson finished speaking at 10:05 he pushed his way through the mob to the waiting car. In the scrimmage Harris managed to tell him what Hogg had said. The car drove off, a metal grille slammed down behind it, and the Labour leader was whisked to the Albany Hotel. He went straight up to his suite with Harris, Alfred Richman, Marcia Williams and Brenda Dew. From this suite Harris put through telephone calls to the *Sun* and the *Daily Mirror* asking them not to report Hogg's remarks to the heckler.*

---

* The call to the *Daily Mirror* caused some chaos. No executive was on duty with authority to give an answer one way or the other. The final decision to "publish and be damned" was taken by Hugh Cudlipp—eventually located in Edward Heath's Albany flat.

Next day both newspapers ignored this request. The *Sun* reported what Hogg said, while the *Daily Mirror* splashed its front page: "HOGG BLOWS HIS TOP . . . He makes a fantastic smear against Labour Party Front Bench." It was the Conservative newspapers that shied away from the story. The *Daily Telegraph* used the story down column one on the front page. *The Times* gave it equivalent space on its main news, or bill, page. But the *Daily Mail*, which had given enormous prominence to Hogg's views on military operations, gave not one line to his views on adultery. The *Daily Express* prepared an edition with Hogg as the front-page splash, but, after a conference, dropped the story entirely.

Next morning Conservative Central Office greeted Hogg's remarks with gloom and anger. The comments of Cabinet colleagues ranged from "unfortunate" to "appalling." They wanted, at all costs, to let the topic drop. So did the Labour Party. Early on Wednesday morning Transport House officials telephoned all regional organizers making it clear that no candidate was on any account to make any reference to the Hogg remarks. That morning Wilson was due to travel by train from Birmingham to London. In case there was any further development which meant that Transport House needed his urgent advice, it was arranged that the Leamington Labour agent should stand by at the station to transmit any message to Wilson when his train stopped there.

Wilson that morning was quite unperturbed by the fuss. At his 10 A.M. press conference in the new A.E.U. building near the Albany Hotel he was in joking, relaxed mood. When asked about Hogg's remark he simply replied, "One can naturally assume that the leader of Mr. Hogg's party will of course make a statement." Under persistent questioning, he did not budge from his attitude that this was a question for Home to answer. In London, at the Conservative press conference, Lord Blakenham was in the chair with Peter Thorneycroft, Minister of Defense, as the guest speaker. A question was asked about nuclear tests, to which Thorneycroft replied with a remark about the need to remove filth in the atmosphere. "Talking of filth in the atmosphere," interrupted Llew Gardner of the *Sunday Express*, had Lord Blakenham any comment to make on Mr. Hogg's statement last night? The unfortunate chairman of the party could only reply, "I personally dislike personalities being brought into politics. From what I have seen it was not of course Mr. Hogg who raised the matter. I think he was answering taunts about the Profumo case. . . . Was he supposed to stand by and accept the idea that human failings are only to be found in one party? They are to be found from time to time in all parties, but we certainly have no allegations to make against any member of the Labour Party."

One politician ensured that the uproar did not die down: Quintin Hogg. He followed up his Plymouth remarks with an attack on the *Daily Mirror*. While congratulating the *Mirror* reporter on his accuracy, he claimed, in a speech at Dulwich, that "the editorial staff of that group of newspapers deliberately put a headline on the report which was a perfectly fair report, to suggest exactly the opposite to what they knew that I was saying." He went on: "I do not suggest that this group of newspapers are simple-minded people. They put that misleading headline on the report knowing there was nothing in the report to justify it, and knowing it was the opposite to what I was saying. And I say that they did it for the worst possible reasons, to smear my character and to try to destroy the chances of the Conservative Party. I say of that group that they are a millionaire corporation. I am only a man with limited means and with a family of five to keep. . . ."*

At the suggestion of Wilson, the unimpeachable Earl Attlee

* Two days later, on October 9, Quintin Hogg was to write to the editor of the *Daily Mirror* saying, "Shall we call it a day? There are more important issues to discuss. Anyhow, it's my birthday." Shortly after the election the *Daily Mirror* retained Quintin Hogg as its standing counsel in libel cases.

was asked to reply to Hogg. In his flat in the Temple where he had gone to live after the death of his wife earlier that year, this venerable but still very astute politician sat down at his desk to type a statement. "Is that the sort of thing you want?" he asked afterward. It was indeed. And Attlee was at his schoolmasterly best when he read out the rebuke to an audience in Southall later that day: "It is time he [Hogg] grew up. . . . He should know that when he has met with a rude interjection he does not lose his temper. He made a very unseemly remark. Mr. Hogg acted like a schoolboy. He made general accusations against the Labour front bench without a shadow of justification. . . . I hope that the Prime Minister will dissociate himself from the railing accusation made by his colleague and administer an appropriate rebuke."

The next day Hogg, and adultery, were the main story in most of the newspapers and the main topic of talk throughout Britain. The *Daily Mail* and the *Daily Express,* which had entirely suppressed Hogg's statement on Wednesday, now gave it thousands of words on Thursday. The readers found themselves reading angry commentary on a remark which from their own papers they cannot have known ever was made. "Hogg's Challenge," screamed the *Daily Mail.* "Hogg Explains," bellowed the *Daily Express.* If Wednesday's *Daily Mirror* had not carried the story under a provocative headline, Hogg would probably not have launched his counterattack and the story for Thursday's newspapers would have been dead. The Labour Party was therefore bitter against the *Mirror,* a usually faithful friend, for having inflamed the incident. This was the first reaction at any rate.

Later in the campaign, many politicians of both parties felt that the Hogg explosion had damaged the Tory side. "A great pity," was R. A. Butler's verdict. "It brings up the past. It reminds people of the last year of the Macmillan Government. I don't think talking about adultery on the front bench is helpful. And anyway the adultery [of Profumo] wasn't

the point. It was the lies." Another front-bench colleague of
Hogg's said some weeks later: "There are some things which
are onside and some things which are offside. This was offside."

Whatever the ethics of Hogg's attack, it turned people's
attention away from what the Tories had hoped would be
the principal topic of the day. On Wednesday both Home
and Peter Thorneycroft delivered major statements on Britain's nuclear deterrent. Arriving, to the surprise of the press,
at the morning Smith Square press conference, Thorneycroft
said: "All our information is that the voters over a wide
cross-section, and including people who previously voted
Labour, are all one way of thinking in this matter in that
we should not lay down these weapons." He said that because
of the nuclear issue, the nation was on the Tory side. This
had of course always been Sir Alec's view. That same day,
on a whistle-stop tour of Hertfordshire, Home was more
vehement than usual on the consequences of a Labour Government: "If the life of Britain is at stake at any future time,
then the decision of what will be done will be not the decision of the British Government but the decision of another
nation. . . . Get that into your heads!" Alas for Home,
people's heads were filled with Quintin Hogg.

Immediately Hogg became a prime target for hatred and
heckling. He had been heckled at Plymouth on Tuesday; he
had been interrupted at Dulwich on Wednesday; on Thursday, at Friends House in Euston Road, he was shouted down.
Of the 2,200 people in the audience less than a half were
Conservatives. The majority were students from London University and they gave Hogg a violent reception. They yelled,
booed, sang the "Red Flag" and chanted "Smear, smear,
smear . . . Profumo . . . Ferranti . . . Rachman . . . We want
Wilson." Although the loudspeaker was turned up full blast,
Hogg scarcely tried to make himself heard. He would say a
few sentences into the uproar, then lean back, with his mouth

open, letting out a series of high-pitched, cracked laughs. Leaving the meeting by the back door, he was surrounded by scores of angry youngsters who yelled, "Name the adulterers!", "Profumo" and other less printable insults. About thirty policemen held back the crowd as Hogg started to get into his car. Suddenly he turned, said, "Where's my wife? I want my wife," and scurried back to the hall. He banged on the closed door with his fists, shouting "I want my wife," as the crowd drew back in mesmerized, perhaps even sympathetic, fascination. At last the Hoggs were reunited and drove off, to the accompaniment of some kicks to the car.

That same Thursday Sir Alec had to face a crowd in the Rag Market at Birmingham where Wilson had been two days before. Police estimated 1,500 out of the 5,500 crowd were opposed to Home, and fifteen minutes before the speech started they were making the great hall rock with shouts of "Tories Out! We Want Wilson! Home go home!" There was one C.N.D. banner and placards complaining "Terror in Ireland," "Tory Rule Means Gestapo Rule in Ireland" and "Stop Ill-Treatment of Republican Irish Women."

Home rose, and the noise began in earnest. He bravely declared, "Let me say at once it's no good trying to drown me down." But it was. This challenge was almost the last thing that anyone heard him say. The interrupters, most of them on the right of the aisle, kept up an incessant uproar. "Get them out!" a steward yelled to a policeman. "I'm not going to have them ruining our meeting." The policeman calmly replied that this was a public meeting and that heckling did not constitute a breach of the peace. And technically he was right. The Conservatives had reserved only 1,000 seats for their supporters. They had not been able to fill the standing room with their own side. Occasionally some scraps of Home's speech floated over the din, like the sound of a single flute in a Wagner storm scene, but 99 per cent was lost.

In the same city of Birmingham sixty-three years earlier, David Lloyd George, the Liberal leader, had to be smuggled out of a hall disguised as a policeman. It was not quite so bad for Home, although he was forced to fight his way up the aisle and he lost touch with his personal detective. "I think somebody aimed a kick at me," he said afterward. Certainly some of the mob kicked and dented his car. A Birmingham Tory M.P., Geoffrey Lloyd, who had sat on the platform with Home, said afterward: "For thirty years I have been used to rough Birmingham meetings with plenty of heckling. For my part I have enjoyed this. . . . But what took place tonight was quite new and un-British." Most of the press and public agreed with him. Indeed, Wilson himself continually urged his supporters not to use this drown-out heckling. But the public must also have noticed that while Wilson managed to ride and even exploit any heckling, Home allowed himself to be shouted down. Few people noticed at the time that this Birmingham effort, a whole week before polling day, was the last big speech Home made in the election.

Things were not going well for the Tories. An N.O.P. poll in the *Daily Mail* of Friday, October 9, showed an 8 per cent swing to Labour in the marginal seat of Doncaster. Like the previous N.O.P. poll on Coventry South, it seemed to suggest that Labour was doing best in just those seats where it needed to do well—the marginal, middle-income constituencies. This would mean that the Conservatives no longer had a built-in 2 per cent lead over the Labour Party. Fears of a Labour victory were revealed in share prices. During the week, £2,000 million was knocked off the stock exchange value of ordinary shares. Losses were particularly grave in "political" shares such as property, insurance and, above all, steel. For instance Stewart and Lloyds were down 7s. over the week, United Steel 7s. and John Summers 6s. The businessmen's own weekly paper not only contemplated but advocated a Labour victory: "It seems to the *Economist* that, on the nicest balance, the riskier choice of Labour and Mr. Wilson will be the better choice for the voters."

It always used to be said of the Conservatives that they can at least hide their differences in time of danger. Even this legend was now to be proved false. Throughout the election campaign, one prominent Tory leader had kept an unwonted silence. Except at a press conference the previous Saturday when he had talked of a "strong undercurrent to Labour," R. A. Butler had not been much in the news. Perhaps he considered this fact when on Friday, October 9, he agreed to be interviewed by George Gale of the *Daily Express* on the afternoon train from London to Stockton. "Matured indiscretions," in Gale's words, "like ripened fruit from apple trees, dropped effortlessly from his lips." How was the election going? "Very close. We're running neck and neck. I'll be very surprised if there's much in it, say, twenty seats either way. But things might start slipping in the last few days." Slipping away? "Yes, they won't slip towards us." What of the Tory campaign so far? "Alec has done very well. Possibly he has spent too much time outside London." Had the Prime Minister been indiscreet when he said there was an Anglo-American draft treaty on the nondissemination of nuclear arms and knowledge? "I don't think there's any such thing. After all I am the Foreign Secretary." And what of Sir Alec's praise for the "young, dynamic" Edward Heath? "That's interesting," Butler replied. "I think Alec's a bit bored by him—not as a Minister, of course."

This interview had been tucked away on an inside page of the *Daily Express*, as though the paper was rather ashamed of the one real scoop of the election campaign. But those few quiet words in a railway compartment rang louder and harsher in Tory ears than any amount of heckling.

"Hogg's outburst on adultery," said a senior Tory official, "was greeted in Central Office next morning with rage and dismay. But people weren't as angry as they were about Rab's remark to George Gale." Sir Alec himself giggled when he heard the news, and he did not reproach Butler afterward.

However, Lady Home did intimate to Mrs. Butler that "Alec had had Gale with him for most of the campaign and that he'd known how to handle him." Other Tory leaders were sympathetic to Butler, who claimed he thought he was speaking off the record. On one thing he also thought he had been misreported. He had not meant that Home was bored with Heath but that everyone was bored to death with the R.P.M. bill. After the poll results, Butler added, "To do me justice, I did get it right, didn't I? I never thought there'd be more than eight or ten in it and that it could go either way. And of course it tipped the other way, as I expected."

The tip was probably due to Labour's next big heave.

13. Into the Sticks

He's the only really competent political TV performer
this country has produced.

LORD POOLE *on Harold Wilson*

ON THE last Saturday before polling both party leaders
were billed to appear at the press conferences. Perhaps drawn
by the double bill, a greatly extended press corps turned up
at both Transport House and the Central Office, some in
weekend sports coats and polo-necked sweaters, several accompanied by wives or girl friends.

This informal atmosphere chimed in ideally with the relaxed mood that now prevailed in Transport House. That
morning it found a triumphant reflection in Wilson's own
performance. It was almost as if the press, which as the campaign went on had come more and more to respect his skill
and sheer professionalism, had decided that for his last appearance in London he deserved to be awarded a benefit
match. If he won the election, would Wilson recommend Sir
Alec Douglas-Home for an earldom? The Labour Party leader
hastily replaced a spontaneous smile with a mock-serious expression and replied as if weighing the question judiciously:
"I don't think, you know, I rate his contribution to the
prospects of a Labour victory *quite* as highly as that." What,
then, about Mr. Hogg? That, it appeared, was a different
matter. It was certainly true that the speaker most in demand
by constituency Labour parties throughout the country was
the Secretary of State for Education; the fact that he could
not appear everywhere was, he feared, already causing a good
deal of jealousy and ill-feeling among the ranks of Labour
supporters. Gone was any sign of the tenseness that Wilson

had occasionally shown at the beginning of the campaign; in its place was a broad, smiling confidence. This even set the tone of his opening statement. The Tory leaders, he claimed, were "rattled and at panic stations, making wild, unsubstantiated charges, suffering from divided counsels—and now even leading Ministers are taking to the boats." This last obvious reference to Rab Butler brought one of the loudest guffaws of the morning, but throughout the whole press conference Wilson scarcely made a reply that failed to bring some form of laugh.

But it was Home who really brought the house down. Across the road in the Conservative Central Office there was no mistaking the mood of gloom. Perhaps because of this, or possibly because of the strange sense of reverence that for some reason comes over British journalists in the presence of a Prime Minister, the Conservative conference opened in an unexpected way. Before anyone on the dais had had a chance to open his mouth, there came a shout from the back, "On a point of order, Mr. Chairman." The interrupter, Mr. Wilfrid Sendall (the political correspondent of that largest selling but scarcely most respected Sunday paper, the *News of the World*), then proceeded to read his colleagues a homily on the way they should, and should not, conduct themselves at a press conference. The substance of his plea appeared to be that people should ask only serious news-gathering questions in order that serious, news-gathering journalists (like himself) might pursue their business without hindrance. If Sendall's intervention had any rationale, it was presumably one aimed at bringing a proper sense of respect into the proceedings.

Its whole effect was ruined by Sir Alec's very first sentence. "I think," the Prime Minister began, "I can confidently say that morale in our party is as high as it could possibly be expected to be." Sir Alec had hardly got out the last three words before a great burst of mocking merriment rang out;

whatever he had meant to say, his qualifying phrase was naturally taken to mean that the Prime Minister recognized the toll that the accidents of the past week had taken in terms of Conservative confidence. After this initial gaffe, Sir Alec rallied and recovered, but in its aftermath his audience seemed to have lost its heart for the business in hand. Although earlier in the campaign there had been indignant demands for the Prime Minister to attend the Tory press conference, when he did finally turn up the proceedings were the briefest on record. Twenty minutes before the usual termination time of one o'clock, Lord Blakenham, with ill-disguised relief, declared the conference closed and the press corps filed out. This was the hour of the Central Office staff. Along the banisters, in the hallway and even from the vantage point of windows, secretaries and officials had been paraded to give the party leader a rapturous send-off. Inevitably the scene had the effect of emphasizing just how remote and distant a figure the Conservative leader had been throughout the campaign; even in his own party headquarters he was obviously regarded far more as a visiting dignitary than as an active participant. The point was not lost on a watching Swedish journalist. "To our way of thinking," he exclaimed, "this is fantastic! They have never seen him before; it is the first time he has been here. Only in England could this happen."

The contrast with Harold Wilson—at that moment busily clearing out his first-floor campaign office in Transport House —could hardly have been more sharp. The plan from the beginning had been that Wilson would spend the last four days up in Liverpool combining meetings in the North with work in his own constituency, and that Saturday lunchtime he left Transport House knowing that by the time he returned to it he would either be Prime Minister or facing another five years as Leader of the Opposition. He was driven first to his home, where he ate a hurried lunch, and then, with his wife, he climbed once more into the Labour Party's hired Humber Hawk for his last London journey to Euston station.

When he arrived there just before 2:15 P.M., ten minutes before the train to Liverpool Lime Street was due to depart, there were no crowds to greet him. Only the accompanying presence of the top-hatted station master, Mr. H. S. Turrill, distinguished him from any other traveler as he made his way down Platform 14 to the now familiar two compartments. The restraint which the British bring to electioneering was maintained right to the end; in less than a week's time he would be returning to that same station as the next Prime Minister, but for the moment he was just an ordinary citizen, entitled to his privacy. Even when, after the train had pulled out, he made his way into the restaurant car, scarcely a head turned; he ate a snack of cheese and biscuits with his staff, and then sauntered back alone to his reserved compartment.

The first interruption of his journey came after an hour and a half at Rugby. For this last train journey that Wilson was to make before polling day the Labour Party had made special arrangements. At each of the three stations where the train stopped the local Labour candidate with a crowd of supporters were waiting to greet the party leader from the platform. Just before the train drew into Rugby, Wilson was reminded of what was expected of him. He pulled a wry face, muttered "I suppose we may as well find out what a genuine whistle stop is really like," and with his wife behind him got off the train to meet a crowd of two or three hundred excited people. There was a good deal of singing and cheering, but Wilson himself seemed embarrassed. In an odd way these three stops—at Rugby, Stafford and then the final one at Crewe—served to emphasize the one area where he was weak as a national candidate. Without the glad-handing gifts of a Rockefeller, or the grand-manner advantages of a Macmillan, he somehow appeared naked and vulnerable as he stood in the center of bright-eyed groups of followers, not knowing quite

what to say. He repeated a few of the jokes he had made at
his press conference that morning, made a routine inquiry
or two about canvass returns and then fell helplessly back on
banalities. First at Rugby and then at Stafford and Crewe
puzzled audiences were exhorted to "have a good campaign
now and enjoy yourselves—I think all over the country people
are enjoying this election, and that's what I want you to do."

This personal shyness had long since ceased to affect Wilson as a public speaker. On the platform, with a microphone
in front of him, he had become by now the complete extro-
vert; with a big audience he established the *rapport* that
often seemed to elude him with groups of individuals. The
first meeting he went to, having left the Liverpool train at
Crewe, was a case in point. Arriving half an hour late at
Queensferry, in the steel-producing constituency of East Flint,
he found a surging crowd of 2,000 people waiting for him,
half of them squeezed into the local secondary modern school
and the other half standing patiently in the rain outside.
Wilson himself was always to regard this as his best meeting
of the whole campaign, and at the same time to acknowledge
the debt that he owed for its success to a small baby in the
front row. The baby proved to be his only interrupter, and
eventually in some embarrassment his mother began to take
him out. Wilson would have none of it. "Don't take him
away," he called out. "This election is about his future. Anyway his contribution to this meeting is much more intelligent
and much more mature than that of any Young Conservative
I've had to deal with." After that, with his audience Wilson
could do no wrong; for once abandoning his prepared speech,
he proceeded to make exactly the type of taunting, teasing
speech that years ago had been Nye Bevan's speciality. It was
the only time at a major meeting during the whole campaign
that Wilson risked this.

On this last Saturday of the campaign it was not just Wilson himself who suddenly seemed confident to the point of

recklessness. "It's hard to remember," said Clive Bradley as the train continued to Liverpool, "that only a week ago we were really sweating it out waiting for those Gallup poll figures, and this week no one's really worried at all." That certainly was an exaggeration. Wilson himself, on arriving from Queensferry at the Adelphi Hotel in Liverpool (his headquarters for the last four days of the campaign), made it his first priority to find out what the Gallup details were. But no one in the carriage was in any doubt what Bradley meant. On the way from Edinburgh to Newcastle a week earlier the Gallup poll figures had seemed to be a matter of life and death; this week they seemed merely an optional extra. It was the Tories, not Labour, who needed to be apprehensive.

For three days the Gallup poll had cast a heavy shadow over Central Office. When the campaign was over Lord Blakenham was to confess that easily the worst period of it for the Conservative Party had been the three days from Thursday, October 8, to Sunday, October 11. "We knew, you see," he explained, "that things were not going too well for us, but there was nothing whatever we could do about it until we'd got through that Sunday Gallup poll. If we'd launched our counteroffensive immediately it would have been killed stone dead by an adverse Gallup poll coming out just after we'd started it. There was nothing for it but simply to sit it out and wait, but it wasn't a pleasant period for us." At the time, nonetheless, the Tories did their best to wear brave faces.

That Saturday afternoon the Conservative Central Office put round to the political correspondents the news of a last-minute blitz attack in which twenty Ministers would make speeches up and down Britain on Monday night. Nearly all of these, it was pointed out, would be members of the Cabinet. This news was, in fact, rather banal, since at any election, two nights before the poll, every possible Minister would normally be making a big speech. Yet on hearing about these twenty ministers, some Conservatives were tempted to ask: "Why not twenty-one?" Why not, for instance, Sir Alec Douglas-Home? His efforts, such as they were, went into whistle-stop tours.

On Saturday, after his press conference, Sir Alec began a tour of London marginal seats, following roughly the same course as Wilson three weeks before. His tour was an almost unqualified disaster. It began badly at Tooting, thanks just as much to supporters as to hecklers. After speaking at a car-park meeting, he passed through the bars of a hotel to visit the stalls in High Street market. Such a throng of well-wishers and ill-wishers pressed in behind him that he and Lady Home were literally pushed along without the help of their own legs. In spite of a cordon of policemen the crowd threatened to crush the Homes against their car. "What bloody silly nonsense this is. Let's get out," said a vexed Lord Oakshott, and Home, wearing a wan smile, was pushed from the market into his car.

The next stop, Clapham, began more peacefully. The loudspeaker was powerful enough to drown out any heckling, and Home got a good hearing. But as he and Lady Home got into their car to go, there were painful incidents. At his press conference earlier in the day, Home had remarked that he had been struck by "the very large number of young people in the audiences . . . and the number of young people that come up to one and talk to one at these meetings." He must have been struck by the young man who peered through his car window at Clapham and yelled: "Why doesn't he stop and answer questions?" to which a friend replied: "Because he hasn't got his matchsticks.* He's afraid." The motorcade was held up by a traffic jam and the

* A reference to Home's engaging confession in a 1962 *Observer* interview: "When I have to read economic documents I have to have a box of matches and start moving them into position to illustrate and simplify the points to myself."

two young men continued to yell political abuse at the by now twitching Premier.

At the next meeting, by Clapham Common, a big crowd of young people had gathered to heckle. These included members of the British Peace Committee, a man from the Hunt Saboteurs' Association and a surly crew of shaggy-haired "rockers" in black-leather jackets decorated with metal buttons. Some of them must have been *Private Eye* readers, for they constantly shouted, "Good Old Baillie," a reference to that magazine's nickname for Home, "Baillie Vass." Others threw fireworks in the direction of the platform. Poor Home did his best: "One of these days, this boy down here who is continually interrupting will do a few days' work for a fair wage," but he seemed to have no heart for the battle. He looked glum, sulky, impatient. It was hard not to think how Wilson, in the same circumstances, would have ridiculed and exploited such a heaven-sent crowd of hecklers. Moreover, Wilson was always eager to take questions after a whistle-stop speech. Not only did Home refuse; he also destroyed the excuse of shortage of time by taking an hour off for tea, after Clapham Common. Observers were amazed that so late in the campaign he spent so little time actually meeting the public and asking for its support. A Conservative journalist, Henry Fairlie, said of this day's meetings: "Sir Alec, in fact, seemed to speak very much as a tired man making a concession. If, his manner suggested, these plain words do not convince you, then I have nothing more to offer you. I have never seen him in such a take-it-or-leave-it mood."

Something in Home's aloof manner seemed to exacerbate hecklers. At Putney Bridge, the next meeting, about twenty young people started to shout the familiar "We want Wilson" and "Home out!" The longer Home soldiered on with his set speech, the angrier they became, and so in turn did the Tories in the audience. Some middle-aged ladies clouted the children with rolled umbrellas. Another took out a bag of pepper and scattered it in their eyes. A purple-faced steward walked up to a scrawny, pale heckler and yelled, "Shut up, you ignorant turd!" straight in his face. More fighting broke out, the police came in, and uproar silenced Sir Alec. At this point a Swiss free-lance journalist who had been shooting the incidents with his ciné-camera walked up to the cluster of hecklers and said to them calmly: "Stop it. You are losing the Labour Party votes." All hecklers stopped at once; and Sir Alec's speech could be heard.

During and after the election, many leading Conservatives argued that Home had done well to tour the country on whistle stops rather than make set speeches to Tory audiences. Quite the reverse is true. When Home had a ticket-only crowd of loyalists he could make quite a tolerable speech on defense, and he could even appear impressive on television. But he never learned how to deal with hecklers, let alone largely hostile crowds. His whistle stops in his own, almost feudal, constituency were a success. They were ineffective, if not damaging, in the cities of the south.

When Sir Alec finished his whistle-stop tour at 5:15 he went home and did no more public electioneering until Monday. Of all the things that distinguish election campaigns in Britain from those in the U.S.A., probably nothing is more surprising than the relative effort given by leading candidates. Johnson and Goldwater, even Humphrey and Miller, campaigned for at least fifteen hours a day and sometimes as much as twenty, during almost every day of a six-week campaign. During a four-week campaign, Home seldom election-eered for more than eight hours a day. He took at least six entire days off. On five out of the six last decisive days he did not campaign at all in the evenings.

By contrast Wilson put in that Saturday one of his longest days of the entire campaign. At the back of his mind there had always been a faint anxiety about his own constituency of Huyton. He knew, of course, that he could not lose it—indeed as long ago as July his agent, Arthur Smith, had told him that he should double his majority of 6,000. But he was worried lest any impression should get abroad that as leader of the party he now had little time to spare for his own constituents. For this reason he had insisted that in the last part of the campaign his outside engagements must be cut down to a minimum so that Huyton could have the first call upon him.

That Saturday night he had arranged to do a tour of the various Labour clubs in the constituency. This had been deliberately arranged in order that the maximum number of people should see him in the shortest possible time. The southern half of England holds no equivalent to the vast, barnlike drinking clubs nominally associated with the Labour Party in the North and the Midlands.* As often as not they are the social centers of the areas that they cover—at least for the married, the middle-aged and the respectable. And on Saturday nights it is normally impossible to get a seat in them after nine o'clock. Their appeal has little to do with politics; what most of the clubs offer is a variety entertainment, a waiter-service of beer, and long lines of tables where patrons can settle down comfortably for an entire evening.

For Wilson, if not for the American television crews who were now following him, the scene on arriving at the St. Agnes Club in Huyton was very familiar. He had done the same round in every election campaign since 1950 and by now he knew exactly how to play it by ear. At the St. Agnes Club he was late—the trip to Queensferry and a short stop-off at the Adelphi Hotel in order to collect his father and eat a sandwich had thrown out his timetable. Waiting for him at the door, Arthur Smith had grown increasingly agitated; he had five clubs to fit in that evening, and the three

* These Labour clubs often have no direct link with the Labour Party, as with the now famous Smethwick Club, which maintains a rigid color bar.

or four hundred people assembled might not take easily to having to wait for their regular entertainment. He need not have worried. From the moment that Wilson's stocky figure could be discerned making its way through the smoke-laden atmosphere it was clear that that night the rest of the bill did not matter. The electric organ blared, glasses were raised and a cacophony of applause and singing thundered forth. Huyton's own hero had come home.

As always in his own constituency Wilson seemed somehow a different individual. Gone entirely was the impressive image of the party leader; in its place was the much more humble M.P.—the man who for fourteen years (and in one part of the constituency for nineteen) had tried to serve a particular body of people. In each of the five clubs in which he delivered a short pep talk he made a point of saying, "I think you'll agree that *I'm* not the sort of member that comes up only at election time."

In Wilson's case this was no idle boast; indeed, that evening, as he moved from variety turns to bingo sessions, what came out was how well he did know his own constituents. By the time he reached the Kirkby Labour club shortly before eleven o'clock, to receive his most rapturous, if also most alcoholic, welcome, all the shyness and hesitancy that he had shown earlier seemed to have disappeared. Here among his own people he was quite simply at home.

Back at last in the Adelphi Hotel Wilson had every reason to feel confident. He had learned that the Gallup poll the next morning was going to show Labour with a lead increased to 6 per cent; nearly all press commentators had begun to take a Labour victory for granted; and in his own entourage the talk, if surreptitiously, had begun to be of a Labour landslide. All this only made Wilson more determined that nothing his own hard work could achieve should be left undone. While his father, eighty-one-year-old Herbert Wilson, sat about in the hotel lobby proudly reciting his son's various majorities since 1945, Wilson himself quietly made his way upstairs to his second-floor suite to start on his last task of the day.

That evening "Ted" Willis, the television scriptwriter nominated by Wilson for a Labour life peerage the previous December, had unobtrusively booked in at the Adelphi. He had come because it was here that all the work would have to be done on the final Labour Party broadcast of the campaign. Wilson had deliberately kept himself out of all party broadcasts since the first one. This decision had been taken partly to counter the Tory gibe of a "one-man band"; but there was also a shrewd calculation that if the final broadcast was to have maximum impact, Harold Wilson himself should not have been overexposed beforehand. From the beginning, the Labour Party had been banking on this broadcast as its main last-minute asset. Certain in its own mind that Harold Macmillan's final television appearance in 1959 had swung hundreds of thousands of votes to the Tories, it was determined to try and turn the same trick in reverse in 1964.

With this aim very much in mind, Wilson sat up till 3 A.M. that Sunday morning working on a script he was not due to deliver until Monday night. By the time he returned to the Adelphi Hotel just before midnight both Clive Bradley and Ted Willis had already gone to bed; but true to Longfellow's vision of a great man, Wilson himself, while his companions slept, toiled upward through the night. Marcia Williams and his research assistant, John Allen, stayed up with him, occasionally putting suggested draft sections in front of him; gradually, though, his own handwriting came to predominate on the various typed sheets. Not until he had achieved a full draft with which he was more or less satisfied did he finally end a day which had begun fifteen hours ago and two hundred miles away in Transport House in London.

The broadcast again dominated the 9 A.M. briefing conference which Wilson held—as he was to do throughout the
next four days—in the sitting room of his suite linked by the
special "Telstar" telephone arrangement to the general secretary's office in Transport House. When Bradley and Willis
arrived at the meeting they were taken aback to find a complete script already in existence. Rather than argue about it
in committee they suggested that they should each work on
it during the day and discuss it thoroughly with Wilson
that evening. As an arrangement this suited everyone, as Wilson himself had a full and busy day ahead of him.

The public part of it started with the normal morning
press conference—from now on held in one of the Adelphi
Hotel's banqueting rooms. No one could have guessed from
Wilson's appearance that he had been up half the night. He
was relaxed, resilient and looked a good deal more refreshed
than did most of his inquisitors. Away on tour these press
conferences had always been much smaller and more intimate affairs than those held in London, but in the last four
days the foreign press (especially a large contingent from
the United States) was to appear in mass. Their questions,
naturally enough, tended to center on foreign policy and
defense, and as their queries became ever more predictable
and repetitive, Wilson himself began to show some irritation:
"You'll find I dealt with that point very fully in my speech
in the defense debate last year"; "If you look at the policy
statement we issued you'll see we put our position very
clearly"; "As I said on March 17—I think column 796 in
Hansard—the party's position on that has always been perfectly plain." To the foreign correspondents (many of whom,
like NBC's Chet Huntley, had come thousands of miles) it
no doubt seemed an unobliging and unforthcoming technique; but Wilson himself was delighted with its effective-
ness. "You know," he was to proclaim later that day, "it's
taken me a long time to realize it, but if you don't like a

question all you've got to do is preface your answer with "As I said in the House of Commons" and everyone goes to sleep and doesn't even bother to write down what you're saying. I ought to have tumbled to it long before, but there's nothing like suggesting it's all stale stuff for distracting attention from an awkward question."

There were few awkward questions at his second press conference of the day, held in the George Hotel, Huddersfield, where he had eaten lunch. It was more like a stroll down Memory Lane. On the drive over from Liverpool Wilson had stopped off to look first at the house he was born in—4 Warneford Road, Huddersfield—and then at Number 40 Western Road, where he grew up until he was fifteen. He therefore needed little encouragement to talk about his boyhood days, even recalling how on the snowy night he was born his mother had missed her potato-pie supper at the Milnsbridge Baptist Church. He was not, he explained, hurt that there was as yet no plaque on the house that was his birthplace. "In this part of the world, you know, they wait until a man is dead." But if Huddersfield had not yet officially remembered him, he certainly remembered everything about it. Out from his wallet came the photograph of Huddersfield Town's cup-winning football team of 1922, and he gleefully corrected "Curly" Mallalieu (one of the town's two M.P.s) as he tried to recall each player's position. Nothing was left out—the names of school friends, what they were now doing, the debt he owed to one particular Milnsbridge schoolmaster. After that, by an easy transition, he began to dwell on the glories of Yorkshire pudding, describing Stanley Holloway's ode on how the first Yorkshire pudding was made as "the most moving poem in the whole English language."* Then it was the turn of books about the North: *Fame Is the Spur* by Howard Spring and *The Crow-*

* Wilson's favorite poem is, in fact, Kipling's "If."

thers of Bankdam by Thomas Armstrong. Both, he thought, admirably summed up the kind of North of England he had known when he was young. The whole monologue had all the marks of prepared display; and the pencils scribbling away in the local reporters' notebooks betrayed its success.

The stop-off at Huddersfield had been arranged so that the Labour candidates in the two borough seats and the one in neighboring Colne Valley might get the maximum advantage out of the fact that the party leader was a local boy. With that end in view Wilson could hardly have put up a more helpful performance, but it was also one that he himself clearly enjoyed. Wilson's allegiance to the North, and his genuine feeling for it, is one of the strongest elements in his whole make-up. Throughout the campaign his best platform performances were nearly always given before Northern audiences, and that afternoon's rally in the St. George's Hall, Bradford, was no exception.

It started a little unhappily. No sooner had the audience sat down after greeting Wilson's arrival with cheers and "For He's a Jolly Good Fellow" than the chairman, in typical, blunt Yorkshire manner, announced: "When Harold Wilson took over the reins following the death of Hugh Gaitskell I am sure there were many of us who thought that he could not possibly measure up to his stature." Even a raucous, loyal shout, "There aren't any now," did not entirely banish embarrassment. It was not that the remark itself was unduly offensive; it was simply that in the circumstances of the recent campaign for the Labour leadership Gaitskell's name was not a tactful one to mention.

But it did not take long for Wilson himself to redeem the blunder. His speech that afternoon was the usual one, but it was flavored and spiced by his now consummate handling of hecklers. From the moment that the first hostile shout came—to be greeted with a warning finger and an admonitory "Now you mustn't, or Sir Alec will be cross with you"—Wilson had his audience eating out of his hand. The worst thing that happened to him that afternoon was, in fact, when his most persistent interrupter ("Don't throw him out—I want him") was ejected from the meeting to an ominous sound of breaking glass. By this stage of the campaign Wilson had come very much to depend on the services of hecklers to establish contact with his audience; it was when he was plowing doggedly through a speech that he ran the risk of seeming remote. But any shout would always bring him back to life. First would come the look of pained surprise, then the mocking half-smile, and finally the retort, often all the more crushing for being genial. His speciality perhaps lay in so devising a dialogue that he frequently seemed to be taking the heckler's side against the rest of the audience. "No, no," he would say cheerfully, "I'm not having that. Our friend here went to a Yorkshire school—he didn't go to Eton—he *can* read." Inevitably the audience would collapse in laughter while the interrupter simply collapsed.

Bradford was to be Wilson's last wholly successful platform appearance of the campaign. He never again achieved the same mixture of warm emotion and cold logic. That same evening, at two schoolroom meetings in his own constituency, all the vigor seemed to have been drained from him. Fiddling with his top coat button, occasionally fumbling for words, saying "finally" three times, he was scarcely the same man who had held the Bradford audience in the palm of his hand. In the last few days of the campaign Wilson was, in fact, to justify the fears that some of his closest associates had expressed all along: the strain told and he grew ever more obviously flat and exhausted.

It was hardly surprising; even when he got back to the Adelphi that Sunday night Wilson had no chance to rest or relax before going to Huyton. Instead he faced a fresh crisis over the script for his TV broadcast the following night. His two broadcasting experts, Clive Bradley and Lord Willis, had been working on it all day, and by no means all their changes and emendations had proved acceptable to the two people who had helped with the original Wilson draft, John Allen and Marcia Williams. Wilson cut through the argument by demanding to see the revised Willis script; he said he liked it (except for a passage on defense which he didn't want to touch), worked through it restoring some of his own original text, and eventually gave it the "all clear" to be taken to Manchester early next morning to be placed on autocue. All this meant that for the second night running he did not get to bed until well past 2 A.M.

The loss of sleep was serious, for the next day Wilson faced probably the most exhausting schedule of his whole campaign. In the morning he was in the market square at Bolton answering questions in the open air; at midday he was at Trafford Park in Manchester taking the traditional mass rally at the Metro-Vickers works; in the early afternoon he held his daily press conference in the Midland Hotel in Manchester. He then went to BBC Manchester studios to do his television broadcast before winding up the day with two mass meetings—one (outdoors) in Stockport's Bear Pit and the other (indoors) in Manchester's Albert Hall. For any man it would have been a harsh ordeal; for a party leader so near the end, it was punishing.

Wilson met it in characteristic fashion, reserving all his strength for the one really important engagement. In the morning, both at Bolton and at the Metro-Vickers works on Manchester's vast industrial estate, he seemed almost deliberately to be holding himself back. This led to his facing some acid questions at his after-lunch press conference. How he was asked, did he think his own meeting at Metro-Vickers compared with the triumph that Hugh Gaitskell had enjoyed there five years earlier? In the size of the crowd, in the measure of enthusiasm, even on the scale of oratory, Wilson probably knew that his own meeting had been a flop compared with Gaitskell's. But he gave not an inch to his questioners, and kept his mind firmly fixed on what he had always said would be his most important single exercise of the whole campaign—his final TV address to the nation.

So tight, however, had Wilson's program been that day that he was already a quarter of an hour late when he arrived at the BBC's Manchester studio in Dickenson Road, Ardwick. This studio—a converted Nonconformist chapel—is probably the most primitive occupied by any television organization in Britain; and when Wilson eventually arrived to do his broadcast against a backing of curtains, a vase of flowers and a fake Louis Quinze clock, he found himself confronting at the other end of the studio a set already arranged for a local "Question Time" program involving Selwyn Lloyd, Anthony Greenwood and the Liberal M.P., Arthur Holt. The whole atmosphere was extraordinarily informal. Around the walls stood practically every BBC official employed in Manchester; at the entrance to the studio were two police constables who had apparently just wandered in from their beat; and in a cluster at the center of the set were no less than half a dozen people who appeared to see it as their duty to advise the Leader on his performance.

Almost lost in the middle of them, Wilson looked suddenly lonely—sitting on a swivel chair in front of a worm-eaten, decayed desk. The BBC producer, bow-tied Stanley Hyland, loaned to the Labour Party for the election period, did his best to bring order out of chaos. "Now I want you at the beginning to smile and look friendly," he said. "You'll have been watching Clem Attlee on the monitor and then you start straight in." At first Wilson objected. "When we finally do it with me looking at the monitor, how is anyone going to know that I've been looking at Clem at all?" Patiently the point was explained that if on television someone turns into camera after a film has gone out, it is automatically assumed that he, as well as the viewers, has been watching it.

Pacified, Wilson made a start, though carefully insisting (before such a large studio audience), "Look, I'm not doing it for expression or sense; I'm just trying to familiarize myself with the words."

It was the first of two run-throughs and three false starts before anyone was satisfied with the finished product. As the time ticked by, Wilson himself remained remarkably patient and composed. But his entourage knew that the studio was booked at 5:15 P.M. and that the G.P.O.'s land line was due to close at 5 P.M. They grew more and more agitated. And even at this late stage there were disagreements over the script. Wilson himself objected to certain passages without apparently realizing that changes now meant a long delay in correcting the autocue. The teleprompter also caused other problems. Always shortsighted, Wilson three times had to stop a recording by saying, "Stanley, I'm sorry I can't read it. You'll have to bring the camera in nearer."

Eventually, at half past four, after a tea break which Wilson used to drink a glass of brandy and to scrape minestrone off his suit with a pair of scissors, he successfully got through a complete script. Everyone on the studio floor waited anxiously for Clive Bradley to come down from the director's box and give his verdict. Bradley, in fact, had not liked the performance; he thought Wilson looked tired and had taken the whole thing too slowly, but in any case the recording had overrun by one and a half minutes. For party political broadcasts a leeway of anything up to a quarter of a minute can be allowed, but this was well outside the limit. There was nothing for it but to start all over again, after making new cuts in the script. A phone call to the G.P.O. brought a promise that the land line would be kept open for one more recording but that nothing could be guaranteed after that.

Reinforced by another glass of brandy, Wilson returned to the set just before five o'clock. All the waits and delays, which had frayed other people's nerves, seemed to have strength-ened his. "All right," he began crisply, "whatever mistakes I make this time, I go on—understood?" In fact there was none; Wilson produced a model, unfluffed performance, and everyone (even those who a few minutes earlier had been bitterly quarreling among themselves) relaxed and complimented each other. There had been nervous moments; but Wilson took only one and a half hours for a broadcast that was to take Home one and a half days.

If it had been a strain, Wilson allowed himself to show it only afterward. Watching his own performance in a crowded BBC dubbing room, he kept puncturing the playback with irreverent comments. "Who's that chap? He looks like the pig we've just seen on the children's program" . . . "No, I don't like the look of him. I wouldn't vote for that fellow myself" . . . "Why does he ask silly questions like 'How are stock exchange prices doing?' . . . Pretty awful at the moment —that's the answer, isn't it?" Only once did the face of the professional politician peep through the cheery mask of the gleeful schoolboy. As the recording ended to a chorus of praise from everyone in the room, Wilson seemed to pay no attention. Instead, suddenly serious, he remarked: "Well, that's that, but what are we going to do now? What I need is a strategy for the last two days. We can't let the initiative slip now."

14. The Rains Came

If you were buying a secondhand car, would you buy it
from Harold Wilson?

ANTHONY BARBER, *former Minister of Health, one year after Wilson's election to the Labour leadership*

THE initiative which Wilson was frightened of losing the
Tories believed they had already gained. In looking back on
the campaign there was not much about which the Conservative Central Office felt pleased, but those in charge were always to believe and proclaim that in the last two or three days
Wilson's comparative inaction enabled them to make up a
lot of lost ground. The Tory "counteroffensive" (as it was
afterward proudly called) really started on October 11, when
Lord Blakenham defied previous Tory practice by actually
calling a press conference on a Sunday. Those who turned
up found a man transformed from the modest, unassuming,
inaudible figure who had until then unobtrusively presided
at the daily gatherings of journalists in the ground-floor hall
of the Central Office. This time Lord Blakenham wore his
fighting boots and stamped around to some effect. For the
first time, at least at top level, Harold Wilson's political
record was introduced into the campaign and compared with
that of Hugh Gaitskell. Shrewdly, Lord Blakenham even
managed to recall a prophecy made by Patrick Gordon
Walker in 1960 that if he were elected leader of the Labour
Party "Mr. Wilson would be the prisoner of the unilateralists." Hugh Gaitskell, Lord Blakenham went on, had "supported the Conservative Government over the nuclear deterrent—but not Mr. Wilson. Hugh Gaitskell wanted to divorce
the Labour Party from commitments on nationalization—

267

but not Mr. Wilson." It was all, naturally, designed to prove
that the Labour Party was "now led by an avowed man of
the Left." When this charge had been first leveled at the
beginning of the campaign by Quintin Hogg, no one had
taken much notice; but somehow the fact that it now came
from the normally cautious lips of the Tory Party chairman
lent it a much greater impact. Whether from a sense of surprise or not, the next morning, Monday, October 12, was one
of the few days in the entire campaign when a press conference actually made headlines.

The second barrel of the Tory counterattack also relied on
an old charge. Very early in the campaign Reginald Maudling had produced his own estimate of the cost of Labour's
program and had challenged Harold Wilson to deny that it
would involve an increase of between £900 and £1,200 million in national expenditure. As a challenge it had fallen
rather flat; Wilson had not even bothered to reply and the
electorate had seemed to dismiss it as a typical piece of election figure-juggling. Now, however, Maudling returned to
the attack and mounted it in a much more vivid way. Carrying out the Labour Party program, he warned, was bound to
involve a ninepence increase on income tax, an extra six-
pence on every gallon of petrol and an additional increase
of six shillings spread between employer and employee in
National Insurance contributions. As an economic forecast
it was soon proved remarkably accurate; and as a political
challenge it was undeniably effective, not least because Maudling deliberately waited to make it until after Wilson's final
broadcast so that there could be no chance of a really formidable comeback.

But in spite of the new vigor that came over the Tory
campaign in the last phase—marred only by Quintin Hogg's
simultaneous outburst that anyone who voted Labour must
be "stark staring bonkers"—any last-minute change in the
electoral temperature could easily have been the result of

extraneous factors. On the morning of Monday, October 12, millions of Londoners found their normal means of getting to work—the London Underground Service—totally disrupted. For Labour it was just the type of industrial stoppage calculated to do maximum damage. That morning new time-tables had come into effect and the drivers, unanimously on two lines and partially on others, had simply downed tools and refused to work them. The result was chaos, not just on the tubes but in traffic-jammed streets as well. Though the Conservative Party made no official move—being more than content to let the lesson sink in—a number of Tory candidates, especially those in the marginal seats served by the District and Metropolitan lines, lost no time in exploiting the situation. Queues at bus stops and crowds waiting outside underground stations found themselves encouraged by loud-speaker to vent their anger and resentment on the political party associated with industrial workers.

The immediate impact naturally fell only in the London area, but the news exposed a vulnerable flank for the Labour Party nationally. The obvious remedy would have been to issue an immediate statement condemning the strike, but inexplicably the Labour Party allowed a whole day to go by before it did so. Equally inexplicably the Conservatives left it to the Liberals to exploit this strange silence. "Why," asked Frank Byers, making exactly the point that Sir Alec Douglas-Home himself should have made on his brief helicopter tour of Essex that Monday, "doesn't Harold Wilson condemn this sort of thing? Is he afraid?" Of course the point was an entirely false one: Wilson was to denounce the strike the next day in the strongest terms ever used by a Labour leader about an industrial stoppage. But his delay in making a move—the result of his absence two hundred miles away in Liverpool—had provided an opening; and the Liberals, not the Tories, had seized it.

It was now that the Conservatives really felt the loss of a

leader as shrewd as Macmillan. Attacks, like those of Blakenham and Maudling, were all very well, but what was really
required now was one last personal push by Sir Alec himself.
No one was more aware of this than the Conservative strategists, and every means had been taken to enable Home to
provide it. Since his unfortunate whistle-stop tour of London
on the afternoon of Saturday, October 10, the Prime Minister
had fulfilled only one other public engagement—his two-
hour tour of Essex on Monday afternoon; otherwise his attention had been given exclusively to preparing and rehearsing
his final broadcast, due to be delivered on the night of Tuesday, October 13, less than thirty-six hours before the polls
opened.

One of the best-kept secrets of the whole campaign was the
two visits that Home made to Associated Television's studios
in Elstree on Sunday, October 11, and again on Tuesday,
October 13.* Normally, all election broadcasts are produced
by the BBC and not by the commercial companies; but in
1959 Lord Poole had broken the precedent, and in the BBC's
view the law as well, by having Harold Macmillan's highly
successful last broadcast recorded on tape at Associated Television and then simply handed to the BBC for putting out
to the nation. Long before the election campaign Lord Poole,
who, as in 1959, had the ultimate responsibility for Conservative Party broadcasts, had decided to follow the same
course again, though fully aware that the challenge facing
him this time was very much more difficult.

Home had never hidden his dislike of television. Almost
the whole of the Sunday visit to Elstree, which ended with
Home doing a run-through which was eventually discarded,

---

* It was such a well-kept secret that even while the resulting broadcast
was being transmitted the BBC Television Center got a call from Rediffu-
sion (ATV's sister London commercial company) complaining of the poor
quality of the picture. This caused great enjoyment at the BBC.

was given over to trying to put him at his ease. Both Norman Collins (the managing director of ATV who produced the program as he had done with the Macmillan one in 1959) and Lord Poole had agreed that there was no chance of getting an actor's performance out of Home; at best it was hoped he would come over naturally as the kind of person he really was. But to achieve this it would be necessary to overcome the tautness and tenseness which had marred his "Election Forum" appearance at the start of the campaign.

For this reason it had been decided that Home should not use a teleprompter. Oddly enough he had never used one in all his years as a politician, and it was justifiably felt that to make him use one now for the first time would only have the effect of increasing his nervousness. Equally it would be impossible to expect him to learn and remember a whole fifteen-minute talk—"even," Lord Poole was to explain afterward, "if he could have managed it, he would have come over like someone reciting a lesson he had learned by heart." That left only one other answer: the whole broadcast would have to be done in separate "takes"—borrowing the technique normally used in film-making for the cinema.

By the time Home arrived at Elstree on the morning of Sunday, October 11, his entire script had accordingly been divided into a half-dozen different sections lasting on average two minutes each. It was only then that the technical difficulties involved were suddenly realized. It is impossible in terms of television production to join together any two clips of film or video tape, no matter how similar the picture, so that they run naturally into each other. The speaker's head is sure to have moved fractionally, and on the join the picture will "jump." To cover the jump the producer "splices in a cutaway," for example to a reaction shot of an interviewer. But here there was no interviewer. Home's performance was, and had to be, a solo effort. To get around the difficulty

Norman Collins proposed that they could always make a linking shot out of the Prime Minister looking at his notes; it could be slotted in between each of the different sections, and only the really knowledgeable would be able to guess why it was there. At first the two party professionals, Sir Michael Fraser (head of the Conservative research department) and Nigel Lawson (who had acted as speechwriter to Home since he became Prime Minister), were appalled. Would not this inevitably emphasize the favorite Labour Party gibe against Home, that he was simply not up to the job and could not even remember his own speeches once they were written for him? Yet Collins's suggestion was accepted, though in the end the linking shot was not needed every time a break in the film came. There was in any case always the argument that it was no bad thing for Home—in terms of identification with the viewers—to make an asset out of his lack of slick professionalism. They might respect Wilson more, but it was always possible that they would like Home better.

But even in order to achieve that it was clear by the time the Prime Minister's party returned to Elstree on the morning of Tuesday, October 13, that Norman Collins would have to do for Home what an American advertising man, Rosser Reeves, had so successfully done for Eisenhower in the 1952 Presidential campaign. Even the methods employed were very much the same. Treating the different sections of his script like "spot commercials," Home would do each one again and again until the professionals were satisfied with the result. Inevitably it was a long and tiring process; and though the original intention had been to get it all done in the course of the morning, in actuality it was late in the afternoon before Home finally left Elstree for the fifteen-mile drive back to Downing Street. For him it was probably the worst day of the whole campaign; for the three personal advisers who were with him, Lord Poole, Sir Michael Fraser and Nigel Lawson (none of the normal Central Office staff concerned with broadcasts had been allowed to be present), it had certainly been the most nerve-wracking.

For no one was in doubt what was at stake. Home's last major platform speech of the campaign had, after all, been made as long ago as the previous Thursday, and after the broadcast the only public part he had left in the election was the courtesy visit to his own constituency. Incredibly, even that Tuesday night while his ministerial colleagues were stumping the country, the Prime Minister himself sat peacefully at home in Downing Street. Originally it had been planned that he should go to London Airport to greet the Queen on her return from her Canadian tour; but even when the Palace, showing an uncharacteristic political wariness, let it be known that "in view of the late hour of her arrival the Queen did not wish any of her Ministers to go to the trouble of meeting her," nothing was done to substitute any other last public appearance for Sir Alec. The whole case for Sir Alec was allowed to rest on this one broadcast; on its impact depended the whole Tory counterattack.

In retrospect it is easy to exaggerate opportunities—especially missed ones. But the situation at this last stage of the campaign was, in fact, a very remarkable one. Having made the running for the greater part of the election, the Labour Party suddenly seemed to have lost steam. It was almost as if a vacuum was there to be filled. But alas for Sir Alec, he failed entirely to meet the challenge. Despite, or perhaps because of, all the effort that had gone into it, his broadcast (in the words of The Times the next morning) "proved to be a symphony in black and white delivered by a tone-deaf pianist, for, though the notes were all there and in the right order, the performance was so totally lacking in style and emotion that its impact was lost on the ear." The missed chance was all the more irritating to the Conservatives because Labour was now wide open to any attack.

For weeks Labour Party officials had been hinting to the press that "Harold would pull something out of his sleeve," that he would startle and thrill the country with a message. In fact, at the very end, Wilson seemed almost to draw away from the national struggle and to become just a simple constituency M.P. It had always been his belief that when in his own constituency he owed allegiance far more to the Huyton party than to Transport House. And on Tuesday and Wednesday and late into polling day itself, he threw himself into such a rush of canvassing that one might have imagined Huyton still a marginal seat.

On Tuesday he went to the shopping center in Kirkby, chatted with housewives and peered benevolently into prams. He inspected a child's teddy bear, had an encounter with an unfriendly dog and accepted the gift of a couple of chips from a small boy's bag. He ate a 1s. 6d. lunch with the old-age pensioners—lamb, carrots, peas and mashed potatoes—and questioned them about pensions and bus fares. He was chased by a French *cinéma vérité* team and persuaded by a G.P.O. film crew to telephone from his car back to the headquarters suite in the Adelphi Hotel. This was unfortunate. He dialed the right number and got through to the Adelphi switchboard, only to find that all his staff were out to lunch.

His two speeches that evening were homely constituency chats about the kind of people and problems he had met during the day. "Today I asked at the Kirkby Labour Club for all the old-age pensioners who had [reduced-fare bus] passes to put up their hands, and then those who hadn't. It was about fifty-fifty." This illustrated Wilson's point about the anomalies of the system for giving passes, and his conviction that reduced fares* are a matter of real importance. "In

---

* The first legislative action of the Labour Government after October was to extend to all local authorities the power to vary fares for old-age pensioners —a power previously enjoyed by only a few municipally owned bus companies.

some ways," he said quietly, "the loneliness of old-age pensioners is more of a problem than their poverty."

Both meetings were held in schools, and on both occasions Wilson spoke a great deal about children. This was inevitable, because hundreds of children followed him around during the day. They asked for autographs, they chanted his name and yelled "Yeah, yeah, yeah," which, in Merseyside, is an honor otherwise given only to Beatles. At one time in the afternoon a crowd of children actually mobbed Wilson and injured his arm. His extraordinary Pied Piper effect on the young is something quite unprecedented in British politics and a little uncanny. For instance children, and sometimes grownups, made a point of touching his car and then gazing at the hand which had received such magical blessing. "The children of Kirkby are some of the luckiest in the country," said Wilson during his first speech, for he admires the local comprehensive schools. They are also some of the noisiest. They banged on the French windows throughout the first meeting. They battled with the police outside the second. There were still scores of them in the streets to yell for their hero when he drove away at ten.

"I haven't seen so many children outside a meeting since 1950 and 1951," Wilson remarked, as though prophesying another electoral dead heat. "I think it's a good sign. This election is about kids." As always when he has no set speech, Wilson allowed his thoughts to wander into all kinds of fascinating byways. The children reminded him of comprehensive schools and this in turn of apprentice training. It was remarkable, only two days before the poll, to hear the Labour leader and probable next Prime Minister giving his views on how to train fifteen-year-olds as chefs and the need to teach them not only cooking but also "a bit of French and bookkeeping." Apprentice training reminded him of how in the last Labour Government he had helped to bring a factory into the Kirkby area. "When I was president of the Board of Trade," he began—and a jaded journalist in the press row, who had heard this boast before, muttered, "He talks of being president of the Board of Trade as though he had been President of the United States." But nothing could check Wilson's proud reminiscence. Still harking back to his days at the Board of Trade, he began to give his views on how to deal with the Russians: "Believe me, it's a slow job getting the Russians to say yes. I had to teach them the word in 1947. It's *horosho* in Russian."* From the Russians, he went on to discuss the Tories. "All they can talk about is us," he confided, and clearly implied that this was a bad thing. "You don't fill an Omo advertisement with a lot of stuff about how bad Daz is." He then neglected his own advice by a series of pot shots at the Conservatives. "I don't know whether you've ever seen Lord Blakenham on TV." He paused. Clearly few in the audience had, so Wilson provided his own word portrait: "Keep death off the road."

These off-the-cuff, rambling addresses show Wilson at his funniest and most fascinating. Unfortunately they seldom contain any great national message. The daily newspaper reporters were glum after the two Kirkby meetings, which they said "hadn't a line in them." Indeed the organization of this stage of the campaign was extraordinarily inept. There were insufficient seats for the reporters. The meetings started late. The Huyton councillor who was supposed to lead Wilson's motorcade around the constituency came to be known as "Cul-de-sac Charlie." It was hardly surprising that Home's broadcast that night, ineffective as it was, dominated not only the TV parlor but Wednesday morning's newspapers as well.

On Wednesday, the eve of poll, Wilson was twenty-five minutes late for his morning press conference. "Sorry I'm

---

* This is actually the Russian for "good." "Yes" is *da.*

late," he said with a snuffle." I've got a filthy cold and I decided to have a lie-in." He made his expected denunciation
of Home's "utterly negative" broadcast, but otherwise he
and the press seemed almost to have lost interest in each
other. Only one question created some stir. Four days before
Wilson had warned "with all the emphasis at my command"
of a last-minute Tory scare. Had that scare materialized?
To this question Wilson gave a peculiar knowing smile but
no answer. He did, however, concede that the campaign had
had "its squalid moments."

The previous and the next Prime Ministers were both in
Liverpool that morning. At a whistle-stop tour Harold Macmillan announced that "this is rather a queer election. It
is going backwards and forwards." To the Wilson entourage it had become, all of a sudden, a dreary election. Such
an air of apathy had descended that only a half-dozen journalists bothered to go with Wilson to Cronton Colliery, in
the nearby constituency of Widnes. This was the pit where
Wilson's agent had once worked, and the visit was therefore
a personal favor. It was a good opportunity for Wilson to be
seen meeting people, but it came too late in the campaign.
This visit on Wednesday was almost the first time Wilson
had gone to see people at work since his election as party
leader.

Perhaps Wilson believed that nothing positive could be
done at this late stage in the campaign. Certainly his eve-of-
poll speech at the St. George's Hall, Liverpool, was a dull
and tired performance. There was nothing dull about the
audience or the immense hall itself, with its brown quartz
pillars topped with Corinthian gilt, and its marble statues
of Gladstone and other Victorian statesmen. But Wilson
arrived late, and Frank Cousins, the union leader, grew more
and more tedious as he played for time in an introductory
oration. It was not until 9:05 that Wilson came onto the

platform and the immense audience rose to sing, in its mass Liverpudlian accents: "For He's a Jolly Good Fellow—and so say all of uzz."

"Comrades and friends," Wilson began, using the word "comrades" for almost the first time since his left-wing days in the Fifties. For the next five minutes he kept looking cautiously at his watch to judge the exact moment—9:16— when he was due to appear on a live ITN newscast. "He'll be saying the bit about people," said one of the party's TV experts, and sure enough, at 9:16 sharp, Wilson paused and began to read out in a loud, Churchillian tone: "We care for people; they care for profit. We care about opportunity; they are preoccupied with inheritance and conserving inheritance. They are concerned with the retention of power; we are concerned to exercise power democratically for the benefit of our people as individuals and our people as families." A few minutes of this and Wilson relaxed again, until, at 9:24, a BBC man in the hall below leaped to wave his arms as a cue for another live broadcast. Once again Wilson's voice got louder and increasingly ponderous. This time he delivered a call for a crusade. The whole speech was dull, nebulous and tired.

The best part of the evening came after the meeting was over. A jostling crowd of 2,000 Liverpudlians marched through the city center accompanying Harold and Mary Wilson back to the Adelphi Hotel. They chanted Wilson's name and "Yeah, yeah, yeah." Somebody flung a glass, and a number of people were kicked in the crush. It was a rough, noisy and typically Liverpool celebration. It demonstrated that this traditionally Tory city was about to swing Left; but it did not give any clue as to how the whole country would vote.

Both sides on this Wednesday evening were badly worried. At his press conference in the morning Wilson had said with surprising modesty that everything would go well if only

Labour could get out its maximum vote (which it had failed to do in the past two elections). Privately, too, he was anxious about the possibility of bad weather; the forecasters were already talking ominously about fog and rain—always more of a disadvantage to the Labour Party than to the Tories. In addition that day gloomy rumors had spread throughout the Wilson entourage that on the basis of last-minute canvass returns, Transport House itself was growing increasingly pessimistic. Nowhere was there any more talk of a Labour landslide.

Labour nerves might have steadied had it been known what was going on in Central Office, or at least in the mind of the one man there who approached the whole business of politics with detachment and dedication mixed in about equal quantities. That morning Lord Poole—the curious, anonymous figure who above any other single person had masterminded the Tory campaign—arrived in his office early. He sat at his desk apparently lost in thought but in reality making a businessman's ruthless assessment of the Tory electoral balance sheet. At the end of an hour he was no longer in doubt; from the beginning he had warned the party that it must expect a minimum loss of thirty-five seats. Surveying in his own mind what had happened in the past three weeks, he was now certain that the party's losses could no longer be contained at that level. The Conservative Government of the last thirteen years was going to go out by somewhere between twenty-five and thirty seats.

For the moment Poole kept his own counsel, saying not a word to discourage the various sanguine statements that were made at that morning's last staff conference of the campaign. Only at the end of the day did he give his professional's verdict to the man with whom he had worked since the internal party upheaval of the previous October. At first Lord Blakenham, always the bluff party crusader, was shocked; he himself had believed from the start of the campaign that it would end in a Conservative victory, if only by ten or fifteen seats. But when Poole (haunted by the 1959 vision of Hugh Gaitskell having under the arc lights forlornly to confront defeat when he had fondly expected victory) urged that Sir Alec himself must be warned, Blakenham did not demur. Bravely he accepted his most unenviable task of the campaign—breaking the news by telephone to Sir Alec in Crieff that he must prepare himself for the worst.

But that night in Crieff, as in many other parts of Britain, rain had already started to fall.

15. In by Four

Oh, we don't discuss nightmares like that.
> HAROLD WILSON *in a TV interview the night he was elected Leader of the Labour Party on what he would do if he had only a threadbare majority in the next Parliament*

AT ELEVEN-THIRTY on the morning of Friday, October 16, Harold Wilson gave a rueful grin, slumped back against the dark-blue cushions of the train compartment and conceded defeat: "It's no good. We shan't make it. I've checked with the slide rule. We've lost by one seat." To make the foretaste of defeat even more bitter, he was aboard what in all the Labour Party's plans had been called the "Victory Special" from Liverpool to London and Buckingham Palace. At 8:15 that morning he and his entourage had caught the train still in a mood of quiet confidence carried over from Labour's gains the previous night. But once on the train Wilson began to think hard—this time as a statistician rather than a politician. The Labour Party, he worked out, was certain of only 309 seats; probably it could hope to pick up three or four more from the traditionally Tory county seats, but where was it going to find the half dozen it needed in order to get the barest of parliamentary majorities? Suddenly the conviction came over him that everyone—the pundits, the computers, even his own party general secretary—had got it wrong: the Tories were going to sneak back after all.

Six hours later he was in Downing Street. The actual victory was as close as the dreaded defeat his slide rule had forecast. If a mere 900 people scattered through eight key constituencies had voted Tory instead of Labour—or indeed had they simply abstained—it would have been Home's right

281

to continue in office. The last day in Wilson's long rise to power passed in a nightmare of alternate hope and terror.

Polling day, Thursday, October 15, got off to a gloomy start. That morning both major public-opinion polls indicated a Labour victory, but only by a percentage lead small enough to be well within their margin of error. The weather, too, had turned wet and misty after three months of almost constant sunshine. Wilson himself was still suffering from his cold, on top of the accumulated fatigue of the campaign. For the first time at his ten-thirty morning press conference, held in the Adelphi Hotel, he had nothing to say to the nation except "The case rests."

The press conference over, Wilson set off for a tour of the constituency. He canvassed houses, dropped in on committee rooms and thanked the party workers. It was clear even then that he would get a massive majority in Huyton. "Bloody marvelous" was the report of a party worker in Huyton village, traditionally a Tory stronghold. In most of the constituency there was a Labour lead even at midday, although Labour does not normally get out its votes until its traditional supporters return from work in the evening. The high poll in his own constituency, and this in spite of a continuous drizzle, probably helped to give Wilson his early confidence. "I'm not worried at all," he told a friend at four o'clock that afternoon, and then went back to his suite in the Adelphi for a sleep.

Later that evening it seemed that Wilson was not so confident. Over drinks with his staff and some journalists in Suite 100 he was cheerful but far from sure. He had heard from Transport House that polling was very high in the marginals, always a good sign for Labour. In fact this report was only half true. More accurately he had been told of the big Liberal vote throughout the country. "Sara* was on just now with the details of one ward in Peterborough. They

---

* Sara Barker, the Labour Party's national agent.

reckon that if we have two hundred off by teatime it's going to Labour. We've got a majority already [6:45]. And polling's high in the Liberal areas. For instance in Brighouse or somewhere she said the polling was very big in the Liberal ward." He mused for a bit: "Quintin is silly; he's annoyed all the Liberals." He gave a laugh; he could afford to laugh at Hogg now, although only the previous week Hogg had been no laughing matter.

"Perhaps you won't be the front-page lead if you *do* win," said one journalist. Even here, over end-of-campaign drinks with the next Prime Minister, the talk was mostly of foreign affairs. It had just been announced that Khrushchev had resigned. Wilson was not certain at first that Mr. Khrushchev had in fact been deposed. "It may have been a stroke, in which case they'll have to have Mikoyan, who's a safe man" —and also an old friend of Wilson's. But if Khrushchev had not been deposed, why had *Izvestia* failed to appear? "There's one explanation which nobody seems to have thought of," said Wilson, suddenly jolly again. "The newspaper may be on strike, or perhaps Roy Thomson's made a take-over bid." Later that night he cashed in on his old acquaintance with the new party secretary, Kosygin. "I knew him very well. He's very tough, very able, very efficient."

Earlier Wilson was asked if his father, Herbert Wilson, would appear on television with him. "We'll let the old man on if its a landslide," he said. By the close of polling that night he did not talk of a landslide, even in jest. "We'll be going to London on the 8:15 train," he told a journalist, "if we win." The journalist was quite frankly astonished. In the sweepstake held by the journalists following Wilson, only one man had guessed a majority of less than ten. "But you will win," he insisted. Wilson, aware now that a belt of rain had since six o'clock blanketed southeast England, looked suddenly grim and withdrawn. "You can never tell with these undercurrents of opinion."

Even at this late hour they had not finally chosen the train.

There was a contingency booking on the 8:15 from Lime Street, Liverpool, to Euston, due in at 12:10. But Wilson was firm that he would not travel down on this early train if things went badly. "If we lose we'll have all the time in the world. You can come with me on the 10:15—and bring the brandy." He was planning, in case of defeat, to spend the whole weekend on the golf course. As the result grew more and more close and uncertain, it was the choice of train which seemed to Wilson a cause of almost neurotic anxiety.

At the end of the little party some of the journalists joined in making Mr. and Mrs. Wilson a presentation of books. "It was a difficult choice," said the journalists' spokesman. "We thought of getting *Mr. Wilson's War* but thought it wasn't really appropriate. Finally, we got these: for Mrs. Wilson a copy of John Betjeman's poems, for Harold Wilson the *Cricketer's Companion,* the *Footballer's Companion* and 'Whatever happens tomorrow,' a copy of Trollope's *The Prime Minister."* Referring to Harold Macmillan in his speech of thanks, Wilson said that he would be the second Prime Minister in the last three "to sleep with a Trollope beside the bed." The gift from the press was unprecedented and a sign of the very real affection for Wilson among the many journalists who have reported him.

The guests left, and the Wilson party settled down in Suite 100 to watch the first results. They included Herbert and Mary Wilson; Marcia Williams and her brother, Tony Field, who was acting as his driver; Brenda Dew and Sandra Gluck, his assistant secretaries; John Harris; researcher John Allen; and the ebullient Hungarian-born economist Thomas Balogh, who had come up to Liverpool to be with his old friend Wilson in this testing time. They ordered a meal of fish and chips to be sent up to the room and settled down to watch television. The noneater, Harold Wilson, was too busy crouched over the telephone in the far left-hand corner of the room to bother about food. The rest chatted nervously in front of the set.

At 10:30 P.M. the first result was flashed onto the television screen. The Tories had held the true-blue borough of Cheltenham, but with a drop in their majority from 9,000 to 5,000. The result caused no missed heartbeat to Wilson, or to Sir Alec Douglas-Home, who was watching the program in No. 10 Downing Street, accompanied only by his wife, two daughters and the faithful lieutenant, Lord Oakshott. Both leaders were waiting for the result from Billericay, an immense Essex constituency of new housing estates and middle-income suburbanites. The Labour Party had hoped to win this seat, but at 10:30, when after a recount the result came out, the Tories were shown to have held it by a comfortable 1,592 votes. It was an anxious moment for Wilson. As Marcia Williams said later on in the evening, "We didn't know whether we were at Hyannisport or Los Angeles." There was good news from the Lancashire cotton town of Accrington, where Labour's Harry Hynd easily held off the challenge of Victor Montagu, the former Earl of Sandwich. There was still better news from the Central London constituency of Holborn and St. Pancras, where the newspaper journalist, Lena Jeger, who had lost the seat at the previous election, had her revenge on Geoffrey Johnson Smith, the Conservative TV interviewer. At this point Wilson was persuaded to leave the television set and to drive the six miles to Huyton High School in his constituency, where his own result was due to be announced at about midnight.

Wilson, his wife and John Harris climbed into their hired Austin Princess at 10:50. They carried with them a portable radio, and on the trip they heard the first real news of a Labour breakthrough, with a succession of victories gained in Liverpool, Bolton, Bradford and both the Stockport seats, which had been Tory even in 1945. The driver, Tony Field, was so engrossed in the results that he took a wrong turning and was held up a further ten minutes on his way to the school, where a huge crowd of Labour supporters, journalists and nearly berserk children had gathered to greet their leader.

He arrived at 11:50, looking tense and with all his com-
posure gone, to fight his way through a hysterical crowd that
had already come to believe in a Labour landslide. Even the
policemen cheered as Wilson was swallowed up in the throng
outside the glass-and-cement contemporary-styled school. "Is
my wife there?" he shouted in the confusion, and was pushed
along through a corridor and into the main hall where the
count was in progress.

At eight minutes to midnight the shock news came through
that Patrick Gordon Walker, Labour's "shadow" Foreign
Secretary, had lost his seat at Smethwick to a Conservative
who had campaigned principally on the issue of colored immigration. As the news was given him Wilson went white.
"God damn Smethwick," somebody shouted. A distraught
Marcia Williams, who had shortly before patted Dr. Balogh's
cheek at the news of a victory, burst into tears. Balogh himself,
who was still cheering a previous Labour gain, was misunderstood by some to be cheering Walker's defeat. "You bloody,
bloody fool," yelled Harris at Balogh, but their argument
was drowned by a new roar of excitement from the count,
where a huge, mostly Labour crowd watched the mounting
mound of ballot papers on the trestle tables.

Suddenly, at 11:58, Wilson seemed to lose all control of his
excitement. Waving both arms, he started to stagger and trot
around the hall like a red Indian warrior working himself up
for the next massacre. A girl photographer slapped his arm
in jubilation and Wilson clutched his hands, boxer-fashion,
above his head. At four minutes past midnight a suddenly
cheerful Harris went over to Wilson, clapped a hand over his
own mouth and burst into giggles. At six minutes past midnight the Clerk to the Council of Huyton stood up to read
the results. Pandemonium. The adored local hero, Wilson,
had trebled his majority and had beaten his Tory opponent
by nearly twenty thousand votes. Still dazed, and in front of
the TV spotlights because the scene was being broadcast live

on the networks, Harold Wilson thanked his party workers and agent, promised to work for the constituency and, at 12:15, gave two hearty kisses to his wife, the second of which was for the benefit of the press photographers who had not been quick enough to catch the first. Throughout the evening Mary Wilson had looked glowing and beautiful with excitement. She clutched the giant toy panda, Victor, which had been given to her at the eve-of-poll rally in Liverpool. "This is the Labour victory!" exclaimed Balogh, pointing in ecstasy to the Labour leader, "and that is the man who won—the man with the intellectual quality and emotional fervor to capture the country."

There was neither clapping nor kissing at 10 Downing Street. Sir Alec watched the results with the same air of aloof distaste that had helped to make them inevitable. He was visited once during the evening by Lord Blakenham and made it clear that he would not issue any statement until the result was certain. The Prime Minister went to bed before midnight. The same mood of reserve had spread to Conservative Central Office. Their mood was downcast but discreet. Even the Smethwick result was a cause of embarrassment rather than jubilation. The reaction of Lord Poole was particularly notable. He was watching the news on television at a party at the Savoy Hotel given by Lady Pamela Berry, the society hostess and wife of the proprietor of the *Daily Telegraph*. When the Smethwick result was announced Lord Poole asked for his coat and walked out of the party—and out of political life.

Other key figures in the campaign watched the results in a less tragic mood. Reginald Maudling had been at the same party. He likes parties, and until he left on Thursday night he had enjoyed himself. He had had a "mad conversation" with Noel Coward and was pleased with the Billericay result, meaning that even if Labour did win it would not be by a landslide. Later that evening he announced, in mock sergeant-major tones, that it was time for him to go up to the "drill 'all" in Barnet, his north-London suburban constituency. As the Labour gains came in he sat impassive and smiling. Then, still smiling and still impassive, he heard his own election result, a majority cut to 8,513. "We're a Conservative country," he said in a typically cryptic manner, "that votes Labour from time to time."

There was nothing impassive about Quintin Hogg, who heard the early results in Marylebone Town Hall, where he was watching his count. The arthritis in his old ankle injury had been "playing up a bit," but the pain could not dampen this one fiery character of the whole campaign. "This is the most casual count of anywhere I've ever seen," he murmured as he paced up and down the Edwardian corridor. "That's why I'm keeping an eye on the tellers." He also kept his eye on a cluster of Liberal supporters with a transistor set. "Any news for me?" he would ask them on hearing of some new Tory setback, and then would add, "We expected that, of course," or "Not very significant, don't you think?" Of one Labour M.P. he said: "I detest the man. He's nothing but an out-and-out Communist. He's the real enemy." And of a Liberal candidate he commented: "Ah well, concern with sewage pays." He did not look pleased with the Smethwick result—merely raised his eyebrows and walked off. His change of mood was mercurial. At one point he broke into song. "There's four-and-twenty piperrrrrs." Then he added, "You must forgive me. At this stage I'm incurably frivolous." In a car driving to the BBC after his own victory had been declared he became rather melancholy. "I hate elections. People think that I love them, but I don't. I hate them. One is always afraid that ultimately they will be decided by irrelevancies. You can't win with the press; they complain that the campaign has not brought out the main issues. As soon as bad heckling or my Profumo retort—a trivial thing, and quite justified—as soon as these occur, who are the first to blow up

but the press? You can't win. . . . I never wanted to go into
politics. I wanted to be a judge. I wanted to add my few
bricks to the Common Law of England." He had already conceded the party's defeat. "People simply thought that thirteen
years was long enough . . . the rational arguments were all
for us, but all one could do was to batter people, cudgel them
over the head with arguments, anything to make them begin
to sit up and consider the choice in rational terms. That was
all I was attempting. I tried to wake people up a bit. I think
I succeeded, don't you?"

The other great firebrand of British politics spent a most
calm election night. After leaving the count at Derby at
1 A.M. George Brown stepped into his chauffeur-driven Daimler and went to New Hall, near Burton-on-Trent, where he
and his family watched television in the tiny parlor of his
friend the vicar. "This gathering," he explained, "is as traditional as Christmas." He felt no particular excitement; he
claimed he hadn't in 1945 either. "I'm not in it for that—I'm
a trade-union man."

The Liberal leader, Joe Grimond, watched the results in
a committee room of the party headquarters, a dingy gray-
stone building across Victoria Street from the Army and Navy
Stores. Occasionally he munched pieces of a green-iced cake
which had been given to him by the Liberal candidate for
Oldbury and Halesowen, whose mother is London's most
fashionable confectioner and baker. The cake had been made
for his birthday on July 29 and had been kept in the Liberal
Whips' office from then until October 15. He remained
throughout the night as calm and cool as Gladstone, whose
portrait looked down at him from the wall above the mantel-
piece. His testy but able colleague, Frank Byers, who had
masterminded the Liberal campaign with great success, was
sufficiently worried by the results to get cross with a reporter.
"You should have done your homework before you got here,"
he snapped. The surprise Liberal gains were not to come until

the following afternoon. This night was punctuated with dashed hopes and falling spirits. The seats at Bolton and Huddersfield fell, and, although Orpington was held, the results in other commuter areas like Finchley had been disappointing. At 1:30 A.M. a quiet and wistful Grimond left for his home in Kew with a terse farewell: "Labour's in. I'm going to bed."

The atmosphere at Transport House was more exuberant. At the prompting of its publicity group the Labour Party had brightened the normally drab Transport Hall by screening off the Doric pillars and faded pre-Raphaelite frescoes. Three television cameras and five sets had been installed, together with boards to mark up the gains and losses of the parties. The vast posters behind the platform had been changed so that the words "When Labour Wins" would not prove painful in the event of Labour losing. Labour leaders like Michael Stewart and Ray Gunter, both of whom had Central London constituencies, arrived during the evening to be interviewed by television commentators who were also present in force. A whole committee room on the third floor had been set up with TV sets and a cold buffet for any member of the National Executive to use if he was in the building. During the whole evening two men made gaffes in front of the TV cameras. The first was the general secretary, Len Williams, who predicted bluntly that Labour would win a thirty-seat majority in the next Parliament. Later that evening the Bishop of Southwark, Dr. Mervyn Stockwood, a long-standing Socialist, told the television viewers that the electors of Smethwick would some day have to meet their Maker, and He would no doubt hold them accountable for their actions.

In Huyton itself Wilson made no such rash statements. Soon after he had heard his own result he went to face the TV cameras which had been set up in one of the small school offices opposite the hall. "I feel moderately happy with the result" was all he would say. When asked if he felt like a

Prime Minister Wilson made what many considered to be the best joke of the whole campaign by replying, "Quite frankly, I feel like a drink." Once or twice he suited the deed to the wish, although he was careful not to be seen doing so on television. The faithful Alf Richman, a Labour journalist and a trusted henchman of Wilson, used his body to screen the sipping party leader from the cameras. At about 12:40 Lord Attlee appeared on television to explain why in 1951 he had resigned with a majority of six. Wilson turned away and said, "It was down to four when G. S. Woods died." The mood in the immediate Wilson entourage was far less exultant than in the crowd outside. At one point, just before leaving the school, a party worker dashed in to say that the Orpington result was about to come in.* More than a dozen people in the TV room paused, in silence, to hear the result. Suddenly Mrs. Wilson exclaimed, "Do you know where my coat is?"

It was the same at the Huyton Labour Club when Wilson looked in to greet his constituency workers. Scores of flushed men and women, clutching their pints of beer, gave him a rapturous victory welcome. "We're thrilled to bits," said the introductory speaker, while from the floor, in true Liverpudlian joy, came a more homely welcome to Harold: "You luvly sod!" But Wilson, holding a half pint of beer, looked preoccupied even while singing the victory songs. When he arrived back at the Adelphi Hotel at 1:33 he had further reason to worry. The Midland results showed only a bare swing to Labour, and even in a few places like Rugby a swing away from Labour. Although the party had won some unexpected seats, it was no longer sure of all the safer marginals. He went back to his suite to discover a somewhat premature magnum of champagne presented by the management, and brooded in front of the television set. It was not until 3:10 A.M. that he plucked up courage to tell Michael Pentreath,

* The Liberals held off the Tory challenge, their 1962 by-election hero, Eric Lubbock, holding onto the seat by a comfortable 3,072 votes.

the deputy press officer, "We're going—the 8:15 train." This meant he was banking on victory. As Pentreath telephoned to a tired but obliging official of British Railways to confirm the reserved compartment, Wilson went upstairs to the press champagne party held in the room of Peter Jenkins, the *Guardian* reporter. Even the holding of this party was a confession of faith in a Labour victory. The organizers had ordered that the champagne should not be brought or opened until it was clear that Labour would win. He lay on a bed, drinking little, during the party until the Gravesend result —a crucial Labour gain—at 4:15, then went back to his room too tired and confused to analyze the final outcome.

At 6:45 next morning Wilson awoke, exhausted and worried, to the big day of his life. He bathed and shaved with his usual meticulous care and breakfasted on black coffee. Just before 8 A.M. he left by car to cover the few hundred yards to Liverpool (Lime Street) station, where a small crowd had gathered on the platform, and a mysterious bag-piper, who had been present the previous evening, arrived once more to greet Wilson with "Highland Laddie." The train whistles screamed, the pipes screeched and railwaymen yelled "Good old Harold" while Wilson himself, conspicuous in the famous Gannex macintosh, waved feebly about him. Beside him, Mary, in a red hat, still hugged Victor, the toy panda.

The Wilson party got into its special compartment: Harold, Herbert, Mary, John Harris, John Allen and Marcia Williams. With one hour to wait until any further results could come through, they settled down to breakfast. What did Wilson eat? The press officer, John Harris, had already acquired the Salinger touch and therefore knew the answer: sausages, bacon and sauté potatoes. With H.P. sauce.

Although Wilson had resolved to sweat out the long wait in silence, he soon became impatient to try and guess where he stood. Incredibly none of the party entourage was sure of the actual overnight figures, even though Wilson himself had stayed up until 4:15. Several journalists and TV men on the train had transistor sets, but these did not work while the train was moving. When it stopped the radio programs were giving music rather than news. In desperation, Wilson dispatched Allen to ask all the journalists if anybody knew the exact overnight score. At last somebody came up with some more or less accurate figures according to regions. It was now, about 10:30, that Wilson got to work with his slide rule, which produced the gloomy prophecy of defeat. Even the news heard at Nuneaton station that Labour had won its first-ever seat in Sussex, the Kemptown division of Brighton, did not cheer the Labour group.

At 11:21 A.M. the train stopped at Bletchley, where a group of some twenty railway workers had assembled opposite Wilson's compartment to cheer. He went to the window and gave them a weak smile, for at this stage his morale was low. Even his calm temper was getting frayed. At 11:49 he still had no comment to make on the results, but he kept his promise to go through to the restaurant car to pose for newspaper photographers. The carriage was crammed with journalists as a frowning Wilson took his seat accompanied by his wife. Would Mrs. Wilson mind putting the panda Victor to one side? asked a photographer. She politely obliged. But Wilson snapped when another photographer asked him to order a drink: "I'm not a performing seal. I've made it quite clear that I'm not going to be photographed eating or drinking." The two police officers and a policewoman who had joined the train at Bletchley moved forward among the journalists. At this point Wilson noticed and did not like a German TV team who had approached with their camera. "This is for press photographers only," he said. The policemen tapped the two Germans on the shoulder and asked them to withdraw. The Germans at first refused, then lost their tempers. "*Armes* England!" one of them cried, then, just to make sure that nobody missed the point, added "Poor England!" The policewoman smiled. "They'll be calling us *Schweinhund* next," she said. At 11:56, as the train went past Watford, Wilson called Marcia Williams to discuss the arrangements for getting from Euston to Transport House in Westminster.

A crowd of about two hundred people was waiting at Euston station to greet Wilson. It included the massive, impassive Len Williams, whose confident boast during the night of a thirty-seat victory had been so sadly overtaken by events. By 12:25, when the train arrived in London, it was not even clear that Labour would get a majority. Certainly Wilson refused to make any statement to the TV teams who had gathered to meet him. With a bleak smile he waved to the crowd of supporters and then got into the car. By 12:45 he was back at Transport House, where he went straight to a press conference in the Labour Hall. "It's still too early to comment on the result," he announced. At 12:52 he remarked rather ruefully to a journalist: "It's getting more like the Kennedy story all along. We'll get the result from Cook County* soon." Although the hundred and fifty members of the Transport House staff were still exultant, the top Labour men had begun to look disturbed. The portly Ray Gunter even forgot to join in "For He's a Jolly Good Fellow" until he was nudged in the ribs by Len Williams. The T & GWU leader Frank Cousins was frowning, while Anthony Greenwood, wearing his usual matinee idol's smile, took a haughty view of the public jubilation. "Do you hear that, Tony?" said an excited colleague. "We've won southeast Derbyshire. Trevor Park is in by 873 votes." "Yes," said Greenwood, "I went up to speak for him."

By late morning Sir Alec was still Prime Minister and indeed still hard at the job. There were still arrangements to be made for the transition next week of Northern Rhodesia into the independent state of Zambia. The Lord Chancellor,

* This was the district of Illinois whose vote for Kennedy in 1960 swung the state to him.

Lord Dilhorne, and the Commonwealth Secretary, Duncan
Sandys, came over to 10 Downing Street to discuss the matter and stayed on for a pre-lunch drink. By the end of lunch
it must have been clear to Home that he had lost the election.
Although he and Blakenham were determined not to concede
defeat until Labour had an absolute majority over both the
other parties, it had grown pretty plain that this was inevitable. On TV, Hogg was explaining why the Labour Party had
won: "I thought it would be very difficult from 1961 onwards.
When you've been in that long, you've got to bludgeon people
into voting for you. They don't want to." At 2:45 the news
came through that Labour, after a recount, had won Meriden,
the last crucial outstanding marginal constituency, and now
were only one seat away from an absolute majority. But at
Conservative Central Office, Lord Blakenham was adamant.
Would he concede? "Absolutely not. I know I've been accused
of sulking, but this has been an absolutely ding-dong battle."
Pathetically he was still hoping that some unexpected Tory
dongs would match the implacable dings of the Socialists. At
2:48 the Labour Party held the Welsh seat of Brecon and
Radnor and had reached the magic figure of 315—enough,
allowing for the speaker to give it an over-all majority of
one in the new Parliament. But even then Lord Blakenham
would not accept the news. He refused to take the TV interviewer's word that the game was up.

There was still no admission from Home. The TV cameras
were trained on 10 Downing Street. The commentators kept
repeating "any moment now," but there was no stir behind
those Georgian windows. At 2:25 a laundry van arrived and
a boy dumped two hampers of Home clothes inside the door.
At 2:45 came a dustcart and at 3:10 three telegrams.* Not
until 3:23, nearly three quarters of an hour after Labour won
power, did Sir Alec, in tails and a top hat, emerge from the

* One of these telegrams, insolently, was addressed to Harold Wilson.

front door of his home for the past year. His last public remarks as Prime Minister were a characteristic and fatuous
glimpse of the obvious: "I'm going to see the Queen." The
commentator remarked rather unkindly: "This is the last
time we shall be referring to Sir Alec Douglas-Home as Prime
Minister."

Since 12:50 Wilson had sat in or paced around Len Williams's room watching the last results coming through on
television. He went out only to greet Lord Attlee, the last
Labour Premier and a loyal friend of Wilson. Shortly after
3 P.M. the Transport House staff laid out a morning coat,
black jacket, striped trousers and wine-colored braces in
Room 113 of Transport House, which had been set aside for
Wilson to change in. It was typical of Transport House that
every time anyone wanted to open the door of this room, it
was necessary to roll back the carpet. At 3:20, just before
Home left 10 Downing Street, Wilson started to change, beginning by announcing, "I won't wear the morning coat"
and choosing the black jacket instead. At this stage, he was
dazed and almost green with excitement. He kept pacing
about the room, uttering almost incoherent phrases. At 3:25,
two detectives arrived who were to accompany the new Prime
Minister. But still no call came from the Palace—only from
Downing Street, to inquire whether Chequers could be made
available to the outgoing Premier and his wife for the weekend. Just before 3:30, Sir Alec saw the Queen. Another five
minutes went by, then ten. Could it be possible that he was
after all insisting on carrying on until the Conservative Government had been formally beaten in the new Parliament?
Five more minutes . . . and then at 3:50 the telephone rang,
not in the crowded general secretary's room but in the "admin. room" next door. A Miss Phyllis Burt took the call and
announced that the Palace was speaking. Immediately Wilson hurried to take the call in a secretary's side office. He
spent nearly five minutes talking, and once again the rumor

spread that something had gone wrong. After thirteen years in opposition, the Labour Party had almost lost belief in the possibility of power. But it was all right. In a few moments Wilson was back in the "admin. room" gleefully repeating to himself over and over again the phrase with which the Queen's Private Secretary had opened the conversation. "Would it," Sir Michael Adeane had inquired, "be convenient for you to come round and see Her Majesty?" "Convenient"—Wilson savored the word and enjoyed it. What else did they think he had been aiming at ever since as a small boy of eight he had first stood on the steps of 10 Downing Street to be photographed by his father? Now, forty years later, he had made it.

Outside Transport House a crowd had gathered. They too had been worried by the delay. "Home's asked to form a dictatorship," said one wag. "Does Harold know the Queen well?" somebody asked. "Of course," said his friend. "He used to see her a lot in his Board of Trade days when he went to film premières." A big black Daimler arrived and was parked opposite the east entrance of Transport House. This was the official car from the Palace and a buzz of curiosity went through the crowd. Suddenly there was a faint cheer from the other side of Smith Square. The crowd turned to see Sir Alec Douglas-Home arrive at Conservative Central Office. The Labour Supporters gave him a few, not unfriendly, boos and some of them rushed across to see the recent Prime Minister in defeat. A hale, elderly man, Herbert Wilson, was leaning against a red Rover car. "Well, we've done it at last!" he shouted to friends, then started to tell a taxi driver all about Harold's childhood.

At 3:58 Harold and Mary Wilson, she in her hound's-tooth suit, appeared on the steps of Transport House. Between them, and squeezed by the crowd behind, stood the stocky, swarthy deputy leader George Brown, who had once hoped that this might be his, and not Wilson's, great day. "Good old Harold," the crowd yelled as Mr. and Mrs. Wilson, with Robin, their twenty-year-old son, stepped into the Daimler. At the same time, as so often in moments of high history, the ludicrous intervened. An elderly and eccentric man rushed forward and bellowed, "What about Manchester? What about Manchester, then?" Even Harold Wilson, the master of dealing with hecklers and House of Commons interrupters, could hardly have answered a question as tough as that. He and Mary, with Robin squashed between, leaned back in the thick cushions and started the long-awaited journey to see the Queen. It was typical of Wilson, and rather touching, that he should have chosen to make this moment of jubilation a family affair.

While Wilson was at the Palace, the center of public interest moved to 10 Downing Street. Everyone in the country knew the famous photograph of Harold Wilson, aged eight, standing cheekily on the steps. They were eager, or certainly fascinated, to see him standing there as a grown politician. Sure enough, at 4:20 P.M. a Daimler drew up at Number 10. But it was not Wilson at all—only Home come back to finish his packing. And Home was still inside when at 4:30 precisely Wilson arrived at his new home. He made a little speech to the TV cameras—"we are facing great problems but there is nothing we cannot do"—and stepped inside.

Sir Alec and Wilson never met during their forty-seven minutes of joint tenure. "I was upstairs clearing up," Sir Alec explained afterward. He and his wife, both wearing tweed suits, left by the back entrance at 5:17. It was a bad afternoon for Home and he kept an admirably stiff upper lip. His farewell interview on TV at Central Office was just as might have been expected. He was gallant and graceful as any earlier earl on the scaffold. Moreover, he made one bad slip of the tongue and the whole final interview had to be filmed again. Next door at Number 11, Reginald Maudling was saying farewell to a home where he had lived twice as long as Home in Number 10. "I think this country has a sense of history," he mused. "I shall have to look for a job and make some money. It's exciting. It won't be such hard work and I'll probably be better paid." Then, looking out onto the russet trees and Horse Guards Parade, he said, "I'll miss the view more than anything." There was a sound of cheering outside, and Maudling, like the chorus of some historical play, said, "Loud cheers." Seeing out the reporter, he stopped five feet away from the door. "You don't mind if I don't come to the door?" he said, suddenly shy of publicity in this moment of sadness.

There was no hint of sadness in Number 10, least of all from Wilson's father, Herbert, gazing around with the triumphant, proprietary air of a man who has seen a dream come true. The new tenant was quickly regaining his nerve and his natural sprightliness as he came at last to a realization of power. He chatted away, dictated speeches, tried out the new scrambler telephone and at one point in the evening actually ran downstairs to take a congratulatory message from President Johnson. For others the grave, grandiloquent aphorisms about taking on the highest responsibilities in the realm. The sardonic Yorkshireman, Harold Wilson, looked around him, then said to a friend with a grin: "Nice place we've got here."

16. The Man Who Made It

"I think I was born with politics in me;
I think the influence of friendly teachers and others
has been considerable, but merely in guiding me in
the direction I wanted to go anyway."

HAROLD WILSON *in an interview in the* Listener, *October 29, 1964*

THE new Prime Minister is a plump, medium-tall, gray-haired man with a scar on his left temple and jagged front teeth which make it awkward for him to smile. He is short-sighted but does not wear spectacles except in a motorcar. As a result his blue eyes have an intense stare, which enemies call cold, and his shoulders have become hunched from the effort of peering before him. A former long-distance runner for Oxford University, he still has an athlete's typically slow heartbeat and calm metabolism. He sleeps well and long and as often as possible. He very seldom loses his temper even when most angry. His tastes are simple rather than austere. He dislikes fresh salmon, rich sauces and champagne but has to fight back a weakness for sausages, lamb chops and chocolate. He drinks very little alcohol except for a lager at meals and a glass of brandy to soothe his nerves before an important ordeal such as a big TV broadcast.

Such is the physical Wilson. His personality is either totally simple or totally subtle, but even his best friends cannot decide which. Certainly he is a very different man from his public reputation. For one thing, the public does not very much like him, but those who know him do. He has the basic likable quality, very rare in famous politicians, of at least seeming to take an interest in other people besides himself. From the start he remembers people's names and, later on, a great many more things about them. Much as he likes to talk, he will also listen with interest and sometimes sympathy. He is kind, almost certainly too kind, with his staff. He can be ruthless and rude when necessary to a parliamentary colleague, but he would take great pains not to slight or wound a junior typist, researcher or press officer.

In private life Wilson is kind and warmhearted. He spends as much of his time as possible with his wife and two sons. After the Scarborough conference in 1963 his very first act was to drive his son Robin to start the new term at Oxford, and he used to start the day by driving his other son, Giles, to school in Hampstead. Most politicians would parade such little acts of fatherly care, but Wilson has always shied away from any attempt to exploit his family. He likes to retreat into private life as into a cave, and none of his close friends today are politicians. The two who were died soon after he was chosen leader of the party. Typically, he gave up countless hours to comfort the families of these two men. Typically, he took care that no word of his kindness was reported in the newspapers.

He is cool and nerveless but also shy. For his first ten years in politics he scarcely ever revealed his wit and brilliance simply because he feared that they might not pass the mark. Lacking confidence, he would try to impress by sheer knowledge and reasoning and by the rather irritating displays of memory about dates and figures. He was particularly silent and diffident in the presence of Bevan, whom he admired, but not without qualifications. At the time of the 1951 walk-out from the Government, Dalton and other ministers referred to Wilson as "Nye's little dog." It was not until the late Fifties that he began to show off his wit and realized that it was good. There had always been a streak of diffidence in him, a North Country fear of "smart," "sophisticated" people, of the fatuous and supercilious fops that he first met at Oxford. For all his fondness for big talk, he has no small talk and therefore dislikes cocktail parties. He is extremely shy of letting people see his emotions. While most politicians wear their ideals on their sleeves, he hates to discuss his faith in the Labour Party with strangers. His faith, like his family, belongs to his private life.

Partly because Wilson does not boast of his principles, there are many people who think that he has none. Certainly he is no idealogue. Abstract ideas like Socialism or the Working Class mean little to him. Even in Oxford, during the Red Thirties, he never felt drawn toward communism because of his Liberal-Labor background and the "public-school Marxists" he met. His beliefs are a mixture of Fabianism, nonconformity, the Boy Scouts code and what might be called Northernism. Most of his speeches sound like the perorations of Lancashire Liberals in the early part of the last century. Emotionally, he is not so much *for* the oppressed workers as *against* the fitted aristocracy of the south. He is *for* factories and against great landed estates. He is against unearned wealth, but he believes that management, just as much as the men, are entitled to benefit from hard work. He is not a visionary Socialist like Morris, Owen, Bevan or, in his way, Gaitskell. Although genuinely concerned about old-age pensioners, widows or crippled ex-miners, Wilson does not believe that socialism will mean the end of sorrow. He wants to improve the machinery of government, not throw it away and get another. Even when he seems to act like a doctrinaire—as for instance his putting steel nationalization into the first year's legislation—he is generally acting for some pragmatic reason. In the case of steel, he wanted to rally his own party by moving straight to the attack. As a pragmatist who wants power, Wilson is prapared to compromise when the need comes. There is probably only one principle that he would not compromise even at the risk of defeat. This is the question of racial equality, about which he feels with almost fanatic violence. In the autumn of 1963 he led the small minority within the "shadow" cabinet who fought successfully to prevent Labour capitulating entirely to the Government's Commonwealth Immigration Act. If this lost the Labour Party Smethwick, then, in Wilson's view, so much the worse for Smethwick. On almost every political issue Wilson belongs to the moderate, hedging, pragmatic side of the Labour Party. On the question of race he is one of its dozen extremists.

Wilson does not like to be called an intellectual, and in the English sense of the word he is certainly not one. The Labour Party intellectual of caricature is a public-school man in reaction against his environment. He is passionate against militarism, sport, the Empire, religion and public schools. In the old Thirties joke "he gets his politics from Moscow, his cooking from Paris and his morals from Port Said." By nature Wilson has nothing in common with men such as these; the left-wing intelligentsia, in turn, has long since deserted the Labour Party for CND or apathy. Nothing better illustrates Wilson's variance with the "intellectuals" than his attitude to foreign countries. The left-wing intellectuals, reared on hatred of Rudyard Kipling, have always deprecated king-and-country patriotism. They used to dislike the Empire and now deprecate Britain's role in the world. But Wilson is patriotic almost to the point of chauvinism. His childhood hero worship of Lord Baden-Powell still shines through his concern for the Commonwealth and his earnest talk of Britain's role and purpose in the world.

There is a strong streak of belligerence in Wilson. His speeches and conversation are full of fighting metaphors such as "strong cutting edge" "storming the frontiers" and the metaphoric "military operations" to which Hogg took exception. He will talk about "having so-and-so's guts" or "I'll cut him about the face a bit." It was unfortunate that when he volunteered in September 1939 he was sent into the Civil Service instead of the Army. He would have made a superb soldier. He has a cool head, an aggressive spirit, luck, infinite calculation and a flair for seizing opportunity. Like another Prime Minister, Winston Churchill, he is fascinated by the history of the American Civil War. Like Churchill, too, he takes an almost obsessional pride in the British Navy.

The man who likes "the *Observer Colour Magazine* but the *Sunday Times* newspaper" is an unashamed middle-brow. He likes the novels of Thomas Armstrong—mostly trouble-at-mill Yorkshire sagas—and he has read Sayers' *The Nine Tailors* between fifteen and twenty times, or neck and neck with the number of times he has seen the ballet *Swan Lake*. He likes *Coronation Street, Steptoe and Son* and film comedies. He thinks Margaret Rutherford is "the greatest British actress on stage or screen" and does not like painting at all. While Macmillan and Home took their holidays fishing or shooting in Scotland and Gaitskell traveled to Yugoslavia or Italy, the Wilson family, year after year, go to the Scilly Isles. Here Wilson climbs in the hills, plays golf or potters around in boats. To the intellectuals of the Labour Party it is an annual cause of distaste that the conferences have to be held in places like Scarborough or Blackpool. But Wilson and the mass of the delegates actually likes both Scarborough and Blackpool. In his likes, dislikes and attitudes, he is so representative of the statistical average man that any good advertising agency would pay a fat fee for his depth interview.

Enemies label him as a Puritan. Certainly he admired Stafford Cripps and was brought up in a devout Congregationalist home and community. Whatever his actual religious views, there is no doubt of his highly moral approach to life. He is shocked by waste—of money, talents or even time. He is psychologically averse to gambling, drunkenness or crime. Although he sometimes makes mildly daring jokes, he frowns on the use of four-letter words or really obscene stories. During the whole Profumo argument he confined his attack to the question of security, but there is no doubt that he felt a strong distaste for the whole seamy world of Ward, Ivanov and Keeler. This streak of prudery, as well as a binding sense of family loyalty, made all the more hurtful the slanderous fabrications about his private life that were whispered about during election year.

If Wilson has a prudish streak, he is nevertheless no prig. Few politicians have so much capacity to laugh at themselves. The famous displays of memory—"You're quite right. I made that point to Kosygin June 12, 1963"—are said in a mocking way. He is always prepared to make fun of his own identification with Roosevelt and Kennedy, his own chopped logic, his own fake indignation.

"I'm not a Kennedy, you see," he once told a reporter. "I am a Johnson. I fly by the seat of my pants." It is a sound piece of self-analysis. He once described how he had dealt with a minor revolt from the left wing of the Labour Party after he had offered to have secret talks with Home on defense. "Hugh [Gaitskell] would have held a meeting of the Parliamentary Party and the whole subject would have been thrashed out and the minority would have been defeated in a vote. I let it be known that if any of them [the rebels] wanted to talk about it they could come and see me privately." In private, of course, he was able to talk them around with a mixture of reason, cajolery and soft soap. Here he is very like Johnson, while Gaitskell was more like Kennedy. The former President had almost permanent trouble with his own party. The present one has almost none.

Sometimes Wilson's cleverness can decline into mere cunning. On January 31, 1963, the day of the memorial service for the late Hugh Gaitskell, the House of Commons was debating defense and particularly the recent Nassau agreement with the United States. The then Prime Minister, Harold Macmillan, who had negotiated the acquisition of Polaris, was putting the main argument for the Government.

In order to back up his case for Britain's independent nuclear deterrent, he quoted an extract from a speech made by Hugh Gaitskell in 1960. The extract he read was a clear and cogent argument for Britain to have her own nuclear weapons in case she fell out with America and was, at the same time, threatened by Russia. Rather proudly and smugly, Macmillan read out the passage, which not only supported his own case but reminded the Labour Party of the old divisions. (The Conservatives hoped that Brown rather than Wilson would take on the leadership from Gaitskell.) Suddenly Wilson leaped to his feet: "I thought that the Prime Minister would give that quotation," he said. "We all remember the speech very well, on March 1, 1960. The right honorable gentleman should, however, be fair. He should point out that at that time Hugh Gaitskell was putting the argument on both sides, for and against the nuclear case. This was part of his fair, balanced argument as he saw it for an independent deterrent. He also put the case against." Here he paused, still on his feet, while Macmillan hemmed and hawed in some embarrassment. Clearly the Gaitskell extract had been handed to him, and he could not remember its exact context. After a short pause Wilson threw in his second attack, aiming to play on Labour grief at the thought of the dead leader: "I must say that the Prime Minister's choice of a quotation is very repugnant to some of us."

In spite of protests from the Government benches, Wilson had made his point. He had made Macmillan look callous. He had diverted attention from his own previous quarrel with Gaitskell about defense to his present championship of the dead leader's memory. After the debate, a journalist said to Wilson, "But Gaitskell wasn't giving both sides of the question. It was a perfectly fair quotation." At this Wilson permitted himself a smile: "I knew that, but I also knew that Macmillan wouldn't be sure. That gave me the chance to make the second point, about referring to Hugh on the

day of the memorial service. I had to show that what he'd
said was false first—and then knock him out by saying it was
repugnant too. It wouldn't have worked the other way
around." Even the details of this tiny incident are characteristic of the man. "I thought the Prime Minister would
give that quotation. We all remember that speech very well,
on March 1, 1960." In all probability nine tenths of the
House had forgotten the speech altogether. In all probability
Wilson himself did not remember much more of it than the
date. But the use of the date proved devastating to Macmillan.

It is also typical of Wilson that he should have claimed
afterward to have planned the sequence of his attack. He is
often credited with infinite care, with never saying a word
by accident. He himself likes to encourage this story. In fact,
more than most politicians, he shoots from the hip. His
weapon is as often the sten gun as the marksman's rifle.

In retrospect it is extraordinary that so vivid and complex
a man could ever have seemed dull. Yet Bevan spoke of him,
jokingly, as "all bloody facts and no vision," and another old
colleague called him "dull and devious—God, he's devious—
diligent and deliberate." This was the public image of Wilson when he took the leadership of the party. Yet in eighteen
months he had established himself as the most positive and
talked-about political figure in Britain. He had been helped
to some extent by poster campaign, the constant TV appearance and by his own zest for publicity. "I photographed him
once in his shirt and underpants while he was shaving," a
newspaperman recalled recently, "but later in the day he
said to me 'that was an Ernie Marples trick. Do me a favor
and destroy that picture.' When you ask him to do ridiculous
things he often puts his finger along the side of his nose and
says, 'Would Ernie Marples do that?' "

As his public image changed, so did the Tory attacks
change their target. In 1963 he was always portrayed as a

cold, sly, insincere intellectual. Toward the end of the general election they began to portray him as a dangerous firebrand. The *Sunday Telegraph* even compared him to Lloyd George. The cold, dull schemer suddenly reappeared as a magical orator and a dynamic radical. In fact the Anglo-Saxon Wilson is far removed in temperament from the Celtic Lloyd George. His favorite Prime Minister from the past is Sir Robert Peel, another hard-working, hard-thinking Northerner with a taste for plain living and economic reform. But the very comparison with Lloyd George shows the fantastic impact that Wilson had made on the British imagination.

Then why, after thirteen years of Conservative rule, could he manage to win by only four seats?

Politicians, like generals, have much less influence on campaigns than they like to admit. Just as Napoleon's invasion of Russia was beaten by General Winter, so was Wilson's bid for power very nearly frustrated by General Summer. The surveys and interviews will show no such thing. Nobody likes to admit to a questioner that his views on politics have been influenced by the weather. But anybody who was in Britain during June, July and August and in the balmy Indian summer which continued to polling day was aware of a general mood of well-being and relaxation, a psychological suntan after the holidays. The cloud of bitterness and disgust which had hung over 1963 had vanished. Gone were the scandalous stories, the satirical TV shows, the sense that Britain was now just a sick joke. When historians of the future come to write of this general election they should ignore the opinion polls and study the chart of noon temperatures on the Air Ministry roof. It is a fair guess that the weather cost Labour twenty seats.

There are four charges that can be made against Wilson's handling of the campaign. The first was his determination to do it the opposite way from Gaitskell, and above all to make big set speeches rather than whistle-stop tours. This was particularly odd, because Wilson is not nearly so good a set-piece orator as Gaitskell but much better in dealing with small outdoor meetings and hecklers.

The second was his decision to spend most of his time in London and to hold press conferences. Some colleagues believed that his time would have been better spent in visiting marginal seats like Reading or Eton and Slough. He got a good press, admittedly, but not because of the press conferences. Most of his answers to questions were rambling in-jokes or sarcastic witticisms that simply did not make news. The one outstanding exception was his disastrous intervention in the Hardy Spicer dispute. By the end of the campaign, most of the journalists were too bored even to ask questions.

The third charge follows on from the others. He is accused of fighting a one-man campaign. It was not just that he took the press conference each day but that he hogged too much TV time. This charge had some justification earlier in the year. The poster and advertising campaign of the Transport House publicists dwelt remorselessly on Wilson's face and personality and fully deserved the jibe of the "one-man band." In the actual campaign Wilson did try to share some of the limelight. He appeared in only one of the actual party political broadcasts, and Transport House did its best to publicize Brown, who indeed proved Labour's best campaign performer. But this was too late in the day. The public suspicion that Labour consisted of nobody but its leader was well and truly formed even before the campaign started. It was too late to revive these sapling popularities of the other Labour leaders. They had withered from lack of sun under the spreading shake of the leader.

The fourth charge is one of weak timing. In the last four days of the campaign Wilson was left with nothing more to say. Naturally he cannot be blamed for failing to pull a rabbit out of his hat. There was no rabbit to pull. But he

might perhaps have spaced out his effort so as to keep the
Labour Party on the top of the front page in the last few
days of the campaign. Ironically it was exactly in this respect
that Wilson's campaign was like Gaitskell's. He too had
sagged during the last few days and allowed the initiative
to be snatched by Macmillan's broadcast. Although Wilson's
broadcast on the final Monday was excellent, it was followed
by two days of inaction.

There is some weight to all these charges but not enough
to explain Labour's poor showing. Whatever his errors, Wilson had established himself in the public mind as the more
vigorous of the two big party leaders. More than half the
country, if the polls are to be believed, thought he would
make a better Prime Minister than Home. If the American
Constitution had been in force in Britain, Wilson would
almost certainly have defeated Home by a big majority. It
was not Wilson but his party that the public distrusted.

How far was Wilson to blame for the dim, rather old-
fashioned reputation of the Labour Party? He once said in
an interview that his three weaknesses were overworking,
being too frank with the press and a dislike of hurting
people's feelings. The first two did him no damage. The third
was very nearly his undoing. In the twenty-one months that
he was leader of the Opposition he made no real changes in
Transport House, the regional parties or the list of parliamentary candidates. In the first days after defeating Brown
he was anxious to avoid a quarrel with Brown's loyal supporters, and it was therefore diplomatic to avoid a drastic
shuffle of personnel. But he could have done so in the summer of 1963 or even as late as the summer of 1964. Instead
he confirmed dull men in their jobs and failed to search out
bright newcomers. Both the Parliamentary Labour Party and
Transport House were older, slower and less efficient than
their Tory counterparts. The public recognized this and remembered it on polling day. It is significant that the party

which talked so unendingly about technological advance has in its own headquarters at Transport House a telephone switchboard of such extreme age and ineptitude that it is scheduled to be sent to a science museum. The same applies to some of the human apparatus of the party.

Although Wilson had studied the Kennedy campaign, he never acquired a similar group of New Frontiersmen. There was no sign of a Sorensen or a Schlesinger or even a Salinger. An octogenarian father Herbert is no real substitute for a younger brother Bobby. Transport House staff men like John Harris, John Allen and even Len Williams all gave good advice in their way, but they could not provide that note of style and freshness which was so badly needed in Wilson's speeches and press statements.

It is curious to speculate whether Hugh Gaitskell would have done better. The Labour Party proportion of votes was only 3 per cent higher in 1964 than in 1959. In total numbers its vote was actually down. But although Gaitskell has been much praised by Tories and Liberals since his death, he was, when alive, never particularly popular. Although he was a better speaker than Wilson and much more capable of arousing emotion, he never came over in quite the same way as a strong leader. The same goes for George Brown, who, for all his great qualities, never inspired the same confidence. All the evidence shows that what Labour needed was not a new leader but a new party.

Would the result have gone differently with a different Conservative leader? The answer is almost certainly yes. In a way Home was a good choice to oppose Wilson just because he was so different. His apparent gentlemanly candor was a foil to Wilson's reputed cunning. He was strong on the issues of foreign affairs and defense, where Wilson was most vulnerable. He undoubtedly got a heavy vote from the women, who were captivated by his boyish charm and wistful, aristocratic shyness. The young ladies looked on him as a father, the old as a son, and a few, it was jokingly said, as a Prime Minister. And Home should be given credit for reuniting the Tory party after the miseries of 1963. Much of this can be attributed to events. The Government ran into a patch of luck. There were no spy scandals, errant ministers or catastrophic failures of policy such as the Common Market and Skybolt. The very approach of the general election was enough to still most of the Tory discontent. But Home, too, helped with his tactful and unassuming leadership.

Yet all Home's advantages had an obverse side. The amateurish charm often appeared just as incompetence. If he was strong on foreign affairs, he was weak on domestic issues. And it was these that interested the public. If he was popular with the women, he was disliked by the men, who respond more to forcefulness than to charm. It may be true that a cricketing crowd loves the amateur captain—but only if he is good. The amateur who never reaches double figures will be far more rudely savaged than any professional. Because Home and Wilson were so very dissimilar, the general election inevitably became a more than unusually personal combat. There is no doubt that Wilson won. In American terms he led his own ticket. And under an American Constitution, Britain would surely have gone into 1965 with a Labour President and a Conservative Congress.

Index

Abrams, Mark, 164, 166, 231
Adeane, Sir Michael, 112, 297
Aitken, Jonathan, 106
Aitken, Sir William, 106
Aldington, Lord, 81-82, 108
Allen, John, 228, 258, 263
Allen, Ros, 164-165
Amery, Julian, 89, 105, 106, 195
Anglo-American Skybolt project, 35
Argyll, Duke of, 76
Attlee, Clement, 17, 19, 36, 240-241, 291

Bacon, Alice, 149, 164
Balogh, Thomas, 21, 33, 219, 284
Barker, Sara, 282
Beaverbrook, Lord, 161
Benn, Anthony Wedgwood, 166
Bevan, Aneurin, 17, 36, 39
Bevin, Ernie, 19
Bevins, Reginald, 108
Birch, Nigel, 95, 101
Blackman, Honor, 233
Blakenham, Lord, 168-169, 279
Bligh, Timothy, 58
Bonham-Carter, Mark, 233
Bowden, Bert, 36
Bowden, Herbert, 15, 45, 137
Boyd-Carpenter, John, 90
Boyle, Sir Edward, 66, 88, 108
Bradley, Clive, 166, 258
Brandt, Willy, 49
Bray, Jeremy, 39

Brooke, Henry, 81, 88
Brown, George, 15-16, 18-19, 23-27, 49-50, 135-137, 203, 297, 311; defeated as Prime Minister, 28-42; reaction to election results, 289-290; speech at Lea, 205-208
Brown, Mrs. George, 215
Butler, R. A., 68-70, 85-89, 94, 172, 181; campaign for leadership, 96-97
Byers, Frank, 233, 289

Callaghan, James, 24-25, 28-35
Case for Conservatism, The (Hailsham), 93
Castle, Barbara, 27
Central African Federation, 118
Central Office (Conservatives), 168-170
Chamberlain, Neville, 117
Churchill, Randolph, 58, 102-103; Fight for the Tory Leadership, 103, 142
Churchill, Sir Winston, 54, 117, 126, 304
Clark, John, 39
Clark, Percy, 165, 218
Clark, William, 71
Cliffe, Harry, 53
Cobbald, Lord, 108, 110
Cohen, Lewis, 216
Collins, Norman, 271
Common Market, 13, 35
Conservative Party: relationship

Conservative Party (cont'd)
to Labour Party, 176-177; propaganda, 170-172; slogans for, 171; split in, 168-169
Corbett, Harry, 178
Cousins, Frank, 294
Cripps, Stafford, 304
Crosby, John, 136
Crosland, Anthony, 22-23
Crossman, Richard, 21-22, 29, 196-197
Cuba: crisis, 36; fleet of British buses to, 150-151

Day, Robin, 201
Deakin, Arthur, 19
Deedes, William, 57, 81
Denning, Lord, 75
Denning Inquiry, 65-66, 75-77
Derby Evening Telegraph, 26
Dew, Brenda, 207
Dewey, Thomas E., 139
Diamond, Jack, 23, 27, 29
Dilhorne, Lord, 98, 103, 295
Donnelly, Desmond, 23, 39, 46
Douglas-Home, Sir Alec, 90-95; in Belfast, 152; on BBC's "Election Forum," 201-202; career in Parliament, 116-118; farewell interview, 298; initial refusal to run, 101-102; introduced in House of Commons, 129-131; Kinross by-election, 127-128; as opponent to Wilson, 311-312; at Perthshire, 121-127; as Prime Minister, 116; the Queen's Commission, 113-115; reaction to election results, 285-287; speech at Birmingham, 243-244; speech at Bradford, 236-237; speech at Elstree (TV), 271-273; speech at

Leeds, 235-236; on television debates, 201; on 3% mortgage, 213; visit with Queen at Balmoral, 190-191; visit to Swansea, 146-148; visit to U.S., 149-151
Driberg, Tom, 27
Drury, Allen, 204

Ede, James Chuter, 38
Eden, Anthony, 118
Edgecombe, John, 56
Eisenhower, Dwight D., 193, 272
Election results, 286-299
Elizabeth, Queen, 79-115 passim; visit to Macmillan, 112-115
Erroll, Frederick, 88, 108, 110

Fairlie, Henry, 254
Fight for the Tory Leadership, The (Randolph Churchill), 103
Foot, Michael, 48
Forrester, Andrew, 124
Fraser, Sir Michael, 173, 272
Fraser, Sir Robert, 35
Fraser, Tom, 28

Gaitskell, Hugh, 8, 14-18, 305-306, 311; death of, 15-16
Galbraith, Thomas, 64
Gallup poll, 217, 252, 257
George, David Lloyd, 243, 308
Gilmour, Ian, 89, 105
Goldman, Peter, 92, 212, 216
Grayson, Victor, 52
Greater London Council, 157-159
Greenwood, Anthony, 39, 49
Griffiths, Eldon, 134, 152
Grimond, Jo, 199-200, 232-233, 289
Gunter, Roy, 290

Hackett, Maurice, 49
Hailsham, Viscount, *see* Hogg, Quintin
Hall, John, 71
Hardy Spicer strike, 217-218, 221, 224-225
Hare, John (Lord Blakenham), 168-169, 279
Harris, John, 23, 164, 238
Hayday, Fred, 23
Healey, Denis, 28, 46, 149
Heath, Edward, 68, 80-81
Hetherington, Alastair, 29
Hill, Herbert, 225, 226
Hobson, Sir John, 57
Hogg, Quintin McGarel (Viscount Hailsham), 85-86, 88-95; attack on the *Daily Mirror*, 240; campaign for Prime Minister, 102-106; *Case for Conservatism, The,* 93; speech at Birmingham, 194-195; speech at Plymouth, 237-238; reaction to election results, 288-289
Home, Lord, *see* Douglas-Home, Sir Alec
Howell, Dennis, 23
Howie, William, 129
Huddersfield, 51-54
Huntley, Chet, 259
Hutchinson, George, 212
Hutchinson, Harold, 153

Immigration Act, 197
Ivanov, Commander, 55-56

Jeger, Lena, 285
Jenkins, Jennifer, 23
Jenkins, Peter, 292
Jenkins, Roy, 23
Johnson, Lyndon B., 149, 150, 153, 214, 297, 305

Joseph, Sir Keith, 83
Junior Carlton Club, 105

Keeler, Christine, 55-59, 160
Kennedy, John F., 163, 305; assassination of, 133-136; visit to England, 67
Khrushchev, Nikita, 61-64, 77, 283
King-Lewis, Dr. Frederick, 83
Kingsley, David, 164

Labour Party, 8, 13-19; relationship to Conservative Party, 176-177; first press conference, 209-210; propaganda, 163-167, 170-171; slogan for, 165
Lambton, Lord, 71-74
Lancaster, Colonel, 101
Lawson, Nigel, 152, 212, 272
Lee, Fred, 36
Lewis, John, 56
Liberal Party, 8
Lloyd, Selwyn, 101, 106
London Underground Service strike, 269
Longford, Lord, 215

McKenzie, Robert, 216
Macleod, Iain, 57, 58, 65-66, 80-81, 84-85
Macmillan, Harold, 35, 277, 305; hospitalization of, 82-97; the Profumo Affair and, 57-58, 59, 64-65, 75; Queen Elizabeth's visit to, 112-115; resignation of, 112-115
Making of the President 1960, The (White), 7
Manchester Guardian, 29-30, 51

Marples, Ernest, 88
Maudling, Reginald, 70-74, 157, 212, 287-288, 298
Mellish, Robert, 13
Mikoyan, Anastas, 283
Millar, Duncan, 126
Morrison, Herbert, 144
Mortgage problem (3%), 205-218
Murphy, Brian, 164-165

Nabarro, Sir Gerald, 89
National Union of Conservative and Unionist Associations, 86-87
New York Council of Foreign Relations, 14
Nicholas, Harry, 27

O'Brien, Gerald, 212

Pannell, Charles, 46, 149
Parken, Bert, 53
Parkin, Ben, 43
Pearson, Frank, 193
Peel, Sir Robert, 308
Pentreath, Michael, 182-183, 185, 291-292
Phillips, Morgan, 208
Plummer, Dick, 39
Poole, Lord, 72, 74, 81 105, 169, 270-271, 279
Powel, Enoch, 72, 108
Prentice, Reginald, 23, 31
Profumo, John, 55-58
Profumo Affair, the, 55-65, 75, 304-305
Propaganda, 163-167, 170-172

Queen's Commission, the, 79-115

Racial prejudice, 176-177, 197-198
Radcliffe Report, 50
Rawlinson, Sir Peter, 57
"Red Duchess of Atholl," 125-126
Redmayne, Martin, 97-98, 101, 109-110
Rees-Mogg, William, 108
Reeves, Rosser, 272
Regency Council, 14
Rent Act, 197
Resale Price Maintenance, 141
Reynolds, Gerry, 39
Rice-Davies, Mandy, 75, 160
Richman, Alf, 291
Rodgers, Bill, 23
Royle, Anthony, 89
Russell, Bertrand, 19
Rutherford, Margaret, 304

St. Aldwyn, Lord, 109
Salisbury, Marquess of, 115
Sandys, Duncan, 104, 106, 295
Scarborough party conference, 22
Scilly Isles, 304
Scottish Hydroelectric Board, 124
"Sutch, Screaming Lord," 227
"Shadow" Cabinet, 45-47
Shore, Peter, 167
Soames, Christopher, 88, 104
Soskice, Frank, 24
Space program, 62-63
Stewart, Michael, 24, 290
Stockwood, Dr. Mervyn, 290
"Stop Wilson" Campaign, 22-23, 32-34
Strachey, John, 28
Strikes, 217-218, 221, 224, 269
Swingler, Stephen, 49

Taverne, Dick, 23
Television debates, 201